CONTEMPORARY SOCIAL RESEARCH SERIES

General Editor: MARTIN BULMER

5

Secondary Analysis in Social Research

CONTEMPORARY SOCIAL RESEARCH SERIES

Secondary Analysis in Social Research

A Guide to Data Sources and Methods with Examples

CATHERINE HAKIM
Foreword by Michael Posner

London
GEORGE ALLEN & UNWIN
Boston   Sydney

George Allen & Unwin (Publishers) Ltd,
40 Museum Street, London WC1A 1LU, UK

George Allen & Unwin (Publishers) Ltd,
Park Lane, Hemel Hempstead, Herts HP2 4TE, UK

Allen & Unwin, Inc.,
9 Winchester Terrace, Winchester, Mass. 01890, USA

George Allen & Unwin Australia Pty Ltd,
8 Napier Street, North Sydney, NSW 2060, Australia

First published in 1982

British Library Cataloguing in Publication Data

Hakim, Catherine
   Secondary analysis in social research. –
(Contemporary social research series; 5)
1. Social science – Methodology
I. Title
300′.72 (expanded)   H61
ISBN 0-04-312015-6
ISBN 0-04-312016-4 Pbk

Library of Congress Cataloging in Publication Data

Hakim, Catherine
   Secondary analysis in social research.
(Contemporary social research series; #5)
Bibliography: p.
Includes indexes.
1. Great Britain – Statistical services – Handbooks, manuals, etc.
2. Great Britain – Census – Handbooks, manuals, etc. 3. Social surveys –
Great Britain – Handbooks, manuals, etc. 4. Social sciences –
Research – Great Britain – Handbooks, manuals, etc. I. Title.
II. Series.
HA37.G7H333   300′.72   82-4046
ISBN 0-04-312015-6   AACR2
ISBN 0-04-312016-4 (pbk.)

Set in 10 on 11 point Times by Rowland Phototypesetting Ltd,
Bury St Edmunds, Suffolk
and printed in Great Britain
by Biddles Ltd, Guildford, Surrey

Contents

Foreword

From its very earliest days the Social Science Research Council has shown a particular concern to foster the type of work that forms the subject of this book. The most obvious expression of this was its initiative in setting up in 1967, jointly with the University of Essex, of a national archive of sample surveys in order to ensure that data collected by this expensive method did not disappear into oblivion (as tended to happen before then) but remained available for exploiting more fully. As an earnest of its belief in the value of such work the SSRC has ever since required recipients of its grants to offer the resulting data to this archive, which partly as a consequence has now grown to an impressive size.

At times when the funding climate for research veers towards the wintry – as, unhappily, is the case just at present – we look to the squirrels of social science to turn to such carefully accumulated stores with a more than ordinary relish. For it is at these periods that secondary analysis, so refreshingly inexpensive compared with almost all other forms of research, can be expected to come into its own.

Dr Hakim's book could not therefore be better timed. I have read it with great interest and with much admiration for her thoroughness and for her grasp of the intricacies of a complicated subject. If it leads to greater use, and more imaginative use, of the vast quantities of data that lie to hand already, it will have fulfilled its purpose more than amply.

MICHAEL POSNER
Chairman, SSRC

Editor's Preface

The structure of the social sciences combines two separate elements, theory and empirical evidence. Both are necessary for successful social understanding; one without the other is barren. The *Contemporary Social Research* series is concerned with the means by which this structure is maintained and kept standing solid and upright, a job performed by the methodology of social research.

The series is intended to provide concise introductions to significant methodological topics. Broadly conceived, research methodology deals with the general grounds for the validity of social scientific propositions. How do we know what we do know about the social world? More narrowly, it deals with the questions: how do we actually acquire new knowledge about the world in which we live? What are the strategies and techniques by means of which social science data are collected and analysed? The series will seek to answer such questions through the examination of specific areas of methodology.

Why is such a series necessary? There exist many solid, indeed massive, methodology textbooks, which most undergraduates in sociology, psychology and the other social sciences acquire familiarity with in the course of their studies. The aim of this series is different. It goes beyond such texts to focus upon specific topics, procedures, methods of analysis and methodological problems to provide a readable introduction to its subject. Each book contains annotated suggestions for further reading. The intended audience includes the advanced under-graduate, the graduate student, the working social researcher seeking to familiarise himself with new areas, and the non-specialist who wishes to enlarge his knowledge of social research. Research methodology need not be remote and inaccessible. Some prior knowledge of statistics will be useful, but only certain titles in the series will make strong statistical demands upon the reader. The series is concerned above all to demonstrate the general importance and centrality of research methodology to social science.

MARTIN BULMER
*London School of Economics
and Political Science*

Author's Preface

Probably the most widely held stereotype of the social scientist is of the academic in a university or polytechnic, engaged primarily in teaching a particular discipline, and engaged to some extent in research on a topic of his or her choice. There is, however, a much larger body of professional social scientists engaged in research and its interpretation and application in central and local government, commercial research agencies and independent research institutes. Collectively, their contribution to empirical social research greatly outweighs that of the academic community, with nationally representative surveys being the norm rather than the exception. After the establishment of the Social Science Research Council Survey Archive in the late 1960s, the great body of research data collected by professional social scientists became accessible to the whole research community, both in Britain and in other countries. Secondary analysis of national surveys and other quantitative social datasets available in archives has now become an important research method in Britain, as it has been for some decades in North America, where data archives were established much earlier. It is a method which is crucially dependent on a high degree of organisation and co-operation in the research community.

This book offers the first review of the secondary analysis potential of major British datasets; the practical and methodological problems and the solutions developed by analysts; and the range of secondary research currently being carried out, highlighting some notable examples. The main reference is to the population censuses and social surveys carried out by the Office of Population Censuses and Surveys, for a number of reasons. These social inquiries are in many ways designed for secondary analysis, and their potential is perhaps the greatest. Household census and survey data are widely used in secondary analyses by government departments, quangos, local government, academics and independent researchers, market research organisations, commercial and industrial concerns, trade unions and employers' organisations, and thus offer a wide variety of examples of secondary analysis. Finally, these data sources are currently the most accessible, both in terms of published reports on the methods used and the main results, and by virtue of the survey microdata and aggregate datasets available at the SSRC Survey Archive.

In addition to the surveys carried out by OPCS, there are many other surveys carried out by departments themselves or commissioned from research agencies. Many of these are also becoming available at the SSRC Survey Archive, providing a wealth of research data for secondary analysis by academic and other researchers. Finally there are numerous SSRC-funded studies being deposited at the Archive for secondary research by other academics. Since the Archive holds some 2,000 social science datasets, this review of their potential for secondary analysis can only be illustrative.

As the examples discussed in the following chapters demonstrate, secondary analysis is used within all the social science disciplines: sociology, economics, political science, history, demography, geography, education, planning, social psychology, social medicine and labour force studies. Indeed, the same dataset is often analysed from the different perspectives of more than one discipline, contributing to a multidisciplinary understanding of social issues and social processes. The examples presented also illustrate how secondary analysis is used by researchers in a great variety of organisational settings: from the isolated postgraduate student with few or no research funds to well-funded research teams in universities or in government departments. One of the advantages of secondary analysis is that it offers all researchers opportunities for empirical research based on large national datasets that have tended to be the privilege of the few.

My appreciation of the variety of secondary research being carried out in Britain was gained in part through working for a time in the Office of Population Censuses and Surveys where I was often asked to advise on secondary analyses of census and other data. My appreciation of the value of secondary analysis as a research method has been enhanced by working in the Department of Employment, where secondary analysis of existing data is often the only method which allows professional social scientists to meet the tight timetables involved in policy research and advice. I have benefited greatly from comments by colleagues in OPCS, the Department of Employment and other departments, and from the advice and assistance of the SSRC Survey Archive in the preparation of this book. I owe a particular debt to Martin Bulmer, without whose encouragement the book would never have been written, and who provided constructive criticism and advice throughout its development.

I am entirely responsible for any errors of fact or interpretation; the views expressed are personal and do not necessarily reflect the views of the Office of Population Censuses and Surveys or the Department of Employment.

CATHERINE HAKIM

Key to Abbreviations

BMRB	British Market Research Bureau
BSA	British Sociological Association
CSO	Central Statistical Office
DE	Department of Employment
DES	Department of Education and Science
DHSS	Department of Health and Social Security
DoE	Department of Environment
EEC	European Economic Community
ED	Enumeration District
FES	Family Expenditure Survey
GHS	General Household Survey
GRO(S)	General Register Office (Scotland)
IFS	Income Follow-Up Survey (to the 1971 Census)
ILO	International Labour Office
LFS	Labour Force Survey
NCDS	National Child Development Study
NDHS	National Dwelling and Housing Survey
NFS	National Food Survey
NHS	National Health Service
NIESR	National Institute for Economic and Social Research
NRS	National Readership Survey
OECD	Organisation for Economic Co-operation and Development
OPCS	Office of Population Censuses and Surveys
PRO	Public Records Office
PUS	Public Use Sample
QMFS	Qualified Manpower Follow-Up Survey (to the 1971 Census)
RCDIW	Royal Commission on the Distribution of Income and Wealth
RSS	Royal Statistical Society
SAS	Small Area Statistics
SOEC	Statistical Office of the European Community
SPSS	Statistical Package for the Social Sciences
SSRC	Social Science Research Council

For my mother and father

1

Introduction

Most social scientists, when contemplating the initiation of a research project, will automatically think in terms of collecting new data. Few will think of reanalysing existing datasets. Researchers like to think that their idea for a research project is original, and hence to assume that relevant data could not yet have been collected by anyone else. But original research can often be done with 'old' data.

Secondary analysis is any further analysis of an existing dataset which presents interpretations, conclusions, or knowledge additional to, or different from, those presented in the first report on the inquiry as a whole and its main results. Secondary analyses will thus include studies presenting more condensed reports (such as social area analysis based on selected social indicators); more detailed reports (offering additional detail on the same topic); reports which focus on a particular sub-topic (such as unemployment) or social group (such as ethnic minority); reports angled towards a particular policy issue or question; analyses based on a conceptual framework or theory not applied to the original analysis; and reanalyses which take advantage of more sophisticated analytical techniques to test hypotheses and answer questions in a more comprehensive and succinct manner than in the original report.

The rationale for secondary analysis of existing datasets overlaps to some extent with the rationale for regular censuses and for continuous multi-purpose surveys such as the GHS, which (as outlined in Chapters 2 and 7) are designed with secondary analysis in mind. Secondary analysis offers economies of time, money and personnel – advantages that are particularly attractive at times when funds for new research are scarce. It limits the reporting burden placed on the public. A decline in response rates was noted in the early 1970s (Market Research Society, 1976) suggesting that the survey method could become over-utilised, and secondary analysis may provide a reasonable alternative for some topics, eliminating the need to carry out new surveys. These arguments suggest that secondary analysis offers advantages over new research. But there are also types of research that can only be done through secondary analysis, where no comparison can really be made with other research methods. Many of the studies based on secondary analysis of census data, for example, illustrate the unique potential of a unique data source. In some areas of social research, such as the sociology of the labour market, of health and of poverty, major empirical studies at the national level are based on secondary analysis of existing sources, as illustrated by Montagna's (1977) review and the DHSS (1980) review. Similarly Durkheim's *Suicide*, an early classic in the secondary analysis of data derived from administrative records, could not have been carried out by other methods. Much demographic research is based necessarily on secondary analysis of data derived from administrative records and population censuses as well as surveys. Replication studies are more readily carried out through secondary analysis than by collecting new data (Finifter, 1975).

Secondary analysis can also be used as an adjunct to new research, either in the initial stages of research development, or as a complement to new research. For example, secondary analysis of national survey data can be used for a preliminary investigation of the size and characteristics of a particular social group or the broad parameters of an issue that is to be researched independently and in greater detail by other methods, and to provide the framework or national context for presenting the results of the new data – as exemplified in Townsend's study of poverty (Townsend, 1979). As the examples discussed in later chapters will show, secondary analysis can offer an alternative to, and substitute for, primary research; it can be used to inform and complement the analysis of freshly collected data; and there are some types of research that are uniquely based on this method.

The aim of this book is to provide a guide to the secondary analysis of quantitative social datasets available in archives, such as the SSRC Survey Archive at the University of Essex, and the social data and statistics that are available in published reports, on microfilm, or as computer printout. It is thus concerned with the secondary analysis of both microdata and aggregate data. *Microdata* is the term used to refer to datasets containing information on individual respondents to an inquiry, whether these are persons, households, or organisations such as schools and companies. Microdata are normally available only through survey archives, but many archives also hold aggregate data on magnetic tape that is also accessible in other formats (such as published reports). *Aggregate data* consists of statistics or tables produced from microdata, relating to broad groups, areas, or categories, and in which the characteristics of particular respondents are no longer identifiable. (However, both microdata and aggregate data are censored to prevent the identification of respondents.) Much secondary research is based on either one or the other type of data but, as illustrated in Chapters 6 and 8, some studies use both microdata and aggregate data from a particular inquiry.

Secondary analysis is often seen as a relatively new development in social research, resulting from the creation of archives to store and preserve machine-readable data, widespread access to computers for data analysis, and more sophisticated methods for the analysis of quantitative data. Certainly these technical and organisational developments have facilitated access to existing social datasets, enabling researchers to carry out secondary analyses additional to, and commonly very different from, those of the researcher who collected the data. But secondary analysis has a long history in social research, largely because central government has for two centuries been the most important source of social data and has had the longest history of an active role in social research. The population census is the longest-standing type of social inquiry, instituted as a regular decennial exercise in 1801 in Britain and in 1790 in the United States. In the nineteenth century statistics from population censuses and administrative records provided the material for secondary analyses, as exemplified by Durkheim's study of suicide from mortality statistics and Booth's (1886) study of the social structure from census statistics. From the mid-twentieth century opinion poll data and academic surveys offered new types of material for secondary analysis, as illustrated in Hyman's earlier review (Hyman, 1972).

But secondary analysis entered a new phase when central government moved from an emphasis on statistics derived from administrative records towards an emphasis on data from sample surveys. This revolution in the type of social data used by central government emerged earlier in the United States, but only became fully established in the 1970s in Britain as reflected, for example, in sources of data on the labour force. This accounts for the greater development of secondary analysis as an important type of social research, both in central government and the universities, in the United States as compared with Britain (Hakim, 1982). Although access to computers and archives can facilitate secondary research, it will only be carried out if the available data are themselves worth analysing. Unfortunately many researchers outside central government are as yet unaware of the social data revolution of the 1970s and inclined to think that the limitations of social data derived from administrative records still apply to the new government social surveys (Bulmer, 1980b). The significance of the change and its implications for secondary analysis are most apparent in the major multi-purpose social surveys established in the late 1960s and early 1970s: the General Household Survey (GHS), the Family Expenditure Survey (FES) and the Labour Force Survey (LFS) discussed in Chapters 7 and 8, all of which are carried out by the Office of Population Censuses and Surveys (OPCS).

The existence of multi-purpose surveys tends to blur the boundaries between primary and secondary analysis. Hyman's earlier definition of secondary analysis as the 'extraction of knowledge on topics other than those which were the focus of the original surveys' (Hyman, 1972: 1) was formulated with reference to academic surveys and opinion polls. These are designed to provide data relevant to previously specified questions and hypotheses, and the assumption is that the original research report will have exhausted the information relevant to the main topic of concern. In the case of multi-purpose and broad social inquiries, such as the census, the FES and GHS, there is no single original researcher and no single and central focus or theme to report on. In a sense they are specifically designed to offer unlimited potential for secondary analysis, and the primary use is simply that essential application which guides and determines the design and methodology of the inquiry. Thus secondary analysis can be more broadly defined today as any further analysis of one or more datasets which yields findings or knowledge additional to those presented in the original report.

Although OPCS is the most important single office engaged in government research, the majority of government surveys are carried out by researchers in other government departments. An increasing number of these are now becoming available at the SSRC Survey Archive for secondary analysis by other researchers, as illustrated in Chapter 9. The majority of the datasets held at the Archive relate to academic surveys and studies which have more restricted secondary analysis potential, usually for researchers working in the same field as the depositor – such as the British Election Study data extensively used by political scientists. Since the Archive holds some 2,000 datasets, this review of their potential for secondary analysis can only be illustrative.

The broad definition of social data and social research adopted here encompasses all studies of the structure and processes of society which draw on information on people's behaviour, attitudes and beliefs. As the examples discussed in following chapters demonstrate, secondary analysis is used within all the social science disciplines; indeed, the same dataset is often analysed from the different perspectives of more than one discipline. Although widely used, it tends to be invisible. Research reports based on secondary analysis cannot readily be differentiated from those based on specially collected data. Frequently the only clue is that the reader is referred to the original report for details of the methodology used, or the report is based on a much larger dataset than most researchers would expect to collect themselves. One of the advantages of secondary analysis is that it offers all researchers opportunities for empirical research that have tended to be the privilege of the few.

Sources of Quantitative Social Data

Sources of social data can be classified into six categories. Table 1.1 presents a typology of the datasets used in secondary analysis and lists a few examples of each type. At least one example of each type of datasource is discussed in the following chapters, with reference to its characteristics, its current and potential uses in secondary analysis, specific problems likely to be encountered and solutions that have been adopted. The aim is to provide, as far as possible, a description of each type of dataset that can be used in secondary analysis, and a guide to the specific potential and limitations of each.

With the exception of population censuses, which are unique to central government, examples of each type of data can be found both from 'official' sources (that is, central government) and 'non-official' sources (that is, local authorities, market research and opinion poll organisations, universities and independent research institutes). The distinction is not watertight as central government departments commission surveys both from OPCS and from independent research organisations, so that some of the surveys listed in the 'non-official' category have been commissioned and funded (in whole or in part) by government departments – for example, the MSC Cohort Study of the Unemployed carried out by Daniel (1981) and the recent sweeps of the National Child Development study carried out by the National Children's Bureau.

Population censuses are unique to central government, in part because they are obligatory whereas surveys are based on voluntary participation (Hakim, 1979a: 344). A population census is a complete and individual enumeration of all persons in a fixed geographical area at a single point in time carried out by central government. In practice some censuses are based on a sample of the population, but unlike surveys they remain obligatory, as illustrated by the 1966 Sample Census of Britain. The closest non-official equivalent to the census were the household sample surveys carried out by some local authorities after the cancellation of the proposed 1976 quinquennial census. A list of these is available from the DoE (DoE, 1979). These were modelled to some extent on both the population census and the GHS, though they also covered topics of local concern.

Continuous and regular surveys are those that are repeated over time. They include surveys with fieldwork spread out evenly across the calendar year (such as the FES) and those repeated periodically, ranging in frequency from the monthly NOP National Political Surveys to the biennial LFS. Some of the continuous and regular surveys are *multi-purpose* in that they aim to collect data on a wide range of topics of broad interest rather than a single or narrowly defined area of behaviour. The GHS is the most important example among official

Table 1.1   Sources and Types of Quantitative Social Data

Types of data source	Official examples (carried out by OPCS or internally by government departments)	Non-official examples (carried out outside government)
I Censuses	Decennial and quinquennial population censuses* Census Small Area Statistics 1841–81 census records at PRO* 1851 Census 2% sample	NOP National Political Surveys National Readership Survey BMRB Target Group Index* Newcastle upon Tyne household survey* EEC Eurobarometer surveys NFER National Survey 1960 1968 Townsend Poverty Survey 1974 British Election Study 1973 PEP Survey of the Unemployed 1963 Affluent Worker Survey 1963–70 Butler and Stokes surveys on Political Change Local authority and market research surveys
II Continuous and regular surveys	General Household Survey Family Expenditure Survey Labour Force Survey National Food Survey EEC Consumer Attitudes Survey*	NCB 1958 National Child Development Study PIC 1946 National Survey of Health and Development* PSI–MSC Cohort Study of the Unemployed
III Ad hoc surveys	1976 Family Formation Survey 1977 Retirement Survey 1975/6 National Training Survey 1977/8 National Dwelling and Housing Survey 1979 Family Finances Survey 1980 Survey of Women and Employment	1851 Census 2% sample microdata Marriages in Mid-Victorian London Local authority LAMIS-based information systems* Local Authority Databank (York University) Determinants of County Borough Expenditure* CIPFA SIS Community Indicators*
IV Cohort (longitudinal) studies	OPCS Longitudinal Study (1%)* DHSS Cohort Study of the Unemployed	
V Datasets derived from administrative and public records	Hospital In-patient Enquiry* DE Stoppages of Work datasets IR Survey of Personal Incomes*	
VI Multi-source datasets	CSO time-series datasets	

Note:
With the exception of those marked by an asterisk all datasets listed are (or will be) available from the SSRC Survey Archive at Essex University. Those not available at the Archive are available in other forms (such as published reports on analyses of the dataset, or of statistics).

social surveys, and has provided the model for some multi-purpose local authority surveys, of which the Newcastle upon Tyne Household Survey is the only regular survey, repeated biennially. There are also multi-purpose market research surveys, such as the National Readership Survey and the BMRB's Target Group Index. (In the USA there is also a multi-purpose academic survey, the General Social Survey described in Chapter 10.)

National *cohort (or longitudinal) studies* are still comparatively rare, with only five examples altogether in Britain to date. Of the five, only three follow up the cohort in question for longer than two years: the OPCS, NCB (National Children's Bureau) and Population Investigation Committee (or 'Douglas') cohort studies.

There are many examples of *datasets derived from administrative records*, but these are most commonly retained by the government department, company, or other organisation responsible for them and secondary analysis is limited to the data presented in published reports, or special analyses provided by the organisation in question. The SSRC Survey Archive holds a number of datasets on strikes derived from the Department of Employment's records, but no other official or local authority datasets as yet. It also holds datasets compiled by independent researchers; these are usually derived from public records (such as marriage registers), from material available at the Public Records Office (such as the nineteenth-century census returns which become public records after 100 years), and other sources.

Multi-source datasets draw together quantifiable information and statistics from a number of sources, such as the population census, other departmental statistics and local authority statistics. They are of two types: *time-series*, such as the CSO time-series data bank which contains time-series for some 2,000 variables; and *area-based datasets* which contain a range of statistical information for specific types of area, such as local authorities. The Archive holds both types, but area-based datasets are available also in the form of published compendia of local authority statistics, such as CIPFA'S twelve-volume *Statistical Information Service* (see, for example, CIPFA, 1979).

The SSRC Survey Archive holds 'official' and 'non-official' examples of all six types of data listed in Table 1.1, but the bulk of its holdings consists of *ad hoc surveys and studies*. These consist of data from personal or postal interviews with a number of respondents at a particular point in time, and usually have a fairly specific focus. This is the most heterogeneous category of data, ranging from surveys based on large randomly selected national samples, to small local inquiries with fewer than 100 respondents identified by a variety of methods.

Most of the examples of secondary analysis discussed relate to datasets that are available at the Archive, more particularly the first three types of data listed in Table 1.1. However, as noted in Chapter 11, the Archive can often obtain the microdata for surveys that it does not already hold, on the request of a prospective secondary analyst. No reference is made to the standard sources of aggregate statistics that are frequently used in secondary analysis. These have been reviewed in some detail in a fifteen-volume series edited by Maunder (1974–81) and elsewhere (Edwards, 1974; Pickett, 1974; Buxton and Mackay, 1977; CSO, 1976, 1978, 1980).

Choosing a Dataset for Secondary Analysis

Some of the more general characteristics that define and differentiate the various types of datasource will have implications for their potential for secondary analysis. These are now reviewed briefly. Survey datasets vary a good deal in size and the degree of geographical detail, the detail and complexity of the topic content, and in their time-specificity. In general, the larger and more complex they are, the greater the potential for secondary analysis as it is unlikely that any single report could exhaust their content, but also the greater the amount of work involved.

The depth of interviewing and topic content varies enormously between social inquiries. At one extreme there is the census, based primarily on self-completion schedules, although census enumerators do provide assistance and advice on how to complete the forms. As the census is addressed to the entire population, the schedules and questions must be straightforward enough to be completed by all heads of households, including those who may have language, literacy, eyesight, or other difficulties. Greater depth is usually achieved when interviewers are used, especially if trained and experienced professional interviewers carry out the fieldwork. The Labour Force Survey is based on interviews with one responsible adult in each household, who provides information about all adults in the household unless they are also present at the time of the interviewer's call. Thus a lot of the LFS data relates to such *proxy interviews*, which are less reliable than personal interviews and yield a higher proportion of missing information. Some academic surveys have been carried out with students rather than professional interviewers doing the fieldwork, though there is an increasing tendency for academic surveys to use the trained field forces of market and social research companies. The depth of interviewing in the two major OPCS continuous surveys – the GHS and FES – is probably unique, although some researchers argue that equally good results can be obtained also in *ad hoc* surveys (Townsend, 1979: 101–4). The depth of topic content obtained through postal surveys can vary from the very shallow to the very detailed. In general, care must be exercised in interpreting the results of data obtained from shallow interviewing as the data are less reliable. Survey datasets offering greater depth of information present the greatest potential, but also greater difficulties for the secondary analyst (although good documentation can remove most of the difficulties).

The sample size, sampling design and response rate for a survey are of particular concern to a secondary analyst. Large, nationally representative and reliable datasets will be of greater interest than data which are more limited in one of these respects. Official surveys often compare favourably with non-official studies on these criteria, as the latter are more frequently based on data for a limited number of areas, or a limited sample size. Data from case studies tend to be of little interest to the secondary analyst, although reports on case studies may provide useful additional detail or background material for a larger-scale study. Official surveys tend to have much larger samples than are used in non-official studies (see Table 1.2), and they can therefore be used to study elusive or small social groups on which separate surveys are not always available or could only be carried out at some cost. The population census offers the most comprehensive and reliable coverage of small and geographically dispersed social groups, and allows more disaggregated analyses than are possible with the GHS and FES. For example, the census is the only standard data collection large enough to provide detailed data on ethnic minority groups, or one-parent families. Even with the GHS, data for two or more years need to be pooled to provide cross-tabulations on small social groups such as these. Survey size also determines the degree of geographical detail available from a datasource. Again the census has the unique advantage of offering data for small areas at sub-regional level, and thus attracts widespread interest from geographers for secondary research. Some regional analyses of GHS and FES data can only be carried out by pooling results for two (or more) years. Thus almost all secondary analyses carried out by geographers and local authorities are necessarily based on census data, and these are described in Chapter 5. Finally, the size of the census allows far greater depth of data content on some topics: for example, as noted in Appendix B, the census occupational classification is far more detailed than in most surveys.

When choosing a dataset, the secondary analyst must consider whether and how *time* will be entered as an additional variable into the research design. This question rarely arises for the primary analyst, except to influence the timing of data collection within the year (for example, by avoiding the summer months when many people are on holiday or out of the home), or in before-and-after studies. The secondary analyst may treat time as a separate variable in the research design, or may ignore it altogether. The time-specificity of the research subject and of the relevant data sources cannot be taken for granted.

Table 1.2   Characteristics of Censuses and Major Surveys

	Population Censuses	Labour Force Survey	General Household Survey	Family Expenditure Survey
Coverage	Great Britain	United Kingdom	Great Britain	United Kingdom
Frequency	decennial[a]	bi-annual	annual	annual
Availability of statistics	1801–1981[1]	1973–81	1971–81[d]	1957–81[d]
Sample size				
No. of households	18 million[b]	100,000	15,000	11,000
Response rate	100%	85%	81–84%	68–70%
Resulting data	data for 100%, 10%, 1% of population	data for 89,000 HHs 180,000 persons aged 16+ grossed up[c]	data for 12,000 HHs 33,000 persons 25,000 persons aged 16+	data for 7,000 HHs 20,000 persons 14,000 persons aged 16+
Data collection	census day (March/April)	6 weeks in spring (May)	continuous throughout the year (January to December)	
Refence period for data on economic activity	week before census day	'last week' and 'usual situation'	'last week'	'current situation'

Notes:
The information presented above gives only a broad description of the characteristics of each data collection. Sample sizes, response rates, timing and results obtained vary from year to year. Relevant publications should be consulted.

a   Plus the 1966 Sample Census.

b   Plus 58,000 non-private institutions (e.g. hotels, prisons, hospitals and other institutions).

c   Results for respondents in households grossed up to mid-year population estimates for the relevant year for the United Kingdom, Great Britain and regions, adjusted to account for the population in non-private institutions (not covered by the survey).

d   Subject to certain constraints, microdata are also available from the SSRC Survey Archive although there is an embargo on access for a number of years after the survey was taken. In spring 1981 the Archive held GHS microdata for 1971–8 and FES microdata for 1961–79.

This needs to be emphasised, as there is a tendency to assume that data cannot legitimately be used once they are a few years old. As some scholars have recognised, new research based on 'old' data may still be very pertinent to current issues, either because there is no reason to believe that the social situation depicted by the data has actually changed, or because data for earlier time-periods shed new light on current issues and the current situation (Mason, Taeuber and Winsborough, 1977; Townsend, 1979: 18–21). Research that is primarily theoretical, concerned with elucidating causal relationships and explanations of social phenomena, is not time-specific in the same way as research geared to descriptive accounts of how society is functioning 'today'. Thus theoretical research, and some types of policy research, do not necessarily have to be based on very recent data; they can well be based on secondary analysis of older data. Alternatively secondary analysis of old data may be concerned precisely with assessing what, if any, the degree and nature of changes over the past few decades have been. Time-series do not always show that there has been a lot of change (Thatcher, 1968). Secondary analysts who have confronted the question of time as a variable in social research with some sophistication have found that a lot of the data in archives are entirely appropriate to their needs, even if such data tend to be regarded by scholars who have only done primary analysis as historic in their antiquity. Hyman (1972) provides numerous examples of this sophisticated approach to time among American secondary analysts, and Finifter (1975) has demonstrated how irrelevant is the time dimension to theoretical research based on replication to test and retest theoretical conclusions derived from earlier research.

The type of factual data available from decennial censuses and, for the inter-censal period, the GHS, are subject to erosion by time, but to a far lesser extent than the subjective (attitudinal) data commonly collected by non-official surveys. The difference in the temporal robustness of the two types of data is attested to by the relative volatility exhibited in the small amount of attitudinal data (on job satisfaction) available from the GHS as compared with the stability of the distribution of household tenure and occupations, for example. The temporal robustness of census data is also attested by the fact that market and social researchers – including those in OPCS – use each census throughout the following decade to check whether respondents are representative of the areas covered by sample surveys. Both the census and the national surveys are frequently used to provide nationally representative secondary data on a topic which is explored in greater detail in a new survey. The census and the GHS are used as alternative or complementary datasources, depending on the topic content or level of detail required.

If a secondary research design requires time-series, then the decennial censuses and continuous surveys are the obvious choice, although more limited time-series can also be obtained from some other sources, such as opinion poll surveys and some of the datasets derived from administrative records. Chapters 6 and 8 describe some of the secondary research based on this type of application. Occasionally two or more *ad hoc* surveys offer data on a similar topic, so that comparisons over time may be possible, as the two graduate surveys described in Chapter 10 demonstrate.

Continuous surveys can also be treated as surveys which provide data for a particular time-period of interest to a project – for example, for a period when a particular policy was in operation, or a particular government in power; for a period when other, complementary, data are available; or for a period when the researcher carried out his own research survey of a more specialised nature. The continuous survey can also be used as a two-stage survey providing data for a before-and-after study of, for example, the impact of the implementation, changing, or abandoning of a policy; the impact of a particular event, such as the impact of a change of government on political attitudes; or the impact of a trend in inflation on attitudes towards pay. In the case of continuous surveys that provide monthly or quarterly data (such as the NOP National Political Surveys or the GHS respectively), the time-period for which data is to be used can be specified fairly precisely as compared with more time-specific surveys (such as the LFS). In much secondary analysis time is entered as an additional variable into the study, and continuous surveys offer control over the time variable.

Datasets and statistics derived from administrative and public records are almost always based on standard definitions and classifications of, for example, unemployment, strikes, crime, or illness. Furthermore, the data obtained from such records may be affected by administrative procedures and concerns, for example, in the extent to which certain types of illness or crime are reported, detected, or recorded. These types of data thus provide information on the workings of administrative systems as much as on the social phenomena connected with them, a point which secondary analysts take into account in their interpretations of the data. These limitations are not found in the data obtained from household censuses and surveys, as they collect information independently of administrative processes, but a number of standard definitions and classifications are applied to many official and non-official surveys. For example, the Socio-Economic Group (SEG) classification is commonly used in many OPCS surveys, including the GHS. A standard definition of head of household is applied to most OPCS surveys, and an equivalent definition of 'chief economic supporter' is usually applied in the census. Some of the definitions and classifications used in official surveys have gained widespread acceptance in non-official research, but there are a number of important standard non-official definitions and classifications, for example, those commonly used in market research surveys.

There are two main implications for secondary analysis. Datasets derived from separate sources, but based on identical, compatible, or comparable definitions and classifications can readily be used to complement each other in multi-source studies. Thus the secondary analyst can overcome the content limitations of a single survey or dataset by utilising others providing compatible information. The second implication is that some knowledge of the characteristics of standard definitions and classifications is required (see Appendix B). With official datasources, the limitations of standard definitions and classifications are well documented, both in the main reports on each datasource, and by researchers who have used the data (see, for example, Hakim, 1980b; Hindess, 1973; Irvine *et al.*, 1979). For example, the definitional and classificatory limitations of data on ethnic minorities in Britain are described by Moser (1972) and OPCS (1979). This information allows the secondary analyst to exercise caution, where necessary, in any interpretations of the data. In contrast, there is often inadequate documentation on how important variables (such as social class) have been defined and coded in the *ad hoc* surveys carried out by academics.

The topic content of official surveys differs from the type of data that are collected in independent surveys. Official surveys are subject to public scrutiny, and must achieve public acceptability. Non-official surveys can obtain a wider variety of data, including topics that may be too sensitive for official surveys. For example, the NOP National Political Surveys and the British Election Study offer data on political views and attitudes to the government that are not available from any official survey. In general, official datasets tend to contain behavioural data in the main, with relatively little data on the attitudes, values, perceptions, beliefs and subjective realities that are frequently available in non-official datasets. Thus official and non-official datasets tend to offer overlapping but often distinctively different types of social data. The lack of income data from British censuses dictates that other sources (all of which are more limited in one way or another) must be used for many of the secondary studies that are routinely based on census data in North America – a limitation which is exacerbated by the lack of Public Use Sample microdata for Britain, as noted in Chapters 3 and 4. If income is a crucial variable in a research design, the FES and GHS are the obvious alternatives, and Chapter 8 describes secondary research based on the FES and GHS which includes income as a variable. Secondary research based on other sources of income data (such as the Department of Employment's New Earnings Survey and the Inland Revenue's Survey of Personal Incomes) is limited to analyses of the published statistics and is not covered here (see Maunder, Vols 6 and 13, for useful discussions). As the Registrar General's and the Department of Employment's occupational classifications are compatible from 1979 onwards (see Appendix B) it may be easier in future to assign income proxy measures to the OPCS occupational and socio-economic classifications (as was suggested by Mayhew and Rosewell, 1978: 246, and, for small area data, by Rothman, 1977: 19–26). The lack of data on ethnic minorities from a direct question in the 1981 Census is most regrettable, but the 1979 and subsequent LFS and, to some extent, the GHS, provide alternative sources (as shown in Table 1.3).

Table 1.3 outlines the major topics covered by the regular surveys. It shows that for some topics, such as labour force participation, a fair

Table 1.3   *Topic Content of Censuses and Major Surveys*

		Population Censuses	General Household Survey	Family Expenditure Survey	Labour Force Survey
Household	– familial structure	X	X	X	—
composition	– age/sex structure	X	X	X	X
	– tax units	—	X	X	—
Housing	– tenure	X	X	X	X
	– quality indicators	O	X	O	—
	– costs	—	X	X	—
Migration	– changes of address	X	X	—	O
	– factors affecting	—	X	—	—
	– country of birth	X	X	—	X
Ethnic minority/race group		O	O	—	X
Father's occupation (social class of origin)		—	X	—	—
Education	– terminal education age	O	X	—	X
	– qualifications	X	X	—	X
	– courses attended	—	X	—	O
Employment	– employee/self-employed	X	X	X	X
	– apprentices and students	X	X	—	X
	– inactive and retired	X	X	O	X
	– unemployment	O	X	O	X
	– second jobs	O	X	O	X
	– full-time/part-time/hours worked	X	X	X	X
	– job change, occupational mobility	X	X	—	X
	– travel to work	X	X	—	O
Household	– sources of income	—	X	X	O
income	– earnings of individuals	—	X	X	—
	– benefits	—	X	X	—
	– other income	—	X	X	—
Household	– total	—	—	X	—
expenditure	– on housing	—	X	X	—
	– on food	—	—	X	—
	– other expenditure	—	—	X	—
Health, disabilities, use of health services		—	X	—	—
Leisure activities		—	X	—	—
Fertility		X	X	—	—

Key:
X   detailed information for two or more years
O   limited information: indirect information, for one year only, or no detail
—   no information in any year

Note:
For further detail on GHS and LFS topics see Tables 7.1 and 7.2; for further detail on population censuses see Tables 2.1 and 2.2.

Table 1.4 *Some Other Major Surveys*

	Frequency	Date	Sampling frame	Sample size	Unit of analysis	Type of respondent	Response rate (%)	Location
National Food Survey	continuous from	1940	electoral register	15,000	households	housewife	52	GB
International Passenger Survey	continuous from	1964	international passengers at ports, airports, etc	260,000	individual traveller	individual traveller	88	GB
New Earnings Survey	annual from	1970	national insurance numbers	170,000	employees	employers	82[a]	GB
Survey of Personal Incomes	annual from	1954/5	inland revenue records	144,000	tax units	local tax offices	95	UK
English House Condition Survey	irregular from	1967	valuation list	9,000	households	household heads	83	E
National Dwelling and Housing Survey	ad hoc	1977–9	valuation list	915,000	households and individuals	one adult in household	85	GB
National Readership Survey	continuous from	1956	electoral register	30,000	individuals	individuals	75	GB
EEC Consumer Attitude Survey	four-monthly from	1974	electoral register	12,000[b]	individuals	household heads	84	GB
National Child Development Survey	ad hoc surveys of cohort	1958	birth records	17,000	individuals in cohort	cohort members and others	87	GB
National Training Survey	ad hoc	1975/6	electoral register	54,000	individuals	working adults	72	GB
Workplace Industrial Relations Survey	three-yearly from	1980	census of employment	2,700	establishments	managers and worker representatives	76	GB
National Travel Survey	regular from	1965	electoral register	15,000	individuals	households heads	85	GB

Notes:

a The NES results are based on returns from employers which are satisfactorily completed in time for processing, but the total response rate is higher. The sample represents about 1% of all employees.

b Total annual sample of 12,000 household heads is the aggregate of three separate surveys: 3,000 households in January, 3,000 households in May and 6,000 households in October of each year.

degree of choice between datasets exists, whereas on other topics, such as health and leisure, there is only one potential dataset. Table 1.4 gives some indication of the data available from other major surveys.

Probably the majority of non-official surveys are simple in that they collect data for a sample of individuals (Townsend's poverty survey and Rutter's study of secondary schools being notable exceptions). Many official surveys are more complex in that the data relate to social entities (most commonly households and families, but also firms, schools and other organisations) as well as the members of these social entities. These richer and more complex datasets offer greater potential for studies of social structure and social processes than do surveys of individuals, but the data processing and analysis problems are also greater, as noted in Chapter 8 and Appendix A.

Secondary Analysis

One advantage of secondary analysis is that it forces the researcher to think more closely about the theoretical aims and substantive issues of the study rather than the practical and methodological problems of collecting new data. The time and effort involved in obtaining funds for and organising a new survey can be devoted instead to the analysis and interpretation of results. Secondary analysis also tends to break monopolies within social research, whether the social research 'oligarchy' observed by Hyman in the United States (Hyman, 1972: 9–10) or the monopoly that government departments in Britain have sometimes exercised over the numerous social surveys carried out by central government at public expense. Secondary analysis permits time to be entered as an additional variable into social research, even when longitudinal studies cannot be carried out. And secondary analysis helps researchers to overcome the narrow focus on individuals and their characteristics, which is so prevalent in much primary analysis of new survey data, in favour of a broader concern with the socio-economic structure and social change.

The simpler types of secondary analysis are based on only one dataset, which may be any of the six types listed in Table 1.1. More complex designs will use data from two or more sources. Different sources may all provide data on a particular social group that is the subject of the study – for example, ethnic minorities, religious groups, one-parent families, social classes or occupational groups, political activists, ideological extremists (such as supporters of extreme political factions or parties), the unemployed, working mothers, trade unionists (members or activists), the highly qualified, and so on. Two (or more) existing sources may be used, for example, to provide comparisons of trends over time, or to provide complementary data on different aspects of the behaviour and attitudes of the group being studied. It may be possible to pool the data from the various sources to create a new and larger dataset, a strategy that is particularly advantageous when the group being studied forms only a tiny proportion of the cases in available datasets. Alternatively the datasets may be used separately to test and replicate the same hypotheses: even if the number of cases in each dataset is small, the reliability of the results will be supported if all the datasets independently yield the same results. (The use of replication as a substitute for significance tests, particularly for small datasets, has been recommended by Hyman, 1972: 136 and Finifter, 1975). In some studies the analysis of a new survey may be complemented by secondary analysis of an existing dataset, with a view to replication, a study of trends over time, or to set the detailed study of a minority or social group in a national context.

It is commonplace for researchers to set the results of new studies in the context of previous research. But earlier studies were often based on rudimentary analytical techniques, especially those based on manual analysis. Some reanalysis of earlier datasets may be necessary to allow direct comparisons to be made. The results of earlier analyses may be confirmed, or it may be found that apparent changes over time are illusory, the product of inadequate analytical techniques. With the rapid development of analytical techniques, statistical measures and related software for the analysis of quantitative social data, much secondary analysis consists of bringing earlier datasets into the current research paradigms and testing out recently developed theoretical frameworks against the mass of potentially relevant evidence accumulated in data archives and statistical compendia – the 'old data for new research' model. Secondary analysis can provide a wealth of data-based research on new topics, issues and policy concerns. It is often a crucial step in the process of getting new issues on to the political agenda, defining information gaps, and hence specifying new research needs. Secondary analysis of existing sources played a part, for example, in the recognition of the one-parent family as a new type of family structure, in putting discrimination against ethnic minorities in council housing on to the agenda, and in revealing the changing pattern of homeworking. However, old issues often resurface in a new form, and secondary analysts may discover that existing datasources provide directly relevant information on a new research topic under an old guise.

Archives increase the likelihood that earlier and later studies on a given topic will be discovered, and thus facilitate the use of secondary analysis for studies of trends over time. For example, the Department of Employment carried out a 1977 survey of 1970 first degree graduates which is similar to a 1966 survey of 1960 graduates carried out by Kelsall. Access to both surveys at the SSRC Survey Archive opens up the possibility of comparing the results of the two surveys, for example, to assess the impact of an increasing supply of graduates and of rising unemployment on the early careers of high qualified manpower.

The existence of continuous national surveys such as the FES and GHS removes at least some of the difficulties involved in trend studies based on collating a number of *ad hoc* surveys – although as Chapters 7 and 8 indicate the data from these too are not entirely comparable across time. The longest time-series can be derived from the population census reports, as Chapter 6 demonstrates. For recent decades there are also independent continuous or regular surveys such as the National Political Surveys, the National Readership Survey and the British Election Studies, providing trend data that can be utilised singly or in conjunction with other surveys. Opinion poll data have been utilised far more extensively by North American social scientists, especially political scientists, than in Britain – but the American literature gives a good indication of the potential in these datasets (Hyman, 1972: 209–55). An example in Chapter 10 shows how secondary analysis of opinion poll data from Gallup surveys was used to complement new research on secondary school students.

Longitudinal (or cohort) studies constitute a separate category of social research, often combining survey data and other types of data on the cohort in question. Now that data from the National Children's Bureau 1958 cohort study (the National Child Development Study) are deposited at the SSRC Survey Archive (and possibly also in due course the Douglas 1946 cohort study), the potential for secondary analysis of this type of data is extended. However, an approximation to cohort datasets can also be constructed from continuous and *ad hoc* surveys, and even the census. These 'constructed' cohort datasets can be developed for generations and time-periods not covered by the specially designed longitudinal studies, which have been initiated only within the last few decades. For example, the 1901–81 censuses can be used to construct four approximate adult cohorts: 1901–51, 1911–61, 1921–71 and 1932–81, each covering a ten-year age group (Table 1.5), for example, to study the work profiles of women in each cohort. Similarly the FES has been running long enough for three (partial)

Table 1.5   *Cohort Data from Decennial Censuses*

	1901	1911	1921	1931	1941	1951	1961	1971	1981
	15–24	15–24	15–24	15–24	15–24	15–24	15–24	15–24	15–24
	25–34	25–34	25–34	25–34	25–34	25–34	25–34	25–34	25–34
Age	35–44	35–44	35–44	35–44	35–44	35–44	35–44	35–44	35–44
of	45–54	45–54	45–54	45–54	45–54	45–54	45–54	45–54	45–54
person	55–64	55–64	55–64	55–64	55–64	55–64	55–64	55–64	55–64
	65+	65+	65+	65+	65+	65+	65+	65+	65+

adult cohorts to be identified, each covering a five-year age group (Table 1.6). Though the GHS has only been running ten years, it could be used to follow small cohorts of particular interest – such as the transition from school to work among the cohort aged 16 in 1971 and 25 in 1980; or the return to work after a period of child-rearing among women in their thirties and forties. Approximate cohort data are not as good as true longitudinal studies, but they provide a valuable complement (or even alternative) to purely cross-sectional analyses of each dataset. Surveys such as the GHS are also large enough for crosssectional analyses by single years of age to offer approximate cohort data, as illustrated in Figure 1.1. Basic data on a cohort (or age group) from household censuses or surveys can be supplemented by data from public opinion polls, *ad hoc* surveys and other sources. Opinion poll data have also been used to develop cohort studies of the alternative effects of ageing and generations upon political attitudes and behaviour (Hyman, 1972: 275). A methodology for distinguishing age, cohort and generational effects in the analysis of data on, for example, fertility, earnings, political opinion and behaviour is now emerging from research based on secondary analysis (Hyman, 1972; Mason *et al.*, 1973; Glenn, 1976).

Cross-national studies, while generally relatively scarce, are more common in certain areas, such as political science, demography and studies of the labour force and of educational systems. There are difficulties in designing cross-national comparative research based on the secondary analysis of *ad hoc* surveys, not the least being the location of suitably comparable datasets, but examples discussed in Chapter 10 illustrate the potential. The activities of international organisations such as the UN, OECD, EEC and other regional organisations have facilitated this type of secondary research, both by collating comparative data on given topics of interest, and in working towards the harmonisation of population censuses, labour force surveys and statistics, health data, fertility surveys, demographic statistics, household budget surveys and, most recently, multi-purpose

Table 1.6   *Cohort Data from the Family Expenditure Survey*

	1957	1962	1967	1972	1977	1982
	20–24	20–24	20–24	20–24	20–24	20–24
Age	25–29	25–29	25–29	25–29	25–29	25–29
of	30–34	30–34	30–34	30–34	30–34	30–34
person	35–39	35–39	35–39	35–39	35–39	35–39
or	40–44	40–44	40–44	40–44	40–44	40–44
head	45–49	45–49	45–49	45–49	45–49	45–49
of house-	50–55	50–55	50–55	50–55	50–55	50–55
hold	55–59	55–59	55–59	55–59	55–59	55–59
	60+	60+	60+	60+	60+	60+

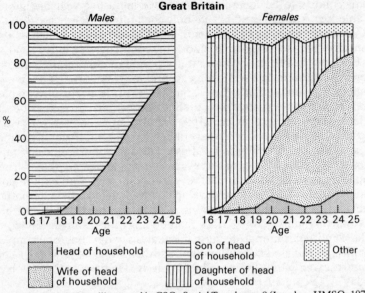

Source: 1975 GHS as illustrated in CSO, *Social Trends*, no. 8 (London: HMSO, 1977), fig. A.11, p. 20.

Figure 1.1   *Cohort date from the General Household Survey. The transition from family of origin to family of marriage: relationship to head of household by age.*

household surveys, across countries. Some opinion poll data, such as Gallup surveys, are available for a number of countries. In addition to the *ad hoc* survey designed as a cross-national comparative study, such as Almond and Verba's five-nation study *The Civic Culture*, there are an increasing number of cross-national comparative studies carried out by research teams in each country who collectively design and co-ordinate their separate surveys with a view to ensuring comparability of both the data collected and the analyses carried out. Cross-national studies based on secondary analysis are greatly facilitated when they are based on datasources that are designed to be as comparable as possible, in purpose and in methodology.

Cross-national studies fall broadly into two types for the secondary analyst: those in which the particular character of countries (their culture, social structure, or political system), is added in as an extra variable in the research, and those in which the aim is to develop and test a theory or set of hypotheses which hold true irrespective of the cultural, social, or political context. In the first case, the choice of countries will be of some importance if not crucial. In the second case, the selection of countries will be less important, so long as those chosen offer datasets that allow replication of the research in question. Thus for example Almond and Verba's selection of countries for their study of the civic culture required that they exhibit variation in the degree of modernisation in order to test the influence of this variable on civic attitudes. On the other hand, labour market stratification theory might well be tested using any industrialised countries for which the appropriate data existed. Whether concerned with differences between countries, or with cross-nationally valid theory development, a variety of approaches can be applied: trend studies, cohort studies, studies of particular social groups, or of theoretical problems. Unless the research specifically includes time as a variable (for example in trend studies), it will not be essential to ensure that the datasets used refer to a common time-period – so that surveys carried out at different times within a decade are often utilised in cross-national secondary analyses, as illustrated in Chapter 10.

How do secondary analysts go about their work, having chosen their research topics and found suitable datasets? In most cases the methods of analysis will essentially be the same as those used in primary analysis, and standard texts on survey analysis or data analysis are readily available. But there are some aspects of secondary analysis that are unique, or at least less likely to feature in standard texts on data analysis: data linkage and the entity problem, and the development of summary measures or indexes. The treatment of time as a variable has already been discussed.

The secondary analyst will often be processing a larger volume of data than the primary analyst, especially in the case of trend studies, cross-national comparative studies, or studies that rely on the complementary use of more than one dataset. The development of summary measures, social indicators and indexes is often a feature of secondary research. As the following chapters should demonstrate, some of the more successful secondary analyses have been based on the development and application of measures that summarise and condense a large volume of data.

Some summary measures are by now standard. For example, economic activity rates and unemployment rates, mortality rates, crime rates, fertility rates and education rates are all taken-for-granted quantitative measures, based on widely differing sources of data, but allowing comparisons across time and countries. Other measures are also being developed by secondary analysts. For example a non-opinionisation index has been developed to analyse data from opinion surveys (Hyman, 1972: 265–73). Measures of net satisfaction have been used to analyse job satisfaction, attitudes to pay, or to the economic climate. Income equivalence scales have been used to present broad measures of poverty (Van Slooten and Coverdale, 1977). A sub-employment index, a discouraged worker rate and measures of labour force attachment have been proposed for the analysis of labour force data (Norris, 1978; Chenoweth and Maret, 1980). Various measures of access to and utilisation of social and health services have been discussed by geographers, economists, sociologists and community health researchers. In the industrial relations field, quantitative measures of industrial conflict or of union penetration at establishment level are being developed. Of course, such measures may be developed and applied by primary analysts – but their measures are frequently *data-specific* in that their definition and design relate closely to the particular dataset or survey generated by the researcher, which is his primary concern. The contribution of the secondary analyst is to extend, standardise and refine such measures so that they can be applied to more than a single dataset for more than one country or time-period.

The secondary analyst is also more likely to confront the difficulties of data integration, the non-comparability and inflexibility of concepts, definitions, and classifications, or what Dunn has termed the 'entity problem' (Dunn, 1974: 141). All social data consist of representations of entities (or social units) and of the states, activities and processes that describe them. Data may refer to single entities (such as individuals, households, or enterprises) or to aggregate classes (such as social classes or socio-economic groups, types of industry, social or ethnic minorities). The concepts and classifications of the states, activities and processes that describe these units, and of the units themselves, tend to become institutionalised, rigid and inflexible, and are subject to a reification bias. The entity problem pervades all social research; if a conceptual framework becomes too ingrained, we lose the ability to perceive changing social realities and to reconceptualise observed phenomena. In one sense, data only become out-of-data when our conceptualisation of an issue or topic has changed, and this may happen within months of fieldwork at one extreme, or within decades at the other extreme. The secondary analyst often confronts the problem of entity concepts embedded in the way data were collected and coded that do not meet precisely his conceptual framework; part of his contribution will be to develop broader entity concepts that allow some variation in the operational definition of his concepts in relation to given datasets. This is particularly necessary when datasets from different time-periods or countries are to be collated or compared. Although the entity problem is highlighted for the secondary analyst, it pervades all social research. As Appendix B indicates, it surfaces even in relation to such basic matters as the classification of household composition, or of occupations, that are used in various datasets. The entity problem is not overcome when microdata as well as aggregate data are available in archives. The discussion of secondary analyses of FES published data and microdata in Chapter 8 shows that microdata offer greater flexibility in secondary data analysis, but not complete freedom.

Dunn's proposed solution to the entity problem is for social data and statistical systems to be designed with secondary analysis and multiple use in mind; for social scientists to professionalise the work of entity representation; and for *ad hoc* data and specialised data from other sources to be linked to continuous and regular data collections – developments which would contribute to an integrated data system as well as to more flexible entity representations (Dunn, 1974: 140–69). He notes also that Stone's work for the United Nations on a System of Social and Demographic Statistics (the SSDS) represents the only social accounting system that is able to deal with the entity problem. The purpose of the SSDS is 'to show what data are desirable on human beings, both individually and in groups, and on the institutions with which they are connected and how these data should be organised in order to provide an information system which will be useful for description, analysis and policy-making in the difference fields of social life' (United Nations, 1975: 3). Both Dunn's and Stone's models for multiple-use social data systems take secondary analysis for granted – indeed, neither author even refers to secondary analysis as such. Similarly secondary analysis is a taken-for-granted feature of the social indicator systems that are being developed by the OECD, EEC, the UN and other international organisations. This points to the wider and long-term role of secondary analysis in social research, and to the central role of multi-purpose data sources (such as the population census, GHS and FES) in the future development of social data systems. The British data sources and datasets reviewed in the following chapters are of particular significance in the development of integrated social data systems: in discussing potential sources of data for the SSDS, Stone made particular reference to British data collections, notably the continuous household surveys and longitudinal studies carried out by, or on behalf of, central government (United Nations, 1975: 23).

Despite a wealth of suitable datasets, secondary analysis has not yet begun to play as central a role in social research in Britain as it does in North America. An examination of the articles in two American journals (the *American Sociological Review* and the *American Journal of Sociology*) and two British journals (the *British Journal of Sociology* and *Sociology*) for 1979 shows that two-thirds of the American articles compared with only one-quarter of the British articles were based on secondary analysis. There are many reasons for this striking difference but one would appear to be the well-established role of social scientists in government research and the close collaboration between researchers in government and in universities in the United States (Sharpe, 1978). The National Longitudinal Surveys and the Family

Income Dynamics Study described in Chapter 7, and the various census Public Use Samples described in Chapter 3, all provide pertinent examples of this collaboration, which exists on an essentially *ad hoc* basis in Britain, although this may now be changing (Hakim, 1982). Because secondary analysis is better developed in the United States, reference is sometimes made to the American literature to supplement the British examples in the following chapters.

So far I have assumed that the analyst is interested in substantive research. However, secondary analysis is also used in methodological and statistical work, for example, to study sampling design, or the validity and reliability of statistical measures (Frankel, 1971; Airey *et al.*, 1976). Examples of this type of application are given in several chapters.

Part One

The Population Census

2

Social Data from the Census

There is a tendency to regard the population census as a demographic data base, but the modern census can more appropriately be regarded as the most important single survey of the socio-economic characteristics of the population. A population census is a government-sponsored, universal and simultaneous individual enumeration of all persons in a precisely defined geographical area. Since the basic headcount is a costly exercise, most censuses maximise the utility of the exercise by collecting basic information on the social and economic characteristics of the population at the same time.

The particular value of census data derives from the fact that it offers complete coverage of the population across a wide range of topics. It thus offers three advantages over other major sources of social data. First, it offers data on topics not covered at all, or only partially, by other sources, such as the self-employed; the unemployed (both unregistered and registered); apprentices; the quality of housing (as reflected in access to, and sharing of, basic amenities); the mode of transport to work; second jobs; people working at home; ethnic minority groups (as indicated by country of birth); and migration. Secondly, the size of the census enables the data on topics covered by other sources to be analysed in greater detail. For example, the census classifications of occupation, household and family composition, and country of birth are more detailed than in any other social survey. Detailed statistics are available on social and ethnic minority groups, such as one-parent families and family workers. The level of geographical detail in census output has no parallel in any other national source. Thirdly, the census offers detailed cross-tabulations across topics. For example, the household tenure distribution of ethnic minorities can be tabulated at sub-regional levels; the precise relationship between educational qualifications and the occupational structure can be explored; the personal and household characteristics of migrants, or the labour force participation of one-parent families, can be examined.

As the census is a unique exercise, and differs significantly from the sample surveys familiar to most researchers, its essential characteristics are noted briefly, but readers are referred to Benjamin (1970) for a full discussion. The Census Act 1920 lays upon the Registrars General of England and Wales and of Scotland the duty of carrying out enumerations at intervals of not less than five years, and specifies the minimum list of topics to be covered. Additional topics can be included subject to parliamentary approval. Consultation with census users in central government, local government and the research community helps to determine the topics covered by a census. The census is compulsory and householders can be prosecuted for failure to complete the census form fully and accurately. The results are published (in whole or part) and laid before Parliament. With the exception of the 1966 Census, the first (and so far only) quinquennial census, censuses have been taken every ten years in Britain since 1801 except in 1941. The decennial census forms are retained for a period of 100 years by the Census Office, during which time they are treated as confidential, and then released to the Public Records Office for use in genealogical and historical research. Thus the census is subject to parliamentary supervision and control, although it attracted very little interest until recently (Bulmer, 1979).

The term Census Office is used throughout for convenience to refer to the organisations responsible for conducting the population census in Britain, that is, the GRO for 1841 and 1851, the two separate GROs (for England and Wales, and Scotland, respectively) for 1861–1966, and the GRO (Scotland) and the Office of Population Censuses and Surveys (OPCS) for 1971 to the present. The Scottish census has always diverged slightly from that of England and Wales, but differences in the resulting data will not be discussed in any detail. The Northern Ireland census is not dealt with at all, as it differs significantly from the British census – for example, religion is one of the topics regularly included, the output and methods of data dissemination differ, and it is carried out by the Northern Ireland Department of Finance. A brief description is given by Buxton and Mackay (1977) and details are given in the Northern Ireland census reports.

The overall advantages and limitations of census data for secondary research were compared with those of other sources in the preceding chapter. In this chapter the subjects and topics covered by census data are discussed in more detail. A broad overview of the topics covered from 1801 to 1981 is given, but the main focus of this and the following chapters is on the recent censuses (1961, 1966, 1971 and 1981) and on census-related social data. The secondary research uses of the earlier censuses (1801–1951) are discussed in Chapter 6. The methodology of census-taking is not discussed at all unless it is relevant to some aspect of secondary analysis. Detailed accounts are given in each census report and also in Glass (1973) for the first censuses, Lawton (1978) for the nineteenth-century censuses, and OPCS and GRO(S) (1977: 11–46) and Benjamin (1970) for the most recent censuses.

Topics Covered by the Census

In the nineteenth century the main restriction on the amount of data collected in the census was the resources required to process the results by hand. With the introduction of punched-card processing in 1911 and, more particularly, the use of computers from 1961 onwards, the amount of information that could be collected and processed increased sharply. Table 2.1 summarises the topics covered by each census from 1801 to 1981. Names are not used in processing the census results, except to inform the coding of relationship to head of household where ambiguities arise, and they are not entered into the computer. However, names (and addresses) are a significant item of information in historians' analysis of the original census records at the PRO (see Chapter 6). All the other information is processed and used to compile the statistical results.

The census only covers topics that are not highly sensitive and on which objective and reliable information can be collected from households and institutions. As Table 2.1 indicates, the main topics are now housing, employment, household composition, migration and country of birth, education and educational qualifications, fertility, the use of cars and transport to work. At the time of the 1851 population census two separate voluntary censuses were also carried out, the Religious Census and Education Census. Neither was ever repeated; education data have since been collected in the population census and other surveys, and religion was agreed to be too sensitive a topic for the census (although it is included in the Northern Ireland census). From 1851 to 1911 data on physical and mental infirmities were collected (on the deaf, dumb, blind, lunatic, etc.) but the topic has since been dropped. In Scotland the census collected information on the number of rooms with one or more windows from 1861 to 1931. With these few exceptions the census has tended to collect increasingly detailed information on the main census topics listed above. However, the census forms provide only a partial guide to the topics on which statistics are available.

The data from each census can be extended by three methods. Separate questions can be inserted on new topics, such as the use of cars in 1966. New or more detailed response categories can be added to existing questions. For example, people working at home were identified by a separate question in 1901, 1911 and 1921, but were identified by a separate code within questions on the workplace address and travel to work from 1951 onwards. A number of derived variables can be created at the processing stage from information on the census forms. Thus although information on relationship to the household head has been collected since 1851, this information has only been used, in conjunction with information on age, sex and marital status, to

Table 2.1 Topics covered by British Censuses 1801–1981

	1801	1811	1821	1831	1841	1851	1861	1871	1881	1891	1901	1911	1921	1931	1951	1961	1966	1971	1981
Name	GB	—	—	—	GB	GB	GB	GB	GB	GB	GB	GB	GB	GB	GB	GB	GB	GB	GB
Sex	—	GB	GB	GB	GB	GB	GB	GB	GB	GB	GB	GB	GB	GB	GB	GB	GB	GB	GB
Age	—	—	GB	GB	GB	GB	GB	GB	GB	GB	GB	GB	GB	GB	GB	GB	GB	GB	GB
Relationship to household head	—	—	—	—	—	GB	GB	GB	GB	GB	GB	GB	GB	GB	GB	GB	GB	GB	GB
Persons absent from household	—	—	—	—	—	GB	GB	GB	GB	GB	GB	GB	GB	GB	—	—	—	—	—
Marital Status	—	—	—	—	—	GB	GB	GB	GB	GB	GB	GB	—	GB	GB	GB	GB	GB	GB
Birthplace in UK or overseas	—	—	—	—	GB	GB	GB	GB	GB	GB	GB	GB	GB	GB	GB	GB	GB	GB	GB
Nationality	—	—	—	—	—	GB	GB	GB	GB	GB	GB	GB	GB	GB	GB	GB	—	GB	GB
Usual residence	—	—	—	—	GB	GB	—	—	—	—	—	GB	—	—	GB	GB	GB	GB	GB
Migration before census:																			
– residence 1 year before	—	—	—	—	—	—	—	—	—	—	—	—	—	—	—	GB	GB	GB	GB
– residence 5 years before	—	—	—	—	—	—	—	—	—	—	—	—	—	—	—	—	GB	GB	—
Language spoken: Gaelic	—	—	—	—	—	—	—	—	S	S	S	S	S	S	S	S	S	S	S
Welsh	—	—	—	—	—	—	—	—	—	W	W	W	W	W	W	W	W	W	W
Occupation of person	GB	—	—	—	GB	GB	GB	GB	GB	GB	GB	GB	GB	GB	GB	GB	GB	GB	GB
Employment status	—	—	—	—	GB	GB	GB	GB	GB	GB	GB	GB	GB	GB	GB	GB	GB	GB	GB
Second occupation	—	—	—	—	—	—	—	—	—	—	GB	GB	GB	—	—	—	—	GB	GB
Work at home	—	—	—	—	—	—	—	—	—	—	—	—	—	—	—	—	—	GB	GB
Workplace address	—	—	—	—	—	—	—	—	—	—	—	—	E,W	—	—	—	GB	GB	GB
Means of transport to work	—	—	—	—	—	—	—	—	—	—	—	—	—	—	—	—	GB	GB	GB

Table 2.1 Topics covered by British Censuses 1801–1981 – continued

	1801	1811	1821	1831	1841	1851	1861	1871	1881	1891	1901	1911	1921	1931	1951	1961	1966	1971	1981
Hours of work (or part/full-time)	—	—	—	—	—	—	—	—	—	—	—	—	—	—	GB	GB	GB	GB	GB
Economic activity status	—	—	—	—	—	—	—	—	—	—	—	—	—	—	GB	GB	GB	GB	GB
Whether unemployed	—	—	—	—	—	—	—	—	—	GB	GB	GB	GB	GB	—	GB	GB	GB	GB
Industry	—	—	—	—	GB	GB	—	—	—	—	GB	GB	—	GB	GB	GB	—	GB	GB
Education at home or school	—	—	—	—	—	GB	GB	GB	—	S	—	—	—	—	GB	—	GB	GB	GB
Age completed full-time education	—	—	—	—	—	—	—	—	—	—	S	—	—	—	GB	GB	—	GB	GB
Educational qualifications	—	—	—	—	—	—	—	—	—	—	—	—	—	—	—	GB	—	GB	GB
Fertility	—	—	—	—	—	—	—	—	—	—	GB	GB	—	—	GB	GB	—	GB	—
Marriage (duration)	—	—	—	—	—	—	—	—	—	—	GB	GB	—	—	GB	GB	—	GB	—
Orphanhood	—	—	—	—	—	—	—	—	—	—	—	GB	—	—	—	—	—	—	—
Infirmities	—	—	—	—	—	GB	GB	GB	GB	GB	GB	GB	S	S	—	—	—	—	—
Eligibility for medical benefit	—	—	—	—	—	—	—	—	—	—	—	GB	—	—	—	—	—	—	—
Housing	GB	GB	GB	GB	GB	GB	GB	GB	GB	GB	GB	GB	GB	GB	GB	GB	GB	GB	GB
Rooms per household	—	—	—	—	—	—	—	—	—	E,W	E,W	E,W	E,W	E,W	GB	GB	GB	GB	GB
Shared accommodation	—	—	—	—	—	—	—	—	—	—	—	—	—	—	GB	GB	GB	GB	GB
Household tenure	—	—	—	—	—	—	—	—	—	—	—	—	—	—	GB	GB	—	GB	GB
Cars and garaging	—	—	—	—	—	—	—	—	—	—	—	—	—	—	—	—	GB	GB	GB

Note:
For further details on topics covered by the 1801–1966 censuses see OPCS and GRO(S) *Guide* (1977); for the recent censuses see Table 2.2.

create derived variables on household and family composition since 1951. Derived variables are sometimes second-best proxies for information that would ideally have been collected through a direct question on census forms. For example second-generation immigrants are counted indirectly in the 1981 Census statistics as people born in the UK with one or both parents born overseas; this derived variable can only be obtained for people who are still living with their parents. The coding and processing of the census results are determined by the time the census is taken; after that it is too late for census users to request the creation of additional derived variables which, while feasible in principle, would entail additional costs for recoding and processing. For example, the 1961 Census cannot be reprocessed to produce tables on one-parent families although the data are in principle available from the census. This type of secondary analysis is currently limited to the early census records available at the PRO (as described in Chapter 6).

The variables for which data are available from the recent censuses are listed in Table 2.2. A comparison of Tables 2.1 and 2.2 illustrates both the potential for extending census results beyond the raw data (or basic variables) to include derived variables, and the non-availability of data in the tabulated statistics. For example, family workers are identified at the processing stage as persons who live in the same household with, and work for, a relative, and statistics on this group are published. On the other hand the 1961 and 1966 censuses collected information on people working at home, but no data on this group are available in the tables produced for these years.

The organisation of the material in the published reports indicates the range of the total available output, and some of its potential research applications. The housing statistics are produced primarily for the DoE and outline the total volume, characteristics and quality of housing in the country, while the headship rate statistics indicate the level of unmet need for housing. The household composition statistics are produced primarily for the DHSS; they outline the familial structure of households and focus on the nuclear families within households which are the social unit of interest for most policy-related studies – for example, in relation to the total number and characteristics of families which are potential clients for various welfare benefits. The economic activity statistics are produced primarily for the DE and outline the size and characteristics of the labour force. The qualified manpower statistics produced for the DES and the DE describe the output of the educational system as a whole and the input into the labour force, indicating the relationship between qualifications and occupations, the utilisation or non-utilisation of qualifications obtained. This topic also merited a number of follow-up surveys (described below). The workplace volumes produced for the DoE and DE describe the geographical distribution of the labour force and (in conjunction with the volumes on usual residence) the implications for travel-to-work patterns and urban and regional development policies. The statistics on country of birth are produced both to identify patterns of migration between EEC and Commonwealth countries, and to provide information for government departments and local authorities on the geographical distribution of ethnic minorities and their housing, education and employment situation compared with the conditions of the population as a whole. Other statistics on the demographic characteristics of the population, fertility and migration provide basic information on population change and its causes. The applications of census data in central and local government are outlined in the White Paper on the 1981 Census (Cmnd 7146, 1978) and in the OPCS *Census Monitors*. The existing policy applications in government do not, however, give much indication of the potential and existing secondary research applications outside the policy sphere which are discussed in the following chapters.

The volume of data on a given topic or population sub-group is not indicated in Table 2.2. In general, the total number of tables, and hence the amount of detail in the statistics on each topic or group, increased from 1961 to 1971, but was reduced somewhat for 1981 as a result of cuts in public expenditure. There are two ways of identifying suitable census data for a particular research topic. If the requirements can be specified fairly precisely, in terms of the variables to be cross-tabulated, the Census Customer Services units at OPCS or GRO(S) can be requested to identify the relevant tables. An index to the 1981 Census tables and statistics, and their equivalents from the 1971, 1966 and 1961 censuses, has been compiled by the Census Office in order to give a quick response to such data inquiries. The index can also identify 'near-miss' tables which satisfy almost all the user's requirements. Researchers who are less definite about their data needs can consult the published census volumes on the given topic and the CSO *Guide to Official Statistics* (which describes the content of each volume and also the unpublished tables), to get an idea of the type of data available. In either case the Census Office must be contacted for information on expected dates of publication or release of the 1981 Census results. Information from the early censuses is identified in the official guide to the published data from the 1801–1966 censuses, which lists, under fourteen headings, all the tables and the volumes in which they appear (OPCS and GRO(S), 1977). The CSO's *Guide* (1976, 1978, 1980) outlines the published and unpublished data from the 1966 and 1971 censuses. Edwards (1974) and Pickett (1974) outline the data from the 1951, 1961, 1966 and 1971 censuses with particular reference to the demographic characteristics of the population, housing and education in the former, and demographic, labour force and

Table 2.2 Data on the Non-Institutionalised Population Available from the Recent Censuses

	1961	1966	1971	1981
Sex	GB	GB	GB	GB
Age (in years and months)	GB	GB	GB	GB
Birthplace (in UK or overseas) of person	GB	GB	GB	GB
Birthplace of person's father and mother	—	—	GB	(GB)
Nationality	GB	—	—	—
Usual residence (in Britain or overseas)	GB	GB	GB	GB
Migration:				
– residence one year preceding census	GB	GB	GB	GB
– residence five years preceding census	—	GB	GB	—
Year of entry to Britain for those born outside UK	—	—	GB	—
Language spoken: Gaelic	S	—	S	S
Welsh	W	W	W	W
Family membership	GB	GB	GB	GB
Household membership	GB	GB	GB	GB
One-parent families/households	—	—	GB	GB
Dependent children in families/households	—	—	GB	GB
Characteristics of chief economic supporter	—	—	GB	GB
No. of earners in each household	—	—	GB	—
Household tenure	GB	GB	GB	GB
No. of cars and vans used by household	—	GB	GB	GB
Garaging for cars/vans	—	—	GB	—
Shared accommodation	—	GB	GB	—
No. of rooms in household	GB	GB	GB	GB
Density of occupation (persons per room)	GB	GB	GB	GB
Basic amenities: bath or shower	GB	GB	GB	GB
inside or outside WC	GB	GB	GB	GB
hot water	GB	GB	GB	GB
whether amenities shared	GB	GB	GB	GB
No. of dwellings and whether inhabited	GB	GB	GB	GB
Age on leaving full-time education	—	—	GB	(GB)

Table 2.2 Data on the Non-Institutionalised Population Available from the Recent Censuses – continued

	1961	1966	1971	1981
Educational qualifications: scientific and technical (of those aged 18 or over)	GB	GB	GB	GB
all higher education	—	GB	GB	GB
all qualifications	—	GB	GB	—
Economic activity status:				
in employment in week before census	GB	GB	GB	GB
out of work in week before census	GB	GB	GB	GB
retired	GB	GB	GB	GB
student (full-time)	GB	GB	GB	GB
inactive	GB	GB	GB	GB
Employment status of the economically active:				
employer	GB	GB	GB	GB
employee	GB	GB	GB	GB
working on own account	GB	GB	GB	GB
family worker	GB	GB	GB	GB
apprentice	GB	GB	GB	GB
Occupation (of the economically active and retired)	GB	GB	GB	GB
Industry (of those in employment)	GB	GB	GB	GB
Workplace (within or outside area of residence)	GB	GB	GB	GB
Working at home	—	—	GB	GB
Means of transport to work	—	GB	GB	GB
Occupation in second job (if any)	—	GB	GB	GB
Working full-time or part-time	GB	GB	—	GB
Weekly hours worked	(GB)	GB	GB	GB
Occupational mobility (occupation one year before the census)	—	GB	GB	GB
Income	—	(QMFS)	(IFS)	—
Work profile	—	—	(QMFS)	—

Key:
GB = Great Britain, E = England, W = Wales, S = Scotland
(GB) = limited information
IFS = Income Follow-Up Survey (see Table 2.3)
QMFS = Qualified Manpower Follow-Up Survey (see Tables 2.3 and 2.4)

education data in the latter. These two sources also consider the advantages and limitations of the census data as compared with other sources on these topics.

Even when certain variables or items of information have been included in the census processing plan, the data may in practice not be available because relevant tabulations were not produced. This happens most commonly in three situations. The data may be available at national level but not for the particular sub-national geographical area of interest; for example, the economic activity rates of women by age group are not available at local authority level. The data may not be available for the particular population sub-group or minority group of interest; for example, tables on the characteristics of one-parent families with dependent children, or on the employment and housing characteristics of ethnic minorities, are available from the 1971 Census, but not from the 1961 Census although the overall size of these two groups can be identified from the basic tables on household composition and birthplace. Thirdly, the variables of interest may not have been cross-tabulated even at the national level; for example, there are no tables on the economic activity profiles of households or families although there are separate detailed tables on the composition of households and families, and on the economic activity of individuals. When data are available in principle, but not in practice, there is the solution of requesting the Census Office to produce the required tables as special tabulations, as outlined in the next chapter.

The lack of census microdata for research purposes is discussed in Chapter 3 (p. 54), but its absence imposes major limitations on the range of data that are available in practice from the census, and hence the secondary research applications of the census. At present such work is limited to analyses of the tabulations produced by the Census Office, and these provide only aggregate statistics for areas of the country and for those population sub-groups identified in census classifications. The tabulations are often referred to as the 'results' of the census, but they are more appropriately regarded as *semi-processed data* which require secondary analysis to yield meaningful results, whether in a policy-oriented or theoretical context. This point is underlined by the fact that the reports on the recent censuses do not contain the commentaries on census results that figured prominently in the reports for 1801–1951 (Hakim, 1980b).

The topics covered by British censuses have tended to be more limited than in other industrialised countries (Redfern, 1981). The main reason appears to be that a wider range of matters are felt to be private than in other countries, and thus unsuitable for a compulsory census. The topics that have been included in censuses elsewhere, but not in Britain, include: religion, languages spoken, duration of unemployment, literacy, location of school or other educational establishment attended, ownership of durable consumer goods, rent paid for accommodation, area of floor space in housing unit, type of sewage disposal system, type of heating and energy used for heating, availability of telephone, number of floors in building and availability of a lift, income, race or ethnic group, holidays taken, child care services used, value of personal property, physical disabilities and number of marriages (Hakim, 1979a: 343). Of these, income and race (or ethnic group) are particularly desirable in a census, as they significantly enhance the research value of all the other data, but it has not so far proved possible to include them in a British census.

Data on immigrants and ethnic minorities have been collected only indirectly through questions on the country of birth of people and (in the 1971 Census) their parents. The inadequacy of the information was widely recognised, and a variety of new direct questions on nationality and ethnic group were tested for potential use in the 1981 Census, but were eventually not included (Sillitoe, 1978). Similarly a question on income was tested prior to the 1971 Census, but was not eventually included in the census. It was allocated instead to a voluntary census follow-up survey.

From Headcount to Census Survey

The earliest censuses (1801–31) took the form of simple headcounts, with the census enumerators responsible for recording the number of people and families at each address by sex and family occupation. Self-completion forms were first issued to households in 1841, so this is regarded as the first modern census (as defined by the United Nations), in allowing for individual enumeration. The purpose of the census as a survey of social and economic conditions was stated on the 1851 Census form:

> The Return is required to enable the Secretary of State to complete the Census; which is to show the number of the population – their arrangement by ages and families in different ranks, professions, employments and trades – their distribution over the country in villages, towns and cities – their increase and progress in the last ten years. (Hakim, 1979b: 135)

For the next century until 1951 the census remained virtually the only national survey of social conditions. The range of data collected was broadened, reflecting the widening responsibilities of government in housing, education, public health, transport, employment and regional development – until 1971, when the topic content of the census was at its broadest, and was further extended by two voluntary census-linked follow-up surveys. This progressive expansion of topics covered by a compulsory census was questioned in the 1970s, and it was argued that the regular and continuous national sample surveys developed since the 1950s might more appropriately supply some of the data collected through the census (Kish, 1979). The policy of household sample surveys providing both complementary and alternative data sources to the census became more explicit and formalised in the 1980s, with the 1981 Census meeting only those information needs that could not be met by national surveys – and the primary purpose of the census became recognised as supplying the need for comprehensive 'benchmark' data that provide the framework for the more regular but smaller surveys. Thus for the period 1801–1951 there are no alternatives to the census social statistics: from 1961 onwards there are an increasing number of complementary and alternative surveys and the census became the 'benchmark' data source rather than the primary source of social data.

Until 1951, in Britain and most other countries, the census was always a 100 per cent enumeration of the population. Since the 1950s sampling has featured increasingly in census work in most countries. In Britain census sampling has taken different forms in the 1961 and successive censuses. For the 1961 Census sampling was carried out in the field: enumerators were required to deliver an extended census form to every tenth household and a basic, or short, form to the remainder. Thus data from the 1961 Census consists of 100 per cent data on the basic topics covered in all forms and 10 per cent sample data on the additional topics covered in the longer form only. The quinquennial census taken in 1966 was a Ten Per Cent Sample Census, with sampling carried out in the field by enumerators, following a complete enumeration of addresses. Thus all the data from the 1966 Census is 10 per cent sample data. In order to avoid the errors involved in field sampling, the 1971 Census was based on 100 per cent enumeration with a single household form. Two samples were taken at the processing stage by the Census Office, a 10 per cent and a 1 per cent sample, and all the information on these forms was coded and processed. The coding and processing of the remainder of the forms was limited to those items on the census form that are defined as easy-to-code, excluding items such as occupation, industry and the location of the workplace. Thus the data from the 1971 Census include 100 per cent data on all the basic topics, plus 10 per cent and 1 per cent sample data on the hard-to-code topics: employment, household composition, travel to work, fertility and migration. A complex design of interlocking samples was prepared for the cancelled 1976 Census, but it is unlikely to be revived for any future census as it presented processing problems. The sampling for the 1971 Census was repeated in 1981.

The use of sampling in censuses illustrates the increasing methodological overlap between censuses and social surveys and highlights the fact that the compulsory nature of the census helps distinguish it from sample surveys (Hakim, 1979a: 344). In Germany the annual microcensus is based on a sample of households and is compulsory, while in some countries sample census questions may be allocated to a separate questionnaire or even to a separate second stage of the census after the main enumeration. For the secondary analyst, it means that checks should be made to ascertain precisely how census sampling was carried out and whether the sample data was collected as part of the compulsory census or as a separate voluntary follow-up survey. In general, census samples selected at the processing stage, and those which share the compulsory nature of the census, will provide more reliable data, and the British census samples share both these features. For further details see Newman (1978). One implication for the secondary analyst relates to the use of significance tests. These are not required for 100 per cent census data; they are rarely used by scholars even in relation to 10 per cent and 1 per cent sample data, because the size of these samples is so very much greater than the samples used in even the largest official national surveys (such as the GHS or LFS), and also because they are drawn from a universal enumeration which does not include any element of non-response. However, Census Office assessments of the degree of sampling error in the census samples (OPCS, 1978a: 63–78) suggest that this can be significant at sub-regional level, and statistical tests of significance should be applied to assess correlations and associations – a further indication of the methodological overlap between census and survey data.

Census-Related Social Data

Although separate from the compulsory census, follow-up surveys provide supplementary data which greatly extend the research applications of the data on particular topics. Substantive follow-up surveys must be distinguished from the coverage and quality (validation) checks that have been carried out immediately after each of the 1961–81 censuses (Gray and Gee, 1972), and from the occasional use of the census as a sampling frame for surveys that are otherwise unrelated (Hakim, 1979b: 146). So far substantive census-linked follow-up surveys have only been carried out on income and on qualified manpower (Table 2.3). The decision not to allow any follow-up surveys to the 1981 Census suggests that those carried out after the 1961, 1966 and 1971 censuses will remain the only sources of such data for some time to come.

The Income Follow-Up Survey (IFS) to the 1971 Census was carried out because questions on income were thought unsuitable for a compulsory census but acceptable in a voluntary sample survey. The exercise was postponed for a year and carried out as a postal survey in

Table 2.3 1971 Population Census and Voluntary Follow-Up Surveys

	Population Census 1971	Income Follow-Up Survey 1972	Qualified Manpower Follow-up Survey 1973
Sample characteristics	100% coverage of all persons in 18 million HHs and in all institutions	usually resident persons aged 15+ in a 1% sample of HHs (180,000 HHs) and a 1% sample of residents in institutions	1% or 2% samples of 5 groups of persons aged 18 or over: 3 groups of qualified persons and 2 groups of non-qualified persons[a]
Sample sizes	54 million persons	310,000 persons	5 samples of 2,800–21,000 persons[a]
Response rate	100%	40%	41%–65%
Results	100%, 10%, 1%	grossed up[b]	weighted[c]
Data collection	census day 24 April 1971	June 1972 (postal survey)	June 1973 (postal survey)
Reference periods for data on:			
– economic activity	week before census day	as for census	as for census plus employment history before the census for some samples
– income	—	year ended 5 April 1972	year ended 5 April 1972
– qualifications	whole life[d]	—	period after age 18

Notes:

The methodology of the two follow-up surveys is complex; only broad descriptions of the surveys are presented here.

a The QMFS covered people who, at the time of the 1971 Census, fell into one of five groups. See Table 2.4 for details.

b Results grossed up to 100 per cent response rate for follow-up survey on the basis of census information for non-respondents, thus correcting for differential non-response.

c Results weighted for differential sampling, with no adjustments made for differential response.

d Information on qualifications obtained at any age for all persons aged 15–70 and for those aged 70 or over who were still working.

June 1972, collecting information on personal and household income for the 1971/2 tax year which was merged with the census records for respondents. The response rate was poor, with full or partial information obtained from 50 per cent of the potential respondents. To correct for differential non-response, income data were imputed for non-respondents by matching them with respondents with similar characteristics as identified in the census. Thus the IFS data are presented for 100 per cent of the census sample of 1 per cent of all usually resident persons aged 15 or over living in households or in institutions. The size of the total sample is variously reported as 310,000 potential respondents, 345,000 forms sent out, and 407,466 persons aged 15 and over. Further details on the methodology of the exercise are given in the main report, which also assesses the reliability of the IFS data in comparison with other sources of data on earnings and income (including the 1971 and 1972 FES), and lists the tables available (OPCS, 1978b). The 1 per cent census sample used for the IFS was also used to produce the *1% Sample Summary Tables* published in 1972 (Edwards, 1974: 41). This report thus provides additional tables on the age, sex, marital status, birthplace and economic activity profile of the national sample for which IFS tables are presented, and can be used in conjunction with the IFS data. The IFS statistics can be used directly as a source of data on the incomes and earnings of persons or households, in particular for those groups that are inadequately represented in smaller surveys, such as students or the self-employed. It can also be used to supply additional information on the income correlates of census-derived social indicators, such as access to cars, basic amenities and tenure.

The Qualified Manpower Follow-Up Survey (QMFS) to the 1971 Census was carried out in June 1973. Samples of people in five categories were asked for further information on their work histories, qualifications and (in some cases) income in a postal survey, and the results were merged with census records on respondents. The sampling fractions, sample sizes, response rates and additional information collected varied between groups, but the survey was designed to allow comparisons between the groups described in Table 2.4, in particular between groups A and D, between groups B and E, and to provide additional information on group C. The results were not adjusted to account for differential response within each group, but were weighted up to yield data on the total within each group. The survey was carried out for the Department of Employment to provide supplementary data for research on the utilisation of qualified manpower, for example, to answer questions on the rate of return to higher education; the career paths, in-career training and deployment of qualified manpower; whether qualifications obtained were fully used; and the movement of qualified married women into and out of employment.

Table 2.4 *Qualified Manpower Follow-up Survey to the 1971 Census*

	Sampling fraction[a]	Sample size	Response rate	Response	Weighted results[b]
A qualified people aged 18–29 in employment:					18,190
– qualifications level a and b[c]	2%	10,767	47·8	5,144	
– qualifications level c only[c]	1%				
B qualified people aged 30 or over in employment:					58,160
– qualifications level a and b[c]	2%	21,443	61·9	13,280	
– qualifications level c only[c]	1%				
C qualified married women aged 30–59 not working (qualifications level a, b and c)					12,225
– original sample	not known	2,379	65·2	1,552	
– with booster sample	not known	4,517	65·2	2,811	
D non-qualified people aged 18–29 working in managerial and professional occupations[d]	1%	2,769	41·5	1,150	10,630
E non-qualified people aged 30 or over working in managerial and professional occupations[d]	1%	8,527	51·9	4,427	44,160
All respondents		48,023	55·8	26,812	143,365

Notes:

a Samples were taken from the 1971 Census 10 per cent sample with fully coded data.

b Results weighted for differential sampling, but with no adjustments for differential non-response, to yield 100 per cent data for each population sub-group.

c A qualified person is one holding at least one qualification at level a, b, or c:
  level a – high university degrees,
  level b – first degrees and equivalents,
  level c – post-school higher education qualifications below first degree level, including most teaching and nursing qualifications.

d Persons in Occupation Orders 24 and 25 in the Registrar General's *Classification of Occupations* (OPCS, 1970). The two samples of non-qualified people were incomplete by about 55 per cent in the case of group D and 33 per cent in the case of group E.

The OPCS report on the survey contains a list of available tables. The 1973 QMFS had a larger sample, a more complex design and more detailed information than the equivalent 1968 earnings follow-up survey to the 1966 Census (DES, 1971), which is regarded by Morris and Ziderman (1971) as the precursor to the 1972 IFS.

The Longitudinal Study (1%) is based on merging 1971 Census information for a 1 per cent sample of the population with other information already held by OPCS, for example, birth and death registration, notifications of cases of cancer, internal and overseas migration as reflected in change of address in national health service records. The study aims to provide a dynamic population sample by updating the original sample with a 1 per cent sample of those recorded as being born in or migrating to Britain after 1971, and information on the sample from the 1981 and future censuses will be added to the dataset. The Longitudinal Study is designed to provide a source of national statistics on fertility, mortality, migration and occupational mobility (OPCS, 1973b). So far few data have been published from the study, although a study of mortality is in preparation (Goldblatt and Fox, 1978; Fox, 1979). It is noted here because it will be an important and unique source of longitudinal data in future decades, that will be of particular interest for certain types of secondary research. In the shorter term, after the 1981 Census data are added to the study, it will provide information on changes in the circumstances of individuals over the decade 1971–81. As the majority of the variables in the dataset are census-derived, the research potential of the study is determined by the content of future censuses. Some indication of the size and characteristics of the LS sample can be obtained from the 1971 Census report *1% Sample Summary Tables*; although the two samples were taken separately, using different methods, they are both 1 per cent samples.

International Perspectives

As noted above, the British census has covered a more limited range of topics than censuses elsewhere, the most notable exclusions being income and race or ethnic group (Bulmer, 1980a; Redfern, 1981). The main implication is that some cross-national comparative research which would rely on census data for other countries would need to use a source other than the British census if income was to be included as a variable, for example, the GHS and FES described in Chapter 7, or, if time was not a significant variable, the IFS data. However, the data available from the IFS are extremely limited in comparison with the income data from the United States and Canada censuses, for example. With this proviso, census-based comparative studies are often easier than with other sources, due to the increasing standardisation of population censuses, in terms of the topics on which basic and additional data are collected, the definitions and classifications applied, and the timing of censuses in the first two years of each decade. International comparisons are facilitated by the official publications of international organisations which collate comparative data from censuses (and other) sources – such as the International Labour Office's *Yearbook of Labour Statistics*, the United Nations *Demographic Yearbook* and *Compendium of Social Statistics*, and EEC and OECD publications. These publications provide minimal notes on the comparability of the statistics and on national differences in definitions and universes, but there is a need for more detailed guides to comparative data from national censuses to complement the guides to census data for particular countries. Blake and Donovan (1971) provide a detailed guide to the published data from the 1960/1 censuses for nineteen Western European countries. Some of the United Nations reports on census work are valuable sources of information on the type of information collected in each country, but they provide little guidance on the available statistical results and how they might be obtained. National census offices do not always produce user-oriented guides to the available data, although there are good guides to the USA censuses (for example, Carter, 1976). Within the EEC, the Statistical Office of the European Communities (SOEC) has been working towards the harmonisation of censuses taken in the member countries, and collates comparative census statistics (SOEC, 1978). It is likely that the SOEC will also publish reports on migration patterns between EEC countries based on census results, and on other topics which require this comparative approach.

3

Census Statistics

Until 1951 all the output of the censuses was published in book format. The number of volumes increased from three in 1801 to eleven in 1901, and then to over a hundred in 1951 with 8,000 pages of tables. After this the formats for the release of census data were diversified to include magnetic tape, microfilm, computer printout and loose pages of printed tables, all of which are commonly referred to as the unpublished tables or data. The total output from the 1971 Census amounted to 1.6 million pages of tables of which only 38,000, or 2·3 per cent of the total were presented in the published volumes (Hakim, 1978d: 8). Users of census statistics are often aware only of one part or type of the whole range of census output.

Types of Census Data

The most widely known and accessible type of census data is the *statistical volumes* published by HMSO and available in libraries. These are divided into the series of national reports which group tables under about a dozen topic headings (housing, economic activity, qualified manpower, and so forth) and the series of county reports which provide a range of census statistics on all topics for each of the counties on a consistent basis. For the 1971 Census there are a number of volumes giving summaries of the census results, such as the *1% Sample Summary Tables* and *Housing Summary*. Separate volumes describe the methodology of each census, and provide documentation on the data produced with details on the definitions, classifications and coding procedures applied. The *General Report* volumes for the recent censuses are essentially methodological and do not contain the commentaries found in the reports for 1801–1951 (see pp. 83ff.).

OPCS has expanded its range of publications in recent years and there are now a variety of other publications which present basic census results, detailed analyses of the census data, reviews of census usage in particular fields and reports on census methodological research. Some of these are available through HMSO; others are only obtainable from the Census Office. A *Guide* available from OPCS (1980a) lists all the 1971 Census published volumes (with brief descriptions of their content) and all other published material from OPCS on the census and resulting data. It is updated and extended by the leaflet 'Publishing Calendar: Censuses' produced annually by OPCS since 1978. This includes references to all Parliamentary Questions on the census and on the availability of census statistics. All major publications on the census are reviewed in the census series of OPCS *Monitors*, a newsletter for census users issued about eight times a year. The *Census Monitors* are also the main source of information on the availability of unpublished census data and they periodically present summary census results on particular topics. Another OPCS guide lists all UK libraries holding census volumes and other data (OPCS, 1980b). All these OPCS guides, leaflets and newsletters are available free on request from OPCS Information Branch in London (see address on p. 60).

Census *Small Area Statistics* (SAS) are the most widely used type of unpublished data. The SAS were originally modelled on the USA Census Bureau's census tract data, and have been developed in response to demand from local authorities, the academic community, market research organisations, central government and related organisations. The 1971 SAS consist of a standard set of tables and statistics (1,600 data cells in total) available for each of the 125,000 enumeration districts (EDs), 17,000 wards or parishes, 1,700 old local authorities, 450 new districts and increasingly large areas including finally the Great Britain totals (Figure 3.1). The census EDs are the basic building blocks of the SAS, consisting of areas with an average population of around 500 and an average of about 160 (120–220) households in urban areas and 100 households (or 50–180) in rural areas. The EDs can be aggregated to produce statistics for standard areas such as parliamentary constituencies and local authorities (Figure 3.2), or *ad hoc* areas defined by the researcher such as social service team areas in local authorities; school catchment areas; council estates; catchment areas for hospitals, railway stations, cinemas, or retail outlets; transport planning areas; or local communities however defined. In addition to the standard 1971 SAS, additional tables (known as Appendix C tables) providing further detail on New Commonwealth immigrants, household tenure and fertility are available for user-specified aggregates of EDs with a population of 2,500 or more; the equivalent Great Britain totals are given in published reports. Hakim (1978b) gives further details on the design of the 1971 SAS and presents the 1971 Great Britain totals. Newman (1978) describes the method of quasi-random error injection applied to the 1971 and (with some modification) 1981 SAS in order to protect confidentiality.

The 1981 SAS are modelled on the lines of the 1971 SAS, but the content of the tables differs: in some respects it is more limited since

Areal units for which census data is produced | Data dissemination sources

GREAT BRITAIN

NATIONAL REPORTS FOR EACH OF THE FOLLOWING TOPICS:-

ECONOMIC ACTIVITY   HOUSING
HOUSEHOLD COMPOSITION   POPULATION
COUNTRY OF BIRTH   MIGRATION
USUAL RESIDENCE   FERTILITY
WELSH LANGUAGE
QUALIFIED MANPOWER
AVAILABILITY OF CARS
NON-PRIVATE HOUSEHOLDS
PERSONS OF PENSIONABLE AGE
WORKPLACE AND TRANSPORT TO WORK
AGE, MARITAL CONDITION AND GENERAL

SCOTLAND   ENGLAND   WALES

There are published, unpublished and special tables for each topic

17 REGIONS

- -

COUNTY REPORTS PRODUCED FOR BOTH OLD AND NEW AREAS

92 COUNTIES   66 COUNTIES
4 CITIES   Metropolitan and Non-Metropolitan
            (Local Government Regions and
            Island Areas in Scotland)

ECONOMIC ACTIVITY LEAFLETS

Abbreviated SAS for new and old Parliamentary Constituencies and for new Counties and Districts

1,765 LOCAL AUTHORITIES   455 DISTRICTS

There are also published, unpublished and special tables for some of the topics listed above

- -

STANDARD SMALL AREA STATISTICS (WARD LIBRARY) AND RELATED DATA PRODUCTS:-

Appendix C tables
Market Research Society Ward Indices
National samples of EDs and Wards/Parishes
Ratio lines
SAS aggregate tapes for both old and new LAs

17,723 WARDS AND PARISHES
(or County Council Electoral Divisions in Scotland)

125,475 ENUMERATION DISTRICTS

There are also some unpublished and special tables for some of the topics listed above

Source: Hakim, 1978d.

Figure 3.1   *Summary of census areas, 1971 and 1981.*

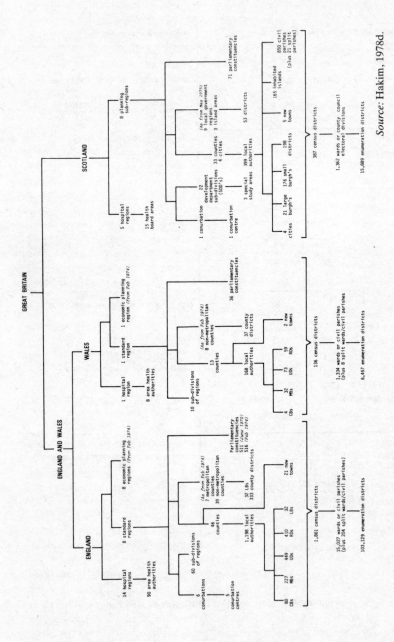

Figure 3.2   Detailed census areas, 1971.

Source: Hakim, 1978d.

less information was collected in the 1981 than the 1971 Census; in other respects the SAS provide more detailed social statistics. As a result of the more extensive consultation with census users the 1981 SAS are geared more closely to the secondary research applications of census SAS. Tables 3.1 and 3.2 illustrate the type of data available in the 1971 and 1981 SAS. Further detail on the 1981 SAS is given in the *Census Monitors*, especially CEN 80/8.

More limited SAS are available for 1961 and 1966. The standard 1961 SAS were produced for all wards and parishes in Britain; they were only produced at ED level when specially requested by specific users, usually local authorities – so the ED level SAS does not offer complete national coverage for 1961. The 1966 SAS provide national coverage at ED level and ward/parish level, but the statistics are limited to the 10 per cent sample results of that census. Thus for some local authorities inter-censal comparisons at either ED or ward/parish level are feasible for 1961–71–81. In practice such comparisons are easier for aggregates of small areas as the boundaries of EDs change almost completely between censuses, and the boundaries of electoral wards and parishes tend also to change over time. The ED boundaries for each census are determined in collaboration with local authorities, and are designed where possible to coincide with socially meaningful neighbourhoods and communities. The ED boundaries for the 1981 Census were also designed (when so requested by local authorities) to be as compatible as possible with 1971 ED boundaries (for example by splitting or combining the 1971 EDs rather than redefining them from scratch) and over half of 1971 EDs were repeated unchanged for 1981 (Denham, 1980: 10). Thus 1971–81 comparisons for small areas within authorities are usually easier than for 1961–71.

The census SAS are released in three formats: on magnetic tape, on microfilm and as loose sheets of printed tables. Data for substantial areas (such as a local authority) are usually supplied on tape; data for a small number of areas are usually supplied as printed sheets of statistics.

For the 1971 Census alone the SAS are also available for national grid squares on magnetic tape only (OPCS, 1977b). The data were produced as standard output for 1km and 10km grid squares and, when specially requested by a user, for 100m grid squares for the area in question. Thus national coverage is not offered at 100m level. Aside from their use in planning exercises at the national level (for example, by the BBC in planning the location of radio and TV transmitters), the data are primarily of interest to geographers. They have been used to produce a 1971 Census atlas for Britain which is of wider interest to SAS analysts, as it presents national maps for a number of widely used social and community indicators derived from the SAS (OPCS, 1980e). The grid square data are not available for the 1981 Census as

SMALL AREA STATISTICS (WARD LIBRARY)   10% SAMPLE   CENSUS 1971

* BIRMINGHAM CB

* CENTRAL PART OUTSIDE C.C.

123   1234/A01   SU 123456

22

ONE YEAR MIGRANTS WITHIN L.A.

Age	S.W.D. Married Males	Married Males	S.W.D. Married Females	Married Females	ONE YEAR MIGRANTS INTO L.A. S.W.D. Males	Married Males	S.W.D. Females	Married Females
1–								
5–								
15–								
25–								
35–								
45–								
65+ 60+								
Total								

FIVE YEAR MIGRANTS WITHIN L.A.   FIVE YEAR MIGRANTS INTO L.A.

Age
5–
15–
25–
35–
45–
65+ 60+
Total

24 HOURS OF WORK OF WOMEN IN EMPLOYMENT

Marr. women with children aged under 5

Women's Age	All women <8hrs 8-30hrs >30hrs	Married women <8hrs 8-30hrs >30hrs	<8hrs 8-30hrs >30hrs
15–			
25–			
35–			
45–			
60+			
Wkg in LAA			
Wkg ex LAA			

26

S.E.G. of h/hold head	HEAD 5 YEAR MIGRANT WITHIN L.A. H/holds Persons	HEAD 5 YEAR MIGRANT INTO L.A. H/holds Persons	TOTAL Cars & Vans
1 2 13			
3 4			
5 6			
8 9 12 14			
7 10 15			
11			
16 17			
Total			
inc. N.C.			

23 ECONOMICALLY ACTIVE OR RETIRED BY S.E.G. OF HEAD

S.E.G.	H/holds Persons	S.E.G. OF HEAD Persons	ECONOMICALLY ACTIVE Males Females	Married Females	PERSONS IN EMPLOYMENT With O/M or school Cert or HND Al level degree in yr.	With change of Occupn in yr.	Wkg ex LA	PERSONS ACTIVE BUT NOT IN EMP.	RET'D MALES
1									
2									
3									
4									
5									
6									
7									
8									
9									
10									
11									
12									
13									
14									
15									
16									
17									
Total									

INACTIVE   NOT IN EMP.

	NEVER ACTIVE
Students	
Women <60	
Others	
Total	

25 NUMBER OF FAMILIES WITH NUMBER OF DEPENDENT CHILDREN

	0	1	2	3	4	5+
Lone parent						
Married couple						

28 INDUSTRY OF EMPLOYED PERSON

Grouped S.E.G.	TRAVEL TO WORK BY Car Bus Train M'Cycle P/Cycle Foot & P/Cycle Other & not stated none	Agri. Mining Manuf. Const. Transport Utilities Distrib. Comm. Services Nat & Loc Govt & Def
1 2 13		
3 4		
5 6		
8 9		
7 10 15		
11		
12 14		
16 17		

CROWN COPYRIGHT

Record 1 consists of Sections 22 & 23.   Record 2 consists of Sections 24 & 28 inclusive.

Table 3.1 1971 Small Area Statistics: Illustrative Extract

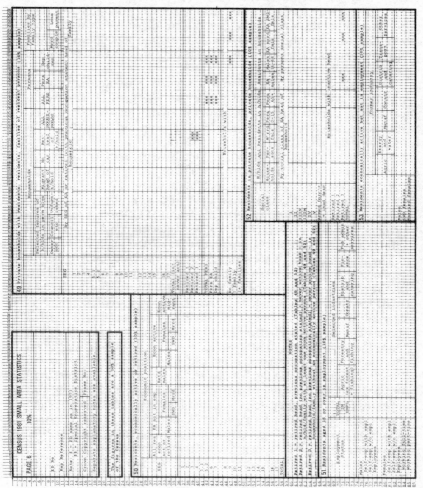

Table 3.2   1981 Small Area Statistics: Illustrative Extract

the level of usage was judged insufficient to justify the production costs.

In the late 1970s the advantages of postcodes for area definition began to be recognised: they offer national coverage and a hierarchy of areal units, and the smallest units cover smaller, and hence more flexible, basic building blocks for the definition of *ad hoc* areas than even the census EDs (Denham, 1980). A computerised postcode directory, relating postcodes to (new) wards and grid references, has been used by OPCS and other government departments since 1980. The directory may be made available to researchers outside central government, thus facilitating the linkage of census SAS to area-coded data from other sources.

Grid square SAS were specifically designed to facilitate area-based studies as at the national level, while the SAS for EDs and wards/parishes are most commonly used for studies at the local level. However, a number of SAS by-products facilitate the use of the data at the national level also.

Two geographically balanced, nationally representative samples of 4,000 EDs and of 4,000 wards/parishes have been produced from the 1971 SAS. These are available as separate sub-sets of the national SAS on magnetic tape. The only equivalent from any other census is the national 2 per cent sample of EDs from the 1851 Census created by the PRO and Anderson *et al.* (1977) (p. 88), and this contains microdata rather than aggregate statistics as in the 1971 SAS samples.

The 1971 national SAS samples were first used by Webber to produce two national socio-economic classifications of small areas, one at ED level, another at ward/parish level. The study was based on multi-variate analysis of a standard set of 40 socio-economic indicators derived from the SAS along lines. similar to the social area analysis studies first developed in the United States (Shevky and Bell, 1955). Once the area classifications (or typologies) had been developed on the basis of the 40 diagnostic indicators, values for a further 260 indicators were added to the dataset, so that the areas can be compared and contrasted on a total of 300 social indicators. The exercise was repeated for SAS aggregates: for all parliamentary constituencies and for all new (post-1974) local authority districts in Britain. Further details on the methodology, results and applications of the four 1971 social area classifications are given in the main reports (Webber, 1977; Webber and Craig, 1978; Webber, 1978a; Webber, 1979) which also list the numerous other publications on the work. It is likely that the national area classifications will be repeated with the 1981 SAS, either independently of, or in collaboration with, the Census Office. Given the high degree of comparability between 1971 and 1981 ED boundaries (noted above), it will be possible to assess changes in the social area classification of small areal units. The 1971 social area classifications are not available from the Census Office but from the census agencies described below (pp. 56–7).

Apart from the *County Report* series, most of the tables in the published census reports present analyses at national or regional level only. A large number of these tables are also available for local authorities and other sub-regional areas in the unpublished formats. *Standard unpublished tables* are those routinely produced for all areal units of a given type, such as parliamentary constituencies, local authorities, new towns and conurbations. Researchers and organisations whose data needs are not met by the standard unpublished tables may request *special (ad hoc) analyses* of census results, all of which are equally available to any other researcher. In most cases the special tables are designed to meet the customer's special needs and they are often produced for just one part of the country, so that they are of restricted interest for secondary analysis. However, some of the special analyses yield national tables that supplement the standard fare of unpublished tables and are of potential use in secondary analysis. The unpublished tables are usually released on microfilm or as computer printout. They are always identified in lists of census tables and in the index to census output described earlier (p. 33) by the suffix U after the table number.

The census *travel-to-work (workplace) and migration analyses* constitute a more specialised type of unpublished data designed primarily for local authorities and so far little used in secondary analyses by other researchers. The published tables on travel-to-work patterns are based on the coding of usual residence and workplace addresses to local authority areas, and hence identify movements between local authority areas. When requested by local authorities or other users, travel-to-work statistics are produced using finer geographical detail in the coding of areas of origin (usual residence) and destination (workplace), allowing daily travel patterns within (as well as between) local authorities to be studied. The unpublished data also include variables (such as sex) which are not distinguished in the published reports, allowing finer detail in secondary analyses – for example, of social class and sex differentials in daily travel-to-work patterns and in the mode of transport used. The unpublished data are released on magnetic tape only, for the 1971 and following censuses, and do not give national coverage. Unpublished data on patterns of migration are available on the same basis as the travel-to-work analyses. These data attract wider interest among secondary analysts, perhaps because migration is an established topic within demography, whereas the travel-to-work patterns arising from the separation of home and workplace and the provision of public transport systems tend to be regarded as the concern of urban and transport planners rather than social scientists.

Unlike the United States Bureau of the Census, Statistics Canada and other census organisations, the Census Office in Britain has never released *census microdata tapes* – that is, tapes for public use containing detailed census information for an anonymous sample of persons, families and/or households. The example of the 1 per cent and 0·1 per cent Public Use Samples released from the 1960 and 1970 USA censuses has led to the suggestion that similar tapes be created from earlier American censuses (Mason *et al.*, 1977) and from the census results for Britain and other countries (Hakim, 1978a; Flaherty, 1979). The Census Office has considered the viability of this type of output in terms of confidentiality constraints, design and potential usage (Hakim, 1979b: 145). There are at present no plans to develop or release sample microdata from any of the recent censuses, although the option is not completely ruled out. Microdata would offer a significant addition to census output, particularly for secondary analysis by social scientists, whose data requirements are less predictable than with the policy and planning applications of census statistics. The flexibility offered by microdata would significantly enhance the census's potential for secondary research on social and ethnic minorities such as one-parent families, the unemployed, people working at home, students and people of New Commonwealth descent. However, the lack of income data from the census would limit the secondary analysis potential of British microdata compared with North American usage. Sample microdata have been created by the Census Office from the 1971 Census. They were used to produce the *1% Summary Tables* published before the full results became available. The 1971 Census 1 per cent sample tape can be regarded as a second-best alternative to microdata. Analyses of the tape still have to be requested from and produced by the Census Office, as the tape is not publicly available – but the cost of special analyses of this tape is much less than with the 10 per cent or 100 per cent data, and the turn-around time is also much less. A similar 1 per cent tape could be produced from the 1981 results (and even the 1961 Census), if there was sufficient demand from census users.

Further information on and documentation for the published reports are given in OPCS (1970), OPCS and GRO(S) (1977), OPCS (1978a) and OPCS (1980c). Further information and documentation on the unpublished data from the census are given in Hakim (1978d), in a number of OPCS papers listed in Hakim (1978c) and in the CSO *Guide to Official Statistics* (1976, 1978, 1980).

Data Dissemination and Related Services

In parallel with the expansion in statistical output from the recent censuses there has been a notable increase in census usage outside central government and in the range of data dissemination and analysis services available from other organisations. The Census Office remains the primary disseminator of census data, but a number of other organisations function as secondary distributors and offer related secondary analysis services.

The Census Office (OPCS in England and Wales and GRO(S) in Scotland) is the main source of information on the design and methodology of each census, documentation for the resulting statistics, the availability of census data (on particular topics and for stated areas of the country) and the primary source of all unpublished data. Statistics released as printed tables or computer printout pose no problems of access. Microfilm versions are released on 16mm and 35mm film, requiring a reader or reader/printer. Magnetic tape versions are released in the form used for census processing within OPCS, currently 9-track tapes. The tapes are not converted to be compatible with the user's computer installation and the tape conversion services of a computer bureau may be required. The Census Office does not provide software for the analysis of census data tapes, as it is considered that such services are more appropriately offered by census agencies and other organisations. The main demand has been for software suitable for analysing the magnetic tape versions of the SAS and SAS derivatives (such as the national SAS samples). Some local authorities produced their own software to handle the 1971 SAS, but there are major differences between the 1971 and 1981 SAS. LAMSAC (the Local Authorities' Management Services and Computer Committee) produced a special package for the analysis of the 1981 SAS, available on subscription.

Unless one uses published reports available in libraries, census data always cost money. The Census Act 1920 requires that the costs of supplying the unpublished statistics be recouped from users. In this respect census data differ from other official data, which are often supplied free of charge (see pp. 107, 111). Costs depend on the particular type and quantity of statistics; estimates can be obtained from Census Customer Services before an order is placed. In general, costs are lowest for widely used output (such as the SAS), and highest for special tabulations produced on request for a particular research project. It should be noted that users of census SAS need also to purchase the census maps showing ED and ward/parish boundaries if a particular locality is to be studied. Up to 1971 the census maps were relatively cheap; with the increased costs of Ordnance Survey maps the 1981 maps are more expensive. Although many types of census data, in particular SAS, are available from other sources, the census maps can only be obtained from the Census Office.

The OPCS headquarters in London also offers a number of services to individuals and organisations engaged in census-based secondary research. A series of *Census Monitors* have been issued since 1978 by

OPCS, providing a link between the Census Office and census users. The *Census Monitors* present information on the development and design of each census and its output; the availability of census output; relevant publications, meetings and research projects; and summaries of the census results. They are circulated free on request to some 3,000 census users inside and outside government by OPCS Information Branch. Research advice can be given on secondary analyses of data from the recent censuses. OPCS occasionally engages in collaborative research with other organisations to develop innovative analyses and applications of census (and other) data, as exemplified by the national social area classifications described above. The Census Use Study provides a bibliographical index of all major published and many unpublished secondary analyses of census data which are of interest both substantively and as exemplars of the methodology of census-based secondary analysis. This index, and copies of the research reports listed, are available at the OPCS library in London by arrangement with the Census Office. This library also holds all published census reports for Britain; national census reports for EEC, Commonwealth and other countries; and related material of interest to secondary analysts. The complete 1971 SAS are held on microfilm at the library and are accessible to researchers who want to extract a limited number of figures from the SAS, or to investigate the SAS content before placing an order with Census Customer Services. Census ED maps are also available for reference on microfilm.

The accessibility of census SAS would be greatly extended if local libraries held copies of census SAS for their localities, but at present few do. Some major libraries, including the British Library Reference Divison (Official Publications), hold the complete 1966 and 1971 SAS. However, most libraries hold only published reports and no unpublished census statistics.

Local authorities usually hold SAS for their area of responsibility, and often act as secondary distributors of SAS or other census data to local water and health authorities – more so in recent years following the Census Office's relaxation of copyright arrangements for local authorities. Some local authorities, such as the GLC, offer a broader census data dissemination and analysis service which is accessible to non-government researchers, and publish methodological reports as well as summaries and analyses of census data for their area of responsibility. The DoE also plays a major role in census data dissemination to local authorities, in the form of methodological guidelines for secondary analysis, the development of software packages for use outside central government, the provision of mapping services for census (and other) data, the national analyses of SAS and other census data which provide the backcloth to local studies.

Census agencies are organisations with an explicit policy of offering census data dissemination and analysis services to all potential users. Some, such as CACI, are commercial organisations; others, such as the SSRC Survey Archive, are non-profit institutions. However, both types are required to collect, on behalf of the Census Office, the basic royalty fees charged for all unpublished census statistics.

The SSRC Survey Archive holds the complete SAS for Great Britain for the 1966, 1971 and following censuses on magnetic tape. The service is limited to data retrieval and no analysis can be carried out for researchers. But the datasets produced for researchers can consist of selected SAS data cells (from which social indicators can be derived) for selected areas or the whole country, or the complete SAS for selected areas (for example, cities). A major advantage is that the data are supplied in a format compatible with the user's own computer installation and in an SPSS file format, a service not offered by the Census Office. The Archive holds a variety of other data files derived from SAS and other census data for 1951–71, including Webber's social area classification, and a number of multi-source datasets containing social, economic, health, electoral and other indicators as well as census-derived indicators for all local authorities. These and foreign census data files are described in the Archive's leaflet *Inventory of Census Holdings*. The Archive periodically holds data-use workshops on the secondary analysis possibilities of its census holdings.

The Archive does not hold the 1971 SAS in grid-square format. The 1971 grid-square data for Britain are available free of charge to all members of the Institute of British Geographers via the Census Research Unit (CRU) at Durham University, which functions as a data archive in this single respect. As the CRU has carried out extensive analyses of the data, and produced an atlas for Britain for the Census Office (OPCS, 1980e), it can also provide advice on the secondary analysis of census grid-square data, some of which are presented in a number of Working Papers available from the CRU.

The London-based CACI is a subsidiary of an American company that offers extensive data analysis services in relation to the United States census output, including the Public Use Samples. CACI holds the complete SAS for the 1971 and following censuses. Its data retrieval package, SITE, allows census SAS to be aggregated for *ad hoc* areas of any shape or size defined by the client, for areas within a specified radius of a specific location, or for standard administrative areas. It is well suited to providing census profiles of catchment areas of, for example, schools, hospitals, railway stations, retail outlets, banks and other public or commercial services. The SITE area profiles include current population estimates compiled by CACI from electoral roll counts and other sources from 1978 onwards, and Webber's four social area classifications. A variety of data analysis services have been developed around the SITE system and Webber's classification of small areas (known as ACORN), all designed primarily for market research and analysis applications, although some could equally be applied in social science research. These and other data analysis services are described in CACI's brochures available from its London office at 289 High Holborn, WC1.

The British Market Research Bureau provides one example of the data services that are being built on to the ACORN classification. The BMRB has extended Webber's social area classification by linking in the results of its national consumer survey (the Target Group Index). The combined dataset contains population, housing and socio-economic indicators derived from the census and measures of consumer behaviour, media usage, leisure activities and financial behaviour derived from the BMRB survey for each of the social area types. It has proved to be an effective dataset for market analysis and also a successful framework for area sampling for market research and social surveys. While BMRB's data analysis services are currently geared primarily to market research, the social area typology has potential applications in social research as well. Existing and potential services are described in a number of papers available from BMRB's London office at The Mall, Ealing, W5.

Further information on census data dissemination and related services offered by OPCS and other organisations is available in Hakim (1978d), the OPCS series of *Census Monitors*, and from the organisations themselves. The OPCS series of Occasional Papers provides additional detail on census methodology, comparisons of the advantages and limitations of census and other sources of data on particular topics, bibliographies on the census and reviews of the secondary research applications of census data including the social area classifications (Newman, 1978; Hakim, 1977, 1978a, b, c, d; OPCS, 1979; Webber, 1979).

Given the wide range of census output and census-derived datasets, the multitudinous publications on census statistics and their secondary analysis applications, the growth of secondary distributors and census agencies and the services they offer, the process of identifying and obtaining the most appropriate data for a secondary research project can be complicated. For most researchers the best starting point will be the published reports, to gain an idea of the type of statistics and the classifications used in them, and also, through the *General Report*, of possible pitfalls in the census concepts, definitions and classifications which may not always suit the research requirements. Previous secondary analyses on a particular topic indicate the solutions to conceptual or practical problems devised by other researchers. When research requires data that cannot be extracted or derived from existing tabulations and must be produced as *ad hoc* output, then the time-lag and costs involved in requesting a special tabulation must be considered. Special tabulations based on the 1971 1 per cent sample offer a cheaper alternative to special runs based on the 10 per cent or 100 per cent tapes. The SSRC provides grants for special tabulations from the census that will then be available to other researchers as well. The datasets and services offered by the census agencies are complementary to those offered by the Census Office, and are of particular interest in relation to the area-based research described in Chapter 5. An important point to bear in mind is that all census output can be regarded as *semi-processed data*. Secondary analysis involves the identification, extraction and processing of the particular statistics relevant to a project. Ehrenberg's (1975) review of approaches to data reduction (that is, abstracting information from statistical tables and the presentation of meaningful summaries in tabular or diagrammatic form) is particularly relevant to census analyses. Data reduction can be a manual process (with a calculator) or be computerised, but either way researchers often fail to allocate sufficient time for this job in their initial research timetable. In this context the speedy turn-around offered by commercial census agencies can be attractive to some census users. Another significant point is that the British census offices do not have the large units specialising in servicing census users that are found in North American and some European census offices. The resources devoted to services for users are limited, and this can lead to delays on complex data inquiries and requests. Due allowance should be made in research timetables.

International Perspectives

The published census reports of all EEC, most Commonwealth and some other countries are available in the OPCS library; comparative statistics are presented in the publications of international organisations (see p. 44). There is one detailed guide, now somewhat dated, to the published data from the European censuses (Blake and Donovan, 1971), and information on census output (and other data sources) is given in the series of reviews of national primary socio-economic data structures for particular countries in the *International Social Science Journal* from 1977 onwards. Relevant information is also contained in the *ISSJ*'s section on socio-economic data bases (see, for example, Goldstone, 1977) and in some texts on sources and methods for particular disciplines (in particular demography). However, none of these sources indicates the extent of unpublished data available from a census, in partciular whether SAS-equivalent data for small areas are produced.

Census offices throughout the world are increasingly disseminating data in machine-readable format as well as in published reports. The SSRC Survey Archive holds a number of foreign census data files (for example, for the USA and Brazil). It has links with North American achives, some of which specialise in international data, with extensive foreign census holdings (for example, for Latin American countries). Census data files for particular countries in Europe or North America can often be obtained through the Archive's contacts with national archives in these countries. Direct contact with the foreign census office in question can be helpful, as some produce guides to their census output (published and unpublished), and some will produce special tabulations if requested. Some census offices, such as the United States Bureau of the Census, Statistics Canada and the Institut National de Statistiques et d'Etudes Economiques (INSEE) in France, have a network of regional data dissemination and user services offices, but international requests are usually handled at headquarters level, or referred to census agencies where appropriate. Within the USA the non-profit DUALabs and commercial CACI are perhaps the most important census agencies, offering data analysis services in relation to the census Public Use Samples that are not available for Britain. In some European countries, such as Norway and Italy, the national archives for social science data (Table 11.1, p. 165) have specialised in developing census-derived datasets and analytical services (Rokkan, 1976; Martinotti, 1978).

One general problem in locating census data for other countries is the lack of standard terminology for the newer types of unpublished census output. In the case of census sample microdata, there is a tendency to use the term Public Use Sample, or to make explicit comparisons with the United States PUS tapes, as these provide the original model for similar output elsewhere, even when the content and structure of the tapes differ. (For example, the Canadian PUS tapes consist of three separate files for persons, for families and for households, so that the hierarchical character of the census microdata is not preserved as in the United States PUS tapes.) But in the case of other unpublished data, there is a tendency for each census office to use its own terminology, and this can inhibit communication. For example, the equivalent to census SAS in Britain is termed census tract data in the United States, and census *sept-pages* in France (because the SAS are printed on seven pages for each small area). It is to be hoped that international organisations involved in census work (such as the UN and EEC) will extend their concern with the standardisation of methods, concepts and classifications to the standardisation of the output from each census and the related terminology for data products.

Contact Points for Census Data and Related Material
Census Information Unit, OPCS, St Catherine's House, 10 Kingsway, London
    WC2B 6JP. Tel: 01-242-0262, ext. 2217.

Census Customer Services, OPCS, Segensworth Road, Titchfield, Fareham, Hampshire PO15 5RR. Tel: Titchfield (03294) 42511, ext. 295/231/296/273.

Census Customer Services, General Register Office for Scotland, Ladywell House, Ladywell Road, Edinburgh EH12 7TF. Tel: Edinburgh (031) 334-6854, ext. 25.

SSRC Survey Archive, University of Essex, Colchester, Essex. Tel: Colchester (0206) 860570 or 862286, ext. 2244.

4

Using the Census: National Studies

The census is used extensively by social scientists in universities and in central and local government as a multi-purpose information base. The aim in this and the following chapter is not so much to offer a review and summary of these research applications as to discuss illustrative examples of the secondary research potential of census output. Here the focus is on studies at the national level, including national studies of regional differences. In Chapter 5 the focus is on sub-regional studies, although many local studies are set in a national context since the census offers data at both levels. The examples have been selected to illustrate the full range of census-based secondary research, and the potential of each type of census output: published reports, unpublished tables, travel-to-work and migration data, follow-up surveys, the longitudinal study and, in the following chapter, SAS, grid-square data and local authority tables. The examples relate to the most recent censuses, including studies of inter-censal change at both the national and local levels; studies using long time-series and comparisons across centuries are discussed in Chapter 6. Readers who wish to obtain further information on the research applications of census data in particular fields should consult the extensive Census Use Study bibliographical index compiled by OPCS and described in the *Census Monitors*, or the OPCS Occasional Papers which draw on this.

Labour Force Reseach

The census is routinely used as a source of data on the size, composition, and industrial and occupational structure of the labour force (as illustrated by articles in the *Department of Employment Gazette* and Payne, 1977). It shares with the major national surveys (see Chapter 7), the advantages of household surveys over administrative records (or surveys of employers based on their records) as a source of labour force data (Bosanquet and Standing, 1972; Hakim 1980a). Until the LFS was instituted the census offered the only source of national data on the self-employed, and it continues to provoke benchmark data on labour force minorities (such as the self-employed, apprentices, the unemployed) to supplement the data from more frequent but smaller-scale household surveys such as the LFS and GHS. It is regularly used as the comprehensive data base for the development of projections for the labour force as a whole or for particular sub-groups, such as highly qualified manpower; and it routinely provides the statistical backcloth on the industrial, occupational and social class structure for primary or secondary research based on other sources. However, the particular interest of the data for social scientists is in the opportunities it presents for studying social factors related to labour force participation, over a longer period than is covered by the relatively recent household surveys, and for social or ethnic minorities that are less well represented by the much smaller-scale sample surveys (Hakim 1980a). The census is also one of the many sources used to study labour market stratification and social stratification and the connections between them (Montagna, 1977).

The published census statistics are often used to study the correlates and causes of labour force participation (or economic activity rates) at a single point in time, or of changes over a period of time. The method may involve the extraction of summary cross-tabulations which pinpoint the association between two factors, or the multi-variate analysis of economic activity rates and a range of other social and economic indicators for a number of areas (such as towns or local authorities), as illustrated by Wabe (1969) and Gales and Marks (1974). The latter study compiled summary tables designed to demonstrate the association between age, the number and ages of dependent children, the socio-economic status (or occupation) of the husband, age on leaving full-time education, the possession of higher education qualifications and the economic activity rates of married women. The variance and skewness of the distribution of economic activity rates for large towns for 1961 and 1966 were examined to show that the impact of the local labour market and industrial mix on women's labour force participation had declined over a five-year period. Finally a regression analysis of married women's activity rates and a range of indicators on the demographic, socio-economic and industrial characteristics of the large towns was carried out. An indicator of the local tradition of women's employment (based on the 1931 Census) was also created, and found to be more highly correlated with the current activity rates than the current socio-economic indicators. Wabe's study was also based on multiple regression analysis of a dataset for local authorities, but the indicators derived from published reports were complemented with two measures of journey-to-work costs (in time and money). Again the census-derived indicators were selected to utilise fully the census information on personal or domestic circumstances (such as the number of children under school age) and on the characteristics of the area of residence (such as the availability of local employment for men and women) which might be associated with the 'dependent' variable of female economic activity rates, and again data for two years (1951 and 1961) were used to assess whether the importance of any factor was stable or changing. The analysis showed that the most important determinant of women's economic activity rate was the availability of local employment and this factor remained stable over time. Other factors were either not important, or their impact declined markedly over the decade – for example, the importance of children under school age showed a marked decline.

A particular advantage of published statistics is that they are readily accessible in libraries, as national census reports, or in the statistical compendia of international organisations, for cross-national comparative studies. There are an increasing number of comparative studies which go beyond presenting single-time country comparisons to examine the degree of convergence or divergence between countries on particular aspects of the labour force. For example, Boserup (1970) used census data in the main to establish three quite distinct patterns of women's employment in industrialised countries, Latin America, Africa, the Middle East, South and East Asia. Hakim (1979c) used published census data alone to establish that a homogeneous pattern of sex-based occupational segregation was found in industrialised countries, but not elsewhere, suggesting that sex as a factor of labour market stratification was the product of industrialisation. Both studies involved the development of statistical measures, or indices, that could be applied to the tables routinely published from most censuses. Boulding *et al.* (1976) developed a number of measures of labour force participation for cross-national comparative studies and many of the UN, EEC and OECD social indicators are derived from routinely produced census statistics for use in comparative studies.

Standard unpublished tables are used in much the same way, though usually to study minority groups identified in less detail in the census reports. For example, Mayhew and Rosewell (1978) had to use unpublished 1971 statistics to study the extent and nature of the 'crowding' into a small number of occupations of eight ethnic minority and immigrant groups: Irish, African, West Indian, Indian, Pakistani, European and other members of the New Commonwealth. Both published and unpublished census statistics and data from other sources (household surveys and statistics based on administrative records) were then analysed to assess the relative importance of various explanatory factors for the degree of occupational crowding observed. In many cases the appropriate census cross-tabulations had not been produced, and the authors had to rely on more partial data. However, they were able to discount some explanatory factors by showing that the *pattern* of variation between ethnic groups observed on one variable did not correspond to the pattern observed on another variable, so that the two variables were not likely to be correlated. In other cases the lack of sufficiently detailed data on ethnic minorities (even in the unpublished statistics) was overcome by developing proxy measures for the required variable, or by using more aggregated data than ideally required.

The census travel-to-work data have been used by academics and two government departments (the DE and DoE) to define labour markets in Britain, along lines similar to the definition of Standard Metropolitan Statistical Areas (SMSAs) in the United States. Smart (1974) analysed the 1961 data to group all local authorities into self-contained labour markets in that 75 per cent of persons working in the area were residents *and* 75 per cent of the residents in employment worked in the area. The exercise was repeated with 1966 and 1971 data to adjust the boundaries of the labour market areas (or travel-to-work areas) where necessary. These functional areas provide the areal basis for the organisation of local employment offices and services, the presentation of statistics on the registered unemployed and the designation of assisted areas by the Department of Industry. A somewhat different approach was used by Hall (1973) to identify functionally defined urban areas on the basis of 1961 travel-to-work and employment data, and the exercise has since been updated with the 1971 data (DoE, 1976; Gillespie, 1977). The urban areas consist of one or more local authorities grouped into three areas interrelated in terms of the supply of jobs and of labour, and the amount of commuting between the industrial and commercial inner urban core and the two rings of residential areas around them. These studies are of interest in their own right in exploring patterns of urban development and change over time. But functionally defined urban areas or labour markets also offer an alternative to the administratively defined areas for which census and other statistics can be published (by the Census Office or other agencies of central and local government) and analysed by social scientists. This alternative is attractive both for theoretical and for policy-related research in that administrative areas often provide a poor basis for research on the organisation of social and economic life at the sub-regional level. The rationale and method of functionally defined areal units for data analysis at the national level has been presented by an SSRC research unit at the University of Newcastle upon Tyne (Coombes *et al.*, 1978). The proposal is being considered by the Census Office with reference to output from the 1981 Census. A study by Flowerdew and Salt (1979) demonstrates the advantages of functional areal units as a basis for the analysis of census data on migration and, potentially, for research on other topics – as demonstrated by the extensive use of data for SMSAs in American secondary research based on census data (for example, Frey, 1980).

A good example of the use of census data in conjunction with other sources is offered by Bain and Elsheik (1979). They created a multi-source dataset by collating 34 variables from four sources: population census data for 1951, 1961 and 1971; census of production data for 1951, 1958, 1961, 1963, 1968 and 1971; employment data derived from administrative records for 1951, 1961 and 1971 (as census of employment data are not available for these years); and data produced from a detailed analysis of the membership records of multi-industry unions. The study adopted the sophisticated approach to the time variable advocated earlier (see pp. 9ff.) in that it recognised that time was not a variable in the analysis and hence data for various points within a two-decade period could be utilised. Regression analysis of the dataset was carried out to examine the factors associated with the inter-industry variations in unionisation. In this case the unit of analysis was the industry (as identified in the Standard Industrial Classification used in most data sources) rather than the individual, the firm, or the occupational group.

In other cases census information is supplemented by information from sample surveys. For example, the DE Unit for Manpower Studies (1977) study of the role of immigrants in the labour force was based predominantly on analyses of published statistics for 1961, 1966 and 1971 and special tabulations on immigrants from the 1971 Census, supplemented by data from a national survey of ethnic minorities and other information.

To date, secondary analysis of the data from the census-linked follow-up surveys on income and qualified manpower has been concentrated in departmental research units, although not all this research is published (but see DES, 1971; Morris and Ziderman, 1971; Butler, 1978: 15). The 1966 Census follow-up survey data were used to estimate the rate of return to different kinds of education, as reflected in the earnings differentials between persons who did or did not benefit from extra education. Both the 1966 follow-up survey and the 1971 Census IFS were used to study earnings relativities and the age–earnings profiles of men and women with different levels of qualifications. But comparisons of the two sources to assess whether the differentials between the qualification levels had changed over the five-year period 1966/7 to 1971/2 were ruled out by the differences between the two surveys. The 1971 Census QMFS data, which offer better comparability with the 1966 follow-up survey data, were not available until the late 1970s, and could well be used for further research in this area.

Census-based research on unemployment has been carried out primarily with reference to estimating the extent and correlates of unregistered unemployment or of total unemployment at the national and regional levels (Stilwell, 1970; DE, 1976; Evans, 1977). However, the secondary research potential of census data on this topic has as yet been little exploited by social researchers: it would allow more detailed

analyses of the personal, household and local labour market characteristics of the unemployed or of particular sub-groups – for example, of
sex, race and social class differentials in unemployment experience, or
of the lower risk of unemployment among the highly qualified (Butler,
1978: 19).

Social Research

The social research applications of census data are broadly of three
types: studies of social stratification, its correlates and consequences;
studies of the changing pattern of social life as reflected in housing
tenure and quality, household and family composition, education and
work; and studies of particular social groups, including ethnic and
social minorities. In all cases the value of the data lies primarily in the
ability to examine in some detail the relationships between aspects of
social life – although more detailed information on any single topic is
usually available from other sources which are used to provide supplementary detail. Each type of study can be carried out at the national
level, or for particular local authorities or even smaller areas. This
flexibility is reflected in government departments' use of census-
derived social indicators for local authorities (and other sub-regional
areas) for resource allocation and planning in relation to housing,
health services, the rate support grant and the personal social services
(see, for example, DoE, 1975; Holtermann, 1975; DHSS, 1976;
Imber, 1977; Salathiel, 1977). It is also reflected in the extensive use of
the data for social research at the sub-regional level described in the
next chapter.

The three types of census-based social research are reflected in the
'Social Commentary' articles published each year in the CSO's *Social
Trends*, most of which use published and unpublished data from the
recent censuses supplemented by more detailed or up-to-date information from other sources such as the GHS and FES. These have
studied young people aged 15–25 in a period of transition from school
to work and in the process of family formation; compared the life-
styles and social situation of men and women and of age groups; and
considered social class differences. The census is also used for research
on children, one-parent families, the various ethnic minorities and the
unemployed (for example, Fonda and Moss, 1976).

The uses of census data in studies of social stratification are illustrated by Reid (1977), who also reviews the various classifications of
social class and socio-economic status used in this and other sources.
His review shows how the census can be used directly, as a source in its
own right, but that the most extensive and sophisticated use is less
direct. The census provides data on social class differences in all the
topics it covers, and 'benchmark' data on the size and distribution of

the social classes and trends over time. It is used, in conjunction with data on deaths in the five-year period around each census, to produce mortality ratios (standardised for age) for each social class and for occupational groups (OPCS, 1978c), and is similarly used to produce studies of the social class gradient in fertility, morbidity and other topics on which OPCS produces data.

The utility of the census (and other) data produced by OPCS is greatly extended by the widespread use of the Registrar General's occupational and social class classifications in other surveys, which allows the results to be compared with the census statistics. In some cases the independent surveys supplement and extend the census information on social class differences. For example, by coding the occupations of (a sample of) divorcing couples to the RG's social classes, and comparing the number of divorces in each social class with the still married population in each class (as indicated by the census) a divorce rate can be calculated (Reid, 1977: 133). Data from the National Children's Bureau's longitudinal study – the National Child Development Study (see p. 148) – have been coded to the RG's social class classification so that the results of the study can be set in a national context and thus extend census information on class differences with information on their impact on people's life experiences – for example, the impact of poor quality housing (as indicated both in the census and in the survey by the lack of basic amenities and overcrowding) on child development, or the impact of social class more generally on the use of health services and educational attainment.

In other studies, comparisons between census and survey data on social class differences inform the interpretation of the survey data, for example, by showing that a particular type of event or experience occurs disproportionately at one or other end of the scale (Reid, 1977; 192, 194). In some studies the social class distribution at earlier censuses is used for comparison with survey information on respondents' fathers in order to eliminate the influence of social mobility on the social class composition of the group studied. This technique was used to show that the over-representation of the lowest social classes among schizophrenics was due to their downward social mobility – that is, that their complaint was the cause rather than the consequence of their social class (Reid, 1977: 119).

The applications of census data in studies of particular social groups and of trends over time are illustrated by the extensive research on ethnic minorities based largely on published, standard unpublished and special tabulations at the national and sub-regional levels (Collison, 1967; Rose et al., 1969; Jones and Smith, 1970; Peach, 1975; Lee, 1977; Stevens and Willis, 1979). In most cases secondary analysis of census data is supplemented by information from other sources such as official statistics on immigration and unemployment, independent surveys (local or national) of ethnic minorities, public opinion surveys and the GHS.

Rose *et al.* (1969) analysed 1966 Sample Census data on the social and economic situation of ethnic minorities compared with the population as a whole, and on changes over the period 1961–6. The analysis is largely descriptive: the census is treated as the source of national 10 per cent sample survey data on immigrant groups (or a complete census for 1961), providing information on total numbers and geographical distribution; their age structure, sex ratios and fertility; family structure; housing conditions; employment and socio-economic status. For example, it is shown that the housing conditions of ethnic minorities were consistently inferior to those of the population as a whole (as indicated by overcrowding, shared accommodation and the lack of basic amenities), but that the level of deprivation varied a good deal between immigrant groups, and had improved for some, but deteriorated for others, over the period 1961–6. In some cases the census statistics were edited and amended (to account, for example, for the inadequacies of birthplace data as a proxy for data on ethnic minorities) and new estimates were presented on the numbers of first and second generation immigrants. The study was based on special tabulations ordered from OPCS, presenting census information on the specified immigrant groups; some of these related to selected areas for which comparable 1961 special tables had been produced for an earlier study. The analyses are significant in that they provided the stimulus and framework for the more extensive statistics later produced as standard output from the 1971 Census, and they offer the only published statistics on this topic from the 1966 (and 1961) censuses. The census analysis was supplemented with secondary analysis of 1966 FES data and the results from a 1966–7 survey on the household income and expenditure of 920 New Commonwealth households in Birmingham. Primary analysis of another 1966–7 survey, on the incidence of race prejudice, was also supplemented by secondary analysis of NOP and Gallup data on attitudes of the British public towards immigrants and immigration. (The conclusions drawn from this 1966–7 survey were subsequently contested and extended in a number of secondary analyses; see p. 149.)

Jones and Smith (1970) also analysed the 1961 and 1966 data but with the emphasis on the economic rather than the social consequences of immigration – although they recognised that in some areas (such as housing) they are indistinguishable. To obtain a broader picture of trends in this period of a sharp rise in immigration the New Commonwealth and indigenous unemployment rates observed in the 1966 Census were extrapolated backwards to 1963 and forwards to 1968. To assess whether the occupational distribution of immigrants differed from that of the total labour force, a variant of the mean deviation was developed and applied to the 1961 and 1966 data. This showed that the occupational concentration of immigrants was generally lower than that of women workers, that there were notable differences between the degree of concentration of West Indian and Asian minorities, and that there were increases for some groups and decreases for others over the period 1961–6. Data from other sources on the average weekly wages in 1961 and 1966 for selected census occupations with concentrations of immigrants were obtained to test the hypothesis that immigration tends to reduce the rate of increase of wages relative to the average or to the past. This showed that the 1961–6 increases in average wage rates tended to be above average in these occupations. The data for 1961 and 1966 were used to obtain figures on the housing of immigrants, both to estimate housing subsidies to immigrants in council housing and to assess their housing capital usage. It was shown that immigrants tend to use social services, housing, education and health services in areas of decline and hence declining use by the indigenous population (Jones and Smith, 1970: 40–3, 56 ff., 109–26, 153 ff.).

Castles and Kosack (1973) drew upon both of these studies, among others, in their study of the impact of immigration on the class structure in four European countries: Britain, France, Germany (GFR) and Switzerland. Noting that even in Britain two-thirds of immigrants are whites, the authors rejected the race relations approach to the study of immigration in favour of a sociological approach with the focus on the social and economic functions of immigrant labour rather than on cultural conflict between racial groups. Six hypotheses were developed in relation to occupational segregation (or crowding), social and residential segregation, social mobility and change in the class structure and its subjective counterpart in attitudes (and prejudice) towards immigrants, and the political economy of labour migration. This broad perspective meant that they had to rely mainly on secondary analysis of existing sources, both quantitative and qualitative. The main sources tapped included the 1966 Sample Census of Britain, the 1968 Census of France and the 1960 Census of Switzerland, as well as a range of other official and independent surveys for the four countries.

By the time the 1971 Census data became available, large comprehensive secondary analyses such as those just described gave way to smaller, more sophisticated, and more purposive studies. The examples offered by Mayhew and Rosewell (1978) were noted above (p. 64). Stevens and Willis's (1979) study of ethnic minority criminality offers a good example in social research, and also reviews other studies in this field that included census data in the analysis. They used two multi-source datasets containing census-derived social indicators and crime rates and provide, in seven appendices, detailed information on the methods used to select suitable census indicators; to match data for census areas (local authorities and EDs) to the police division areas for which crime data were available; the methods used to produce 1975 estimates of ethnic minorities unemployment rates for areas of London; the multi-variate analyses carried out and the significance tests applied to the results. The first dataset was created and analysed at two levels: seven conurbations and about ninety police divisions within them. The results disproved the hypothesis that areas with high concentrations of West Indians or Asians also have high crime rates. The second dataset included arrest rates for ethnic groups compiled from Metropolitan Police District 1975 arrest records in conjunction with ethnic minority population data from 1971 Census special tabulations and derived OPCS population estimates, a number of SAS-derived social indicators and unemployment rate estimates. Multiple regression showed that social factors 'explained' a high proportion of the variance in arrest rates, but that the 'ethnic factor' was also significant. An extensive and sensitive discussion of the interpretation of this 'ethnic factor' is given which offers a notable contrast to the simplistic interpretations of social factors typically given by economists, statisticians and geographers.

As noted earlier (p. 43) the full benefits of the OPCS Longitudinal Study for research on changes in social patterns over time will not be seen until after the 1981 Census data are available. The first major study based on the LS is of the particular social and economic factors contributing to the social class gradient in mortality rates. Studies based on aggregate census data have shown correlations between poor housing and childhood mortality; the LS allows such correlations to be tested on the basis of microdata. Statistics produced from the LS have shown, for example, that mortality is exceptionally high for children and above average for adults living in households which share or have no access to a bath; that mortality is above average for those living in council housing and below average for those in owner-occupied homes; and that mortality is lower among those in employment than among the unemployed (Goldblatt and Fox, 1978; Fox, 1979). An illustration of the wider potential of the LS in the long term is given by Benjamin's (1958) study of inter-generational social mobility based on linking 1951 Census records with birth registration information. Professor Fox's secondary research project at the City University is analysing statistics derived from the LS to assess the impact of unemployment on subsequent mortality among other topics. Statistics from the LS could also be used to explore the dynamics of family and household formation and change over time; to assess the relationship between poverty indicators (such as poor quality housing and unemployment) and the life-cycle; to measure inter-censal social or occupational mobility within the population as a whole, among men, women, ethnic minorities, or age groups; to assess the relationship between geographical mobility, occupational mobility and housing tenure; to study the work profiles of women over the life-cycle and in relation to their family responsibilities; and to identify the determinants of migration within the country. Secondary analyses of data from the Longitudinal Study will provide a valuable adjunct to studies based on cross-sectional data from the census and household surveys.

Data from the 1971 Census Income Follow-up Survey (IFS) was used by Dinwiddy and Reed (1977) in a study for the RCDIW of the effects of social and demographic change on income distribution over the period 1951–71. These years were chosen because the 1951 and 1971 censuses offered the most detailed and reliable data on the social and demographic characteristics of the population, and the 1951–71 changes are analysed in some detail. The IFS and, to a lesser extent, the FES were used as the main sources of data on the income distribution of individuals and tax units. While both allowed incomes to be related to the characteristics of individuals, the IFS had a much larger sample (400,000 persons compared to 14,000) and thus allowed more detailed analyses. For example, the IFS alone provided information on the income distribution of students and other young people aged 15–24 years broken down by single years of age, sex and marital status. The analysis was based on eight special tabulations of the IFS data obtained from OPCS which are now listed in the main IFS report (OPCS, 1978b: 25) as being available to other researchers. Appendix C of the study outlines the methods used to analyse the IFS tables, and Appendix D presents tables showing the 1971/2 income distribution for all persons and tax units in the sample. The analysis shows, for example, that the increase in women's economic activity rates over the period 1951–71 was the single most influential factor on the income distribution and, unlike all others, tended to reduce the overall inequality of the income distribution for individuals, in that it reduced the share of the top percentile and substantially increased the share of the bottom quintile (Dinwiddy and Reed, 1977: 137–45, 156, 161, 99–102).

Political Science Research

The main use of census data by political scientists is in studies of the correlates of voting behaviour. Studies are usually based on multi-source datasets for parliamentary constituencies, although studies of smaller areas (such as electoral wards) or larger areas (such as the larger constituencies for EEC elections) are also possible. Crewe and Payne (1971) outline the rationale and methodology of constituency data analysis. One approach is to divide constituencies into categories on the basis of their voting behaviour (for example, to separate

marginal seats from others) and study the social and economic characteristics of each as revealed by census-derived indicators. Another
approach is to group constituencies on the basis of their census
characteristics, for example, by using Webber's (1978a) classification
of constituencies, and then study the voting behaviour in each type
(Webber, 1978b). Yet a third approach would be to add census-
derived indicators on the social and economic characteristics of the
local ward or constituency to survey information on respondents (and
non-respondents) in national studies of electoral behaviour and political attitudes, in order to assess more directly the relative influence of
the local environment and of personal characteristics on people's
voting behaviour. One study (Miller *et al.*, 1974) compiled a time-
series on the census characteristics of constituencies for 1918–71, to
assess the changing relationship between voting behaviour and constituency characteristics over half a century.

Urban and Regional Studies

The eight standard regions of England plus the two for Wales and
Scotland were retitled economic planning regions after the February
1974 local authority reorganisation. It is thus not surprising that
regional studies based on census (and other) data tend to have an
economic, rather than social, focus. As a good deal of other data are
available at regional level, most studies are multi-source, and rely
primarily on collating data from published reports, such as the CSO's
annual *Regional Statistics*. Because they must rely on ecological correlations for very large areas, this type of study is unable to go beyond
establishing correlations and associations between census (and other)
variables. While they may be of substantive interest or relevant to
regional policies, few studies exhibit innovatory developments in
secondary analysis beyond those discussed above in relation to
national studies or in the following chapter in relation to small area
studies. For example, Cheshire and Weedon (1973) studied patterns of
inter-regional migration and regional differences in unemployment
based on the 1966 Census. Stilwell (1970) studied patterns of regional
unemployment in an attempt to establish whether hidden (unregistered) unemployment varied between regions. Many other examples are to be found in the *Regional Studies* journal.

   Following Moser and Scott's (1961) early study of British towns
based solely on published data from the 1951 Census, there has been
one important development in this area of census use. Studies based on
the 1961 and 1971 censuses highlighted the limitations of administratively defined areas, and there is now a movement towards the
use of functionally defined urban areas, both for studies of urban
change and as a basis for other census-based secondary research. This

research was outlined above (p. 65) as it is based on census data on travel-to-work patterns and employment. Another approach was adopted by Donnison and Soto (1980) for their study of 154 towns (or urban areas) based mainly on 1971 Census data. They copied Webber's cluster analysis technique to produce a typology of towns which was used to explore a number of issues in urban studies.

International Perspectives

As noted earlier, the availability of microdata for census samples greatly extends the secondary research potential of the census, particularly when income data are also collected in the census. Thus much more extensive census-based research is carried out by social scientists in North America, much of it based on the American 1960 and 1970 and the Canadian 1971 PUS tapes rather than on the aggregate data used in all British research. Examples can be found in North American social science journals (for example, Gwartney and Long, 1978; Nakamura *et al.*, 1979). Elsewhere, census-based research is not dissimilar to that found in Britain.

International comparative studies based solely on census data are still rare, though the population census is frequently used for basic information on social and demographic characteristics in comparative studies by political scientists, and is often used for comparative studies of women (Boserup, 1970). Probably the only type of research that is uniquely based on census data is the study of international migration between countries, as most censuses collect data on country of birth or nationality. For example, other countries such as Canada make use of British census data to assess the numbers and characteristics of Canadians in Britain. However, the equivalent data on British emigrants to other countries are obtained from the OPCS International Passenger Survey.

5

Using the Census: Area-Based Studies

Apart from administrative sources, which typically offer information on a single topic, the census is the only source of information on a wide number of topics for small areas or for relatively small and dispersed groups within the population. The census allows not only the size and characteristics, but also the geographical distribution of particular groups in the population to be determined. It is thus of particular interest for local studies and for placing local studies in a national context. In Chapter 4 secondary analyses at the national and regional level were considered. The focus here is on studies at the sub-regional level, in particular secondary research based on the census SAS (see p. 46) and local authority data. Most studies at this level are purely local, but there are also a few national studies based on SAS or local authority data for the whole country (Holtermann, 1975; DoE, 1975; Edwards and Pender, 1976; Imber, 1977; and numerous studies by Webber).

The census SAS deserve special attention because they are the most user-oriented, most accessible and most widely used output. Census data for enumeration districts (EDs) were first requested in 1951 by a group of academics at Oxford University who formed the Oxford Census Tract Committee (which later developed into the Census Research Group) and also by Birmingham City Council. The first SAS were thus produced from the 1951 Census for Oxford and Birmingham only, and resulted in a number of studies by Collison and Mogey (1959) and Collison (1960, 1967) and others. The coverage and content of the SAS from succeeding censuses were extended and developed in response to demand from an expanding group of users. Within this group local authorities remain the most important, because of their influence on the design of the SAS and their use of the secondary analysis of SAS for policy and planning at the local level. Indeed, much of the SAS-based research by social scientists is oriented towards social policy at the local level. Similarly the most important single application of census data in government has recently been recognised as their role in resource allocation, in particular the use of census-derived social indicators for the annual calculation of the rate support grant needs element (Salathiel, 1977). The SAS are also used extensively to plan and monitor service-delivery, for example, by area health and water authorities, the gas and electricity supply industries and transport authorities. In the private sector they are used in market research, to study the catchment areas of existing and potential retail outlets, banks and similar enterprises.

Several factors stimulated SAS-based secondary analysis in the 1970s: a focus on area-based programmes of positive discrimination; the 1974 reorganisation of local government which created the need for the new authorities to obtain a picture of the communities they served; a trend towards corporate planning and information systems within the new larger authorities; and the social indicators movement. Secondary research based on the SAS is a lively area of census use, with local authority, social and market researchers extending the policy, planning and applied research uses of the data, while academic social scientists argue the relative merits of alternative theoretical orientations and data analysis techniques (Gittus, 1972; Johnston, 1976; Knox, 1978; Hakim, 1978b; Carley, 1981). The main issues tend to be the well-known ecological fallacy; the problems of casual explanations from aggregate data; and concern with the way that area boundary definition determines in part the results obtained (much as question-wording partially determines the results of a survey).

The common approach to the analysis of census SAS is the extraction of anything from four to fifty social indicators (or community indicators, as they are often termed when they relate to areas within local authorities) for use in three types of area profile (Hakim, 1977). *Summary studies* are reference works containing summary statistics in the form of tables, diagrams, or maps (for example, Shepherd *et al.*, 1974; CIPFA, 1979; OPCS, 1980e). *Measurement studies* attempt to measure, at a single point in time, the relative position of areas on some dimension such as quality of housing, socio-economic status, social need, or deprivation (Holtermann, 1975; DoE, 1975; O'Dell and Parker, 1977). *Information system studies* are the most sophisticated type of area profile, involving an initial multi-variate analysis to produce a qualitative area typology which then forms the basis for further purposive studies of specific topics such as housing, unemployment, or life-styles. The Liverpool Social Area Study (Webber, 1975) was the first of these, but subsequently many local authorities and other census users have found it advantageous to use the national socio-economic classifications of small areas (p. 52). This allows a local study to be set in a national context, which can be helpful, for example, in establishing the need for additional resources for deprived areas; it allows for comparisons between areas of a similar type across the country, for example, to monitor the relative performance of similar authorities on some policy or to monitor sales performance in areas of the same type; and it allows for purposive area sampling for local (or national) surveys. Another national area classification (Imber, 1977) was rather more purposive and has so far been little used outside central government (but see CIPFA, 1979: 55–68).

The selection of appropriate social indicators is a crucial first step in any secondary research based on the census. A guide to the more frequently used census social indicators is offered in Hakim (1978b); information on their performance at the national level is provided in the reports on the national social area classifications (Webber, 1977, 1978a, 1979; Webber and Craig, 1978). It is likely that the build-up of this body of information on the performance of census indicators as social and community indicators will lead to more discriminating and considered selection of suitable indicators in the 1980s than was commonly observed in the 1960s and 1970s. For example, the percentage of households sharing basic amenities, but not lacking any, provides a useful indicator of bedsitter-type accommodation (and therefore of multi-occupancy and transient populations), but it has not been used as regularly as the more conventional household tenure indicators, even in studies of urban areas (Hakim, 1978b: 10, 13).

The selection of areal units poses fewer problems as SAS are available for a hierarchy of areas ranging from EDs to regional and national aggregates, and EDs are small enough building blocks for other *ad hoc* areas to be reasonably well defined. The aggregation of EDs is advantageous for the SAS 10 per cent sample data, as the reliability of the data is improved. The larger the areal unit used in a study, the easier it is to link in data from other sources, either because area-coding of survey data (national or local) is feasible, or because data from other sources are available – for example, local authority data, electoral statistics, health and education data, or statistics on registered unemployment. The 1971 SAS grid-square data are mainly of interest to geographers. Although an index is available (Visvalingam, 1978) which relates the 1km grid squares to administrative boundaries, no other data are available coded to grid-square format, so that analyses of census grid-square data must be carried out in isolation from all other sources of social data. Very occasionally researchers have geocoded non-census data in order to relate them to the geocoded census data (Jones and Roper, 1974).

Studies Based on Census SAS

Studies based solely on census SAS offer limited scope, and are concentrated in local authorities' policy and planning activities, where they are used to identify communities for area-based action, to plan resource allocation, to identify concentrations of client groups and to provide a general information base which may be updated with, or replaced by, data from local surveys. For example, the analysis of census SAS was recommended by the DoE for the identification of housing stress areas (DoE, 1975; O'Dell and Parker, 1977), and SAS were used in a number of Inner Areas Study projects. Because of their relative accessibility, local action groups and community workers have carried out secondary analyses of SAS to contest the local authority's case for redevelopment plans, and pressure groups such as Shelter have promoted local community use of the SAS.

Sometimes SAS secondary analyses by pressure groups can have national repercussions and lead to reviews of existing policies. The Runnymede Trust's study of the effect of public sector housing policies on the distribution of tenants of New Commonwealth origin in London council housing estates was based on the 1971 SAS. The study first extracted the SAS data for London's large council housing estates by identifying the 2,000 EDs (out of a total of 17,500) where over 90 per cent of the population was in council housing. Detailed analysis of the housing and social characteristics of these EDs was carried out, identifying in particular the proportion of New Commonwealth immigrants (first and second generation) in each estate. Additional information on these estates (age, location, density of occupation, quality of the housing) was obtained from the GLC. The study concluded that the coloured population was under-represented in council housing, and was also in the worst housing on these estates (Runnymede Trust, 1975). This led to the GLC carrying out a similar analysis of the census SAS to establish the social characteristics of the tenants of GLC housing estates, and a lettings survey to establish whether and why coloured applicants were allocated to less desirable vacancies, and finally to a reassessment by the DoE of the desirability of local authorities keeping records on the housing of ethnic minorities.

Other studies have circumvented the limited information on ethnic minorities in the standard SAS by ordering special tabulations similar to the 1971 SAS but for 'coloured households' only, and then comparing the social and employment characteristics and spatial distribution of the 'coloured' and 'non-coloured' groups using standard SAS-derived indicators. Both the SAS and local authority tables have been used to study the residential segregation of immigrants in London and other cities at each of the recent censuses and the degree of dispersal between censuses (for one example and a review of earlier studies, see Lee, 1977). Multi-variate analysis is regularly applied to SAS-derived indicators (in isolation or in combination with indicators from other sources) to map the social geography of cities, for social area analysis and factorial ecology (see, for example, Robson, 1969; Herbert, 1972; Knox, 1975) and similar analyses have been carried out for major towns (Moser and Scott, 1961; Donnison and Soto, 1980). Inter-censal changes in ED boundaries can present difficulties in studies of change over time in the socio-spatial structure of cities. One solution is to do a comparative analysis of samples of EDs from each census for the urban area in question, although this excludes the option of mapping the results (Davidson, 1976). Finally, the SAS are used extensively by social and market research agencies for area-based sampling for surveys, or to check the representativeness of a survey sample *post-hoc*. Webber's socio-economic classification of wards/parishes has proved a highly successful sampling frame for social and market research as well as a classificatory variable for analysing survey results (Bickmore *et al.*, 1980). The 1971 SAS provided the area sampling frame for Smith's national household survey of ethnic minorities: at the first stage EDs with at least 2·4 per cent New Commonwealth immigrants were selected; at the second stage households within these EDs were sampled to construct a sampling frame of adult members of the New Commonwealth ethnic minorities (Airey *et al.*, 1976).

Studies Based on Multi-Source Datasets

The research applications of the census SAS and local authority statistics are greatly extended when they are combined with data from other sources to create multi-source area-based datasets. Many researchers create such datasets on an *ad hoc* basis for particular research projects. But there is at least one published multi-source dataset for local authorities (CIPFA, 1979), and there are a number of others at the SSRC Survey Archive, which combine indicators from recent censuses and a wide range of other indicators for local authorities in Britain (Hakim, 1978d: 48). The secondary analysis potential of these datasets has only begun to be exploited.

Byrne *et al.* (1975) collated a dataset for education authorities containing indicators of educational attainment and performance (such as the percentage of children staying on beyond compulsory education age and the proportion of examination passes) and indicators on the social, economic and housing characteristics of each authority derived from the 1966 Census. Analysis of the dataset showed a strong association between the socio-economic characteristics of an area and the educational attainment variables, suggesting that the educational system failed to counteract and equalise social inequalities. A similar analysis of 1971 Census indicators and selected performance indicators for LEAs led Midwinter (1977) to question whether the principle of equality of educational opportunity squares up with differences between local education authorities in output measures after controlling for the socio-economic character of the area.

This approach – using the census as a source of indicators on the social and economic characteristics of areas, and analysing their association with (or impact on) indicators from other sources on the

behaviour of people in these areas – is also used in studies of delinquency and crime (Baldwin, 1974); studies of voting patterns in
parliamentary constituencies (Crewe and Payne, 1971; Miller et al.,
1974); studies of the social determinants of morbidity and mortality
(Brennan and Lancashire, 1978); and patterns of expenditure and
resource allocation by local authorities (Imber, 1977). This approach
has been facilitated and extended by the availability of Webber's
national socio-economic area classifications based on the 1971 Census
data. Scott-Samuel (1977) has recommended the use of Webber's
social area classifications for resource allocation and service planning
in the health services and community medicine. He found that the
social area classifications discriminated better than the more conventional health service indicators, providing adequate explanations for
differentials in infant mortality, the uptake of vaccination and the
incidence of infectious disease. The social area classification has also
proved an effective summary of the census socio-economic indicators
for studies of voting behaviour (Webber, 1978b) and of life-styles more
generally, as illustrated by the BMRB's continuous survey of consumer behaviour, leisure activities and media usage (Bickmore et al.,
1980). The particular advantage of the social area typology is that it is
available at four levels of aggregation, so that it can be used for local as
well as national studies, as illustrated by Rutter et al. (1979: 148).
Studies with a theoretical or methodological focus are not obliged to
use the most recent available data, so that the 1971 area typologies
could be further exploited for some time to come by social scientists.

All the above studies have linked aggregate census and non-census
data for specified areal units (such as local authorities) and have been
constrained by the relatively limited variety of official statistics available for these areal units. A second approach to the use of census SAS
and other sub-regional data is to link the statistics into survey microdata (whether local or national) which offer more detailed information
on personal and household characteristics and behaviour. In this case
the census is used as a source of information on the characteristics of
the neighbourhood in which the survey respondent lives, with a view to
assessing the relative influence of the neighbourhood as compared
with other factors (such as social class, age and ethnicity) on the
respondent's behaviour and attitudes. For example, the *local* social
class and racial mix may be expected to influence educational or
occupational aspirations, racial attitudes, leisure activities and political views. A high proportion of economically active wives in a survey
respondent's neighbourhood might offer a proxy measure of the
impact of peer group, family, or local attitudes towards working wives,
and/or a measure of the local availability of work for women (Wabe,
1969). The impact of poor quality accommodation on the aspirations
and behaviour of schoolchildren may be exacerbated by living in a

neighbourhood of poor quality housing, as indicated by census data for the survey respondent's locality. In this approach interview data on respondents to a survey are supplemented with information on their neighbourhood characteristics, either in the form of selected census indicators, or as the code for the area type as identified in one of Webber's national classifications – a process that is easy if the electoral register (for wards or parliamentary constituencies) provides the sampling frame for the survey, or if the national area classification itself is used in the sampling design. This type of study is the only means of avoiding the ecological fallacy in testing causal hypotheses about environmental influences on social behaviour (Johnston, 1976).

International Perspectives

Some of the research applications of the census small area data are in fact second-best substitutes for secondary analysis of census microdata (or Public Use Samples) which are not available in Britain, so equivalent census analyses will not be found in those countries – such as the United States – where Public Use Samples are available to social scientists. In other cases the census analyses have counterparts elsewhere – for example, geographers will use aggregate census data to map the social geography of cities and regions even when census microdata are available. However, the volume of equivalent research elsewhere is somewhat limited by the fact that census small area data are a comparatively recent development in most countries, with the particular exception of the United States, where data for census tracts (the equivalent of EDs) have been released since the 1920 Census (largely due to the prompting of the sociologist Ernest Burgess) and are extensively analysed as a standard census product.

National socio-economic area classifications along the lines of Webber's four 1971 Census classifications are as yet unique to Britain; however, it is possible that similar national area classifications may be produced from the 1980 USA Census, but independently of the Census Bureau. Because census small area data are usually unpublished, awareness and use of the data in secondary research outside government is determined in part by the data dissemination infrastructure. For example, in France, where INSEE's regional data centres facilitate access to small area data by non-government users (academics, commercial enterprises, pressure groups, trade unions and the general public), and in Norway, where the national social science archive has built up large files of time-series data for all communes, secondary analysis of census small area data is extensive. The role of archives in the development of research on social ecology and of cross-national comparative studies is illustrated and reviewed in Merritt and Rokkan (1966) and Dogan and Rokkan (1969).

6

The Census in Historical Research

Unlike all other types of census-based research, which are limited to the aggregate data produced by OPCS, there are three types of data available for historical research:

(1) the original census returns deposited at the Public Records Office after 100 years, currently the enumerators' books for 1841–81;
(2) the census commentaries and social reports contained in the published census reports for 1801–1951;
(3) the census statistics presented in the published reports for 1801–1981.

The research applications of aggregate census statistics are well established but they still remain relatively under-used in relation to their potential. The research applications of the original census returns have begun to be exploited in the last decade, and this is the area where rapid and innovative developments can be expected in the future. The value of the census commentaries and social reports as documentary evidence on various aspects of the social structure and social change has only recently been recognised and should be utilised more fully in the future. In this chapter examples of research using each of these three sources of data will be discussed; but the potential for further use is perhaps of greater interest and will also be explored. Few researchers have so far attempted to use all three sources in combination, and this approach can throw new light on the published statistics. Historians have now begun to use census data in combination with other sources of quantifiable data for the nineteenth century to create multi-source historical datasets. It is likely that the census will increasingly become a central data source for this new social history in which quantification and measurement play a central role, as compared with traditional history. Indeed, the terms cliometrics, historical demography and historical sociology are all used to distinguish this quantitative and data-based historiography from traditional history.

Three categories of scholars are now contributing to the development of theoretical frameworks, the methodology, and the compilation of data from the early censuses. Local historians, working individually or in groups, may have a special contribution to make from their facility in interpreting early census data in the light of local knowledge (Beresford, 1963). Historians may be relatively less well versed in social science theory and in data analysis techniques, but they bring a wealth of other historical evidence to bear on the census data. Social scientists can contribute more formal theoretical orientations and sophisticated empirical tests to the study of trends over time and the dynamics of social change. It has been repeatedly found that the application of modern data analysis techniques to historical data can overthrow accepted views and interpretations of the recent past, so that this area of census-based research is likely to see lively debates for some time to come.

Although the focus here is on the secondary analysis of early census data, much of the following discussion will also apply to other sources of quantifiable data, such as the historical datasets at the SSRC Survey Archive and the early surveys held at the PRO (1971), for example, the original tabulations of the Ministry of Labour surveys of the unemployed in the 1920s (PRO, 1975: 75, 78).

The Census Commentaries as Documentary Evidence

The census commentaries are themselves an important illustration of how a data-based approach to writing history can illuminate and overturn accepted views of social change. The commentaries were written at a time of rapid social change, and the authors, most of whom are identifiable, were clearly attempting to clarify the nature of these changes and to offer a more objective data-based contribution to the debates surrounding these changes – discrediting some popular views and lending support to others. The early census reports can be regarded as the precursors of the annual *Social Trends* reports produced by the CSO since 1970. They attempted to collate available data on social trends, though in the nineteenth century the census was the primary if not sole data source on most aspects of society. The census commentaries are a valuable source of documentary evidence because they reveal how the census was developed over the nineteenth century with a view to producing data relevant to issues and questions of the day and how the data were 'applied' to provide answers to these questions. They reveal the census as a social product, and provide evidence on the thinking that lay behind the design of the census as a data collection and the design of the resulting statistics and tables. In addition to presenting the main results of each census, the reports contain, within the commentaries, a number of additional tables which provide inter-censal comparisons and data on trends over time, summary tables, and special analyses on topics that attracted contemporary concern or interest. These are usually commented on at greater length than the main tables and give some indication of the contemporary issues to which the data were applied. If the census is a snapshot of the nation at a particular point in time, the commentaries reveal how and why the camera was angled, how and why the picture was framed in a certain way (Hakim, 1980b: 553).

The commentaries provide information on the changing concepts of work, employment and economic activity: the emergence of the concept of a personal occupation rather than a family occupation, the move towards the narrow economic concept of work as gainful employment rather than productive work more broadly, and the increasing separation of the home and the workplace (Hakim, 1980b). The commentaries throw light on the changing occupational classifications used to tabulate the census results, reflecting a concern to understand a rapidly changing social structure which was crystallised in the Social Class classification in the early twentieth century.

The value of the census commentaries as a documentary source is illustrated by Davies's comparative study of the occupational classification of nurses in the British and American nineteenth-century reports, and Davidoff's study of landladies and lodgers (Davidoff, 1979; Davies, 1980). Both show how changes and ambiguities in definitions and classifications which appear to be methodological weaknesses when the census is used as a statistical source can point to important historical changes. Davidoff uses the census commentaries, as well as other sources, to outline changing views of the practice of taking in lodgers and of shared accommodation; a sample of 1851 and 1871 census returns for Margate and Colchester provides illustrative examples of the types of household that took in lodgers, and evidence also of variations between enumerators in recording landladies as having this occupation or none at all; other contemporary material is also used to study changing views on women's employment and the separation of home and workplace.

Davies uses the census commentaries to document the continuing ambivalence throughout the nineteenth century about the social and professional status of nurses, and the gradual professionalisation of nursing as an occupation. She shows how this change in status is reflected in the occupational classification of nurses, who were grouped with other domestic servants in 1851, and gradually upgraded in status over the century until they were finally allocated, with doctors, to the professional category of occupations in 1921. A similar pattern is found in the United States census's treatment of nurses over the same period. The census commentaries provide insights on the reasoning that lay behind changes in the treatment of nurses, the criteria and information that were taken into account. For example, they show that Florence Nightingale had an influence on the census officials' view of nurses (Davies, 1980: 607).

The census commentaries could be fruitfully studied as a source of documentary evidence on other aspects of social change in the nineteenth and early twentieth centuries, for example, the changing concepts of childhood, family and household, nationality, residence and migration as reflected in census definitions. Changes in the groupings and classifications applied to social phenomena, such as occupation and household composition, and developments over time in the topics selected for statistical analysis and comment, can illustrate the contemporary social concerns to which the census responded over the first one and a half centuries of its development. Similarly the reports on the education and religious censuses of 1851 provide a wealth of material on two important social concerns of the mid-nineteenth century (Lawton, 1978: 224–86). A very closely related, though separate, source of census commentaries are the numerous contemporary articles in the *Journal of the (Royal) Statistical Society* which commented on both the design and results of the population census. These discussed potential improvements in census methodology and problems in the conceptual framework of the census, and presented further summaries and analyses of census data relevant to contemporary issues, as exemplified by Collet's analysis of data on women household heads in relation to the issue of women's suffrage (Collet, 1908).

Census Time-Series and Cliometrics

The value of the published census statistics in offering the longest time-series of social statistics for Britain has long been recognised. However, the work involved in compiling figures from each of the reports, modifying them to improve comparability between censuses, and then carrying out secondary analyses of the data obtained, has discouraged many researchers, so that there is a tendency to rely on any time-series that have already been compiled by others.

All the techniques of statistical analysis and approaches to data analysis that are currently used in relation to recent censuses can be applied to the earlier published census statistics (and also to statistics compiled from reanalysis of the original records), with a number of provisos. The earlier census data is generally less reliable, as data collection methods were less developed and enumerators exercised their judgement in compiling their records to a greater extent than nowadays. Interpretations of the statistics need to take account of the quality of the data, which is poorer the further back one goes in the nineteenth century. This affects the comparability of the statistics from succeeding censuses. Most of the weaknesses of the early census data are now identified and recorded, particularly in relation to the data on labour force participation, the topic which has been most extensively analysed. The OPCS and GRO(S) *Guide to Census Reports, Great Britain, 1801–1966* (1977) collates information on all the major changes in question-wording, instructions to enumerators and coding procedures over this period, providing an important reference work on inter-censal changes in census procedures; but it does not offer a detailed guide to the relative comparability of data from successive censuses. The published reports on each census provide more detailed information and those for the nineteenth century in particular point to inconsistencies between censuses when commenting on the inter-censal tables. Buxton and Mackay (1977) offer the most comprehensive guide to the use of 1801–1971 census data on employment, and they also compiled time-series of labour force data for 1841–1971, with details of the estimation techniques used. Price and Bain (1976: 348) have compiled a 1911–71 time-series on women's position in the occupational structure.

Some scholars have compiled time-series which allow social indicators currently in use to be applied to the earlier census data also. For example, Mitchell and Deane (1971) compiled a time-series for 1841–1966 which allows economic activity rates for the earlier censuses to be computed, and this is reprinted by the Department of Employment (1971). However Hakim (1980b) has questioned some of the procedures they adopted and offers another time-series of economic activity rates for the nineteenth century. Female economic activity rates for 1901–71 have been compiled by Gales and Marks (1974) and, in more detail, Hakim (1979c). Time-series on the social structure, usually derived from the occupational structure, have been compiled by Booth (1886) for 1801–81, Marsh (1958) for 1871–1951, Payne (1977) for 1921–71 and Banks (1978) for 1801–1911. The last offers a good example of how techniques of estimation can be applied to the nineteenth-century statistics in order to obtain broad inter-censal comparisons and to fill the gaps in the less detailed information available from the earliest censuses. Similarly Law (1967) and Lawton (1978) have compiled comparative statistics on urbanisation trends from the 1801–1911 censuses and applied modern mapping techniques to the early data. Lee (1979) provides employment statistics for regions and counties for 1841–1971. Census time-series have been used to study the process of industrialisation and de-industrialisation, the de-skilling of jobs and the de-professionalisation of women. All of these sources offer time-series at the national level, and are frequently used to set the context for similar analyses of census data for individual towns or localities – including many of the secondary analyses of the original census records discussed below. It would be possible to extend the techniques used to the compilation of time-series on trends in housing, household composition and other topics covered by the early censuses. However, the range of topics covered by the census is fairly limited until the turn of the century (see Table 2.1).

It is conceivable that new social indicators and indicators developed specifically to measure change over time will be developed and applied to the early censuses, but the relatively limited number of published tabulations available before 1961 (when computer processing was adopted), and variations between censuses in the design and content of the tabulations, suggest that the most innovative work is likely to be found in secondary analyses of the original records, where these limitations are removed. However, the full potential of the existing statistics from 1801 to 1951 has probably not yet been tapped. Studies by Gales and Marks (1974) and Hakim (1979c) show that relatively sophisticated indicators can be applied to the published statistics to yield measures of social change. The latter study developed a number of measures of the degree of sex-based segregation in the occupational structure. Each of the measures overcame problems of inter-censal comparability in a different way and tapped a slightly different aspect of occupational segregation; together they provided a rounded picture of trends over the period 1901–71. The basic data required for the analysis consisted only of a table giving the total numbers of males, females and all occupied persons in each occupation separately listed at each census. A basic table of this type can be located in each census report from 1841 onwards, so that this type of analysis could well be extended back into the nineteenth century. The census commentaries for the late nineteenth century indicate that the relevant tables were produced in response to public concern at major changes in the sex composition of industries and occupations (Hakim, 1980b). This suggests that the census commentaries may provide useful indications of the topics that would repay further analysis – both because the relevant data were produced and because it is likely to yield significant results on social changes.

An American study based on multi-variate analyses of census time-series indicates the potential for similar analyses of the British statistics (Haber, 1973). One example of multi-variate analysis of nineteenth-century census data is described in the following section, as the data were derived from enumerators' books rather than the published reports.

The Census Records, 1841–81

The 1841 Census organised by the newly established GRO was the first modern census in that self-completion forms were issued to house-holders, and the names and addresses of individuals were recorded. Prior to that census enumerators were required to collect summary information on each household, and the information which survives from the 1801, 1811, 1821 and 1831 censuses is the aggregate statistical data presented in the published *Abstracts*. Very exceptionally enumerators' records from these first four censuses survived in local libraries and it is possible that increasing numbers of these early records may be identified. Harrison (1976) and Lawton (1978: 13, 139) describe some already identified; the Cambridge Group for the History of Population and Social Structure is identifying others. The census returns for England and Wales are treated as confidential for a period of 100 years, but the surviving records for 1841–81 are available for public inspection at the Public Records Office (PRO) (Hakim, 1979b: 141–3). Microfilm copies of the returns are also held in some local libraries (Gibson, 1979; OPCS, 1980b). The surviving records for 1841–1901 consist of the enumerators' books, as the original household schedules were destroyed in 1904 (Lawton, 1978: 16). In due course the household schedules for the 1911 and following censuses will all become available, except for the 1931 forms, all of which were accidentally burnt.

The Census Search Room is now the most heavily used section of the PRO, and the special services and facilities developed to assist users of the nineteenth-century census records have been described by Hakim (1978d). The PRO expects that the use of the census records for historical research will increase in the future, and it is likely that these services will be extended. All the records have been microfilmed, so it is possible for researchers to obtain a complete set of microfilms for the towns or areas they are studying. However, the process of extracting and coding data from the enumerators' books into a format suitable for analysis is still time-consuming and laborious. Computerisation of the records would facilitate research, but this needs to be done as a collaborative exercise between historians and the PRO. So far the PRO has collaborated with Professor Anderson's research team at Edinburgh University to create a datafile for a national 2 per cent sample of enumeration districts in Britain, containing data for about 415,000 persons in 945 clusters from the 1851 Census records. The data have been deposited at the SSRC Survey Archive, and are available to other researchers for secondary analysis. While the computerisation of the complete census records for 1841–81 is a distinct possibility, there are two issues that first need to be resolved. For some studies, nationally representative data are required and national samples would meet this need far better than complete data for individual towns. But for other studies, a particular town or type of area is specifically chosen, and 100 per cent data is often required for these, most particularly for geographical studies of urban development, but arguably also for historical sociology. Equally important is the question of the standardisation of the coding of the information contained in the enumerators' books. The Cambridge Group have gone some way toward developing standardised classifications to be applied to nineteenth-century data, including the census records, but as noted in Chapter 1 the entity problem raises doubts as to whether any single set of standard classifications can meet all users' needs, even though they allow comparability between census years and between studies. In addition, research based on census records is still in its early stages and it is questionable whether it is yet possible to devise a range of standard classifications and definitions which will meet all the innovative research designs that are likely to emerge in future decades. Some of the early approaches adopted by historians are already being questioned. A major advantage of Anderson's 2 per cent sample from the 1851 Census is that predetermined classifications were avoided by entering the complete contents of the enumerators' books on to the computer file (with spelling errors, alternative spellings and enumerators' comments). Users of the data are free to formulate their own classifications, definitions and coding frames, but it also means that coding of the data must be carried out by the secondary analyst before analysis can proceed (Anderson *et al.*, 1977).

There is now an extensive literature emerging on the methodological and practical problems of the analysis of the early census records, including sample design (area-based samples versus random samples of households and the question of whether and how to exclude the institutional population); the relative advantages and disadvantages of detailed manual analysis versus large-scale computer-based analyses; the difficulties engendered by variation in the enumerators' practices at a given census as well as variations in census-taking methods between censuses; the absence of census maps and the relative paucity in nineteenth-century maps generally. A particularly good overview is provided by Lawton (1978). But there has so far been relatively little or only indirect discussion of two issues which in my view are fundamental. The first is the choice between extended analysis and reanalysis, that is, between using the census records in much the same way as they were originally analysed to produce more detailed tabulations than are contained in the published reports but which are comparable with the published tables, and reanalysing the original records using new frameworks with results which may differ significantly from the published reports because they are based on current social science theory and approaches to data analysis. The second and related question is whether the conceptual frameworks applied to twentieth-century data should be applied to nineteenth-century data, thus offering comparability between reanalyses of the early censuses and recent censuses, or whether new frameworks should be devised offering greater historical accuracy – the choice between comparability and historical accuracy.

Two examples illustrate the significance of the issues: the application of the economically active/inactive distinction, and the choice of socio-economic classifications based on occupational classifications. A reanalysis of the early census records might allocate occupations and an 'occupied' (or economically active) status to people with no occupation recorded, for example, landladies who earned income by taking in lodgers. Practice varied between enumerators in recording occupations for women in particular, and a reanalysis need not be bound by earlier definitions. Similarly, early censuses varied in defining people engaged solely in household duties and the care of children (who include males as well as females) as 'occupied' or 'unoccupied' and a reanalysis might adopt a more consistent approach. Reanalysis can also involve applying concepts, definitions and classifications that were never used at the time, for example, of household composition, but in this case there is no visible discrepancy between the new conceptual framework and any that might have been applied in the nineteenth century.

The question of historical accuracy is more salient in the practice adopted by some historians of reallocating working women and children to the economically inactive class (Mitchell and Deane, 1971; Lawton, 1978: 177), a practice of questionable validity (Foster, 1974: 292; Hakim, 1980b: 576). Some scholars have applied twentieth-century census occupational classifications to the nineteenth-century data, thus ignoring the significant changes in the social status of particular occupations over a century. The usual arguments advanced for these approaches are that comparability is improved, but this may be a somewhat spurious and invalid comparability at the expense of historical accuracy. Comparability between censuses does not necessarily involve applying the same unvarying classificatory framework to each census dataset.

Foster's study of three towns, Oldham, Northampton and South Shields, illustrates the secondary analysis potential of the early census records. His study of *Class Struggle and the Industrial Revolution* was based on the 1841, 1851 and 1861 census records, the 1851 religious census, marriage records for 1845–56 and the Registrar General's annual reports, as well as a wealth of other contemporary material. The study is not without flaws, perhaps the major one being the fact that in order to limit the extent of manual analysis required, Foster used small samples of the census records for each town (Table 6.1). As a result the detailed analysis of the samples quickly ran into the problem of inadequate cell sizes, and it appears that many of his tables are based on highly or completely unreliable base numbers of households, thus vitiating the conclusions drawn, despite his frequent use of tests of significance to support his conclusions. The statistical weakness of the study is largely masked in the book (in which base numbers are never quoted in the tables), though apparent in the more detailed information given in the PhD thesis on which it is based. On the other hand Foster's approach is both innovative in terms of the many social indicators developed and applied to the data, and illustrative of the trend towards more theoretical approaches to historical sociology. His thesis is that Oldham's militancy (as compared with the two other towns) was attributable to class-consciousness rather than to other factors, and he thus contrasts the towns on a wide range of factors, including a number of census-derived variables.

Table 6.1   *Census Samples Used by Foster (1974)*

	Total households	Sampling fractions	Number of households in sample
1851 Northampton	5,100	1/20 (5%)	271
1851 South Shields	6,222	1/15 (7%)	433
1841 Oldham	10,992	1/30 (3%)	377
1851 Oldham	11,778	1/35 (3%)	387
1861 Oldham	21,700	1/50 (2%)	434

The occupational structure and industrial mix of the towns are compared with the Great Britain average, using reanalyses of the published statistics and of the original records, to show the comparative levels of industrialisation, the dominance of particular industries and the high proportion of wage-dependent families (Foster, 1974: 74–8). The distribution of household heads with birthplaces within 3 miles radius, 20 miles, over 20 miles, Scotland and Ireland is used to indicate the importance of 'immigrants' to each town and, conversely, the strength of homogeneity of local cultural traditions and perspectives. Two other measures of solidarity and mass class-consciousness are devised: the degree to which wage-earning families (in particular 'craft' and 'labourer' families, i.e. skilled and unskilled workers' families) intermarried and lived next door to each other. The intermarriage analysis is based on marriage records for the towns (which provided data on the occupations of both parents to each marriage), while the neighbouring analysis is based on separate, and much larger, samples of census records than those used for the main study (identified in Table 6.1). The actual incidence of craft–labour neighbouring and intermarriage is then compared with postulated random incidences derived from contingency tables. The resulting index of association shows deviations from random behaviour to which tests of significance are applied. The keeping of servants is used as a social indicator in Foster's study of the bourgeoisie in the three towns. He was able to collate information on particular families identified by name both in the census records and in other contemporary sources to build up a composite picture of their life-styles. Thus he found that the keeping of two or more resident servants by an employer (as identified in the census records) was a good indicator that the employer was worth more than £25,000 (as identified by probate personalty). At the same time the decision to keep less than two servants by an 'upper-class' family was taken as an indicator of Puritan 'abstinence' and was shown to be connected with other life-style characteristics of the wealthy (Foster, 1974; 195, 178, 202).

In his discussion of the economics of class-consciousness Foster attempts to develop estimates of poverty in 1850 by marrying information on wages and prices with data on the composition and employment of wage-earning households in his samples from the 1851 Census. Contemporary sources on wage rates were used to estimate each family's total income and, similarly, rent and fuel costs. Estimates of the subsistence minimum for an adult male were taken from Rowntree's and Bowley's surveys at the turn of the century, and Bowley's food requirement equivalence sales were used to obtain a weighted sum of the cost of food for all members of each family. (The approach is similar to the use of income equivalence scales in the analysis of FES data in the 1970s outlined in Chapter 8.) This allows the proportion of families with collective incomes below or close to their minimum subsistence food requirement costs to be estimated. As the early censuses did not identify the unemployed, Foster also uses contemporary sources of information on unemployment levels in Oldham industries to simulate the incidence of unemployment in his sample of households from the 1851 Census for Oldham, and then re-estimate incomes in relation to subsistence level requirements. This analysis suggests that 41 per cent of Oldham families would have had incomes below subsistence level at a time of high unemployment compared with 15 per cent on the assumption of no unemployment (Foster, 1974: 96; it should be noted, however, that Foster's own interpretation of the figures is misleading). Foster also attempts to estimate the proportion of families below the subsistence level poverty line at each stage of the life-cycle, suggesting that couples with young children were particularly prone to poverty, especially in the minority of families headed by an unskilled labourer, and that these families often shared accommodation in order to avoid poverty (Foster, 1974: 97–9).

Foster's study of poverty in 1850 illustrates the more sophisticated approaches being adopted to the analysis of early census records. These reanalyses go well beyond supplying additional tabulations to those quoted in the census reports. Secondary analyses of the census data can be greatly extended by the use of other complementary contemporary data to fill the gaps in the relatively limited census information on households. Similarly the census records can be supplemented with other data for studies of, for example, migration, trends in family and household structure, and urban change. (See the many examples reviewed in Lawton, 1978.)

Another trend is for the techniques of analysis developed in relation to recent census data to be applied also to the nineteenth-century data. Shaw used multi-variate analysis for a social area analysis of Wolverhampton in 1871, replicating Webber's study based on the 1971 Census Small Area Statistics (see Chapter 5). A systematic sample of 20 per cent of households in the 1871 Wolverhampton census records was taken, and these were allocated to thirty-five modern grid units. Scores were calculated on twenty-six socio-economic variables, chosen to correspond as closely as possible (given the more limited 1871 Census data) to the forty socio-economic variables derived from the 1971 Census SAS. The sevenfold social area typology for Wolverhampton in 1871 was then mapped on to, and compared with, the ninefold social area typology for Wolverhampton in 1971. The results provided a historical perspective on the development of the town over a century (Shaw, 1979a), 1979b). Other census-based contributions to the 'new urban history' are outlined in Dyos (1968) and Lawton (1978).

This discussion has focused on the three types of early census source taken separately, although increasingly most studies use two, if not all three, elements taken together, to provide a composite census picture of social trends in conjunction with the full range of other quantifiable data and documentary evidence. Careful textual reading of the commentaries can assist interpretation and reanalysis of the statistics; secondary analysis of the original records can throw new light on the published statistics; the commentaries are an essential adjunct to analysis of the enumerators' books. The three sources taken together yield maximum returns, as demonstrated by Lawton (1978: 82–145).

The PRO is the primary location for the early census records for 1841–81. Some local libraries hold microfilm copies of the PRO records (Gibson, 1979; OPCS, 1980b), and a few also hold original census records for 1801–31 not available at the PRO. A list of all the published census reports for 1801–1966 is given in OPCS and GRO(S) (1977: 1–10). Copies are held by the OPCS library in London and numerous other libraries (OPCS, 1980b). Some of the reports for 1801–91 have recently been reprinted by the Irish Academic Press in their Parliamentary Papers series. It is possible that all the census reports will be microfilmed in the near future, largely because the condition of the nineteenth-century volumes is deteriorating rapidly; this will make it possible for a far greater number of libraries to hold microfilm copies and thus improve access. For further details see Hakim (1978d: 31–5).

International Perspectives

Secondary research based on the early censuses is developing rapidly in other countries as well as in Britain. In the United States and Canada the original records are released for public use after a seventy-year period only, so that the manuscript census records are available for more recent periods (Flaherty, 1977). The research uses of the data are similar to those described for Britain, and the data are often computerised (Bogue, 1976; Denton and George, 1973; Fogel and Engerman, 1974; Lammermeier, 1973). Some data archives have pursued a policy of creating historical data files and collating time-series from the census and other sources, such as the ICPSR (Bogue, 1976) and the Norwegian Social Science Data Service, which has computerised the complete records of the 1801 Census verbatim (rather than in coded form) in order to ensure that none of the value of the records was lost to historians or linguists (Rokkan, 1976: 452). The Cambridge Group maintain links with researchers in other countries who are engaged in quantitative research based on early censuses and other sources, maintain a library of relevant research reports, and occasionally publish reports on international comparative studies.

Part Two
The Multi-Purpose Surveys

7

Multi-Purpose National Surveys:

The GHS, FES and LFS

Until the 1960s most social data offering national coverage were obtained from relatively infrequent national surveys or derived on a more regular basis from information in relevant administrative records. The 1970s saw a revolution in official social data with the establishment of a number of national multi-purpose surveys carried out on a continuous basis or repeated at regular intervals by government departments or by OPCS as a service to departments. By the late 1970s the secondary research usage of these surveys had extended to include quangos, Royal Commissions, nationalised industries, local government, market research organisations and the academic research community. Access to these and other government surveys was further facilitated when the data were deposited at the SSRC Survey Archive in the late 1970s, and more extensive secondary research based on these sources is likely to feature in future decades.

The continuous surveys (with fieldwork spread out evenly across the calendar year so that the data are not affected by seasonal variations) include the General Household Survey (GHS), the Family Expenditure Survey (FES), the National Food Survey (NFS) and the International Passenger Survey. The main regular survey is the Labour Force Survey (LFS) carried out biennially in May throughout the EEC. As the major national surveys are used by all government departments, the data dissemination system for them is wider and more systematised than for *ad hoc* surveys. Access to them is thus both easier and more controlled than for single-time surveys, where *ad hoc* arrangements with particular researchers are more likely. In this and the following chapter the focus is on the three multi-purpose surveys with the widest interest for secondary analysis: the GHS, FES and LFS.

The General Household Survey

The GHS is unique in having been designed from the start as a multi-purpose social survey that would be used by all government departments, with no single topic or departmental interest dominating the survey as a whole. It is also the newest continuous survey, having started in 1971. The GHS is the brainchild of OPCS Social Survey Division and its design reflects their long experience of carrying out surveys for central government departments. More specifically, the origins of the GHS may be found in four main sources: the obvious utility of multi-purpose surveys in many countries; the time-gaps between decennial population censuses; the growing need for more information than was available from administrative statistics on many aspects of public policies and services in Britain; and the need for a readily available means of examining relationships between some of the main areas of social statistics. The GHS offers a number of major advantages as a social research exercise. It covers a wide range of social topics for relatively small costs. It is flexible, and has been adapted over time to meet changing needs for information among departments. It is a continuous survey, thus allowing trends over time to be identified and facilitating response to new trends. It allows the interrelationships between the main areas of social interest to be studied – for example, data on labour force participation can be related to data on health or education or household composition. (This advantage is offered also by the population census, but the GHS offers more detailed information on a wider range of topics than does the census, and is of a more practical size for *ad hoc* analyses.) Many of the questions are similar to those used in the census, so that GHS data bridge the gap between decennial censuses. As the pace of social change increases, the inter-censal decade may exhibit important degrees of change in behaviour, as illustrated by rising labour force participation rates among women. Again, because it is a continuous survey, it is possible to aggregate data for two (or more) years in order to obtain sufficiently large samples for the study of small groups in the population. Finally, a continuous survey allows a specialised field force and research team to be developed and maintained; the results of experience gained can be used to improve the design and analysis of the GHS itself, and may also be usefully applied to the design of other surveys.

The GHS was initiated in January 1971, and has run continuously since then. From 1971 to 1974 the sample design was the same as that used for the FES, but a new sample design was adopted from April 1975 onwards. The survey is officially sponsored by the Central Statistical Office (CSO) which chairs an interdepartmental committee responsible for the overall development of the survey and for deciding the topic content of the survey in each year. In 1977 a review of the

GHS was carried out jointly by the CSO and OPCS and a formal policy was adopted for controlling the range of topics to be covered by each year of the survey (Durrant, 1978).

The GHS covers five main subject areas, namely, family information, housing, education, employment and health, that are of continuing interest to most departments. With the exception of health, these are also the topics covered by the census, although the depth of information is much greater in the interviewer-based GHS than in the census (see p. 8). Within each subject area there are some 'core' topics and questions that are included every year and change very little over time, thus allowing time-series to be developed; additional topics included periodically or for a limited number of years; and other topics included on an *ad hoc* basis.

Table 7.1 identifies the 'core' topics and the additional questions and topics that have been included in the GHS over the first decade of its existence. It should be noted that the range and form of questions may have varied over time for a given topic, and thus data are not always perfectly comparable across the years of the survey. For example, in 1977 the health section was completely revised to include more detailed questioning about the impact of ill-health on people's everyday lives, and this approach was continued in 1978. The health data for 1977–8 are thus markedly different from those obtained for 1971–6 and for 1979–81. The questions on income have been improved since 1971, and from 1979 were revised to afford comparability with the FES. Thus for 1971–8 the data relate to income over the past twelve months; from 1979 the data relate to 'current' income. In 1972 questions on housing costs were added to the housing section, and questions on smoking habits were added to the health section. In 1978 questions were introduced on housing satisfaction and on drinking patterns. In 1979 the questions on fertility and family formation were extended. Questions on long-term unemployment experience were included in 1975–7. Questions on household theft were included in 1972–3 and repeated in 1979–80. A section on medicine-taking was included on an *ad hoc* basis in 1972–3. The survey included a main section on leisure in 1973 and (in amended form) in 1977 and 1980. The demand from departments for additional questions and new sections has increased over the years and the CSO, in conjunction with OPCS, has to ensure an even balance between competing demands for space in the GHS within the constraints imposed by fieldwork considerations, and to avoid an excessive reporting burden on the public. Most of the data collected by the GHS are factual or behavioural, as this is usually of greater interest for policy purposes than attitudinal data. However, attitudinal data are sometimes collected to complement the more factual data on major policy areas; for example, questions on job satisfaction and attitudes to pay have been included in

Table 7.1   *Topics covered by the General Household Survey, 1971–81*

		1971	1972
Housing	tenure and size	X	X
	amenities	X	X
	telephone and consumer durables	—	X
	housing costs	—	X
	household theft	—	X
	high-rise accommodation	—	—
	satisfaction with housing	—	—
Migration	number of years at present address	X	X
	number of moves in last 5 years	X	X
	potential movers	X	X
	previous housing tenure	X	X
	housing tenure decisions	X	X
	country of birth	X	X
	parents' country of birth	X	X
	colour (white, other)	X	X
Education	type of school, college, etc. attended	X	X
	terminal education age	X	X
	qualifications	X	X
	current education and apprenticeships	X	X
	father's occupation	X	X
	teacher training course experience	—	—
	use of nursery schools, etc. for under-5s	—	—
Employment	occupation (SEG and KOS)	X	X
	industry	X	X
	hours worked	X	X
	job satisfaction	O	O
	reasons for absence from work	X	X
	job-finding methods	X	X
	occupational pension and sick pay provision	X	X
	unemployment (registered and unregistered)	X	X
	unemployment experience (duration, cause)	O	O
	attitudes to armed forces as a career	—	X
	job mobility and change	X	X
	second jobs	X	X
	travel to work (and working at home)	X	X

1973	1974	1975	1976	1977	1978	1979	1980	1981
X	X	X	X	X	X	X	X	X
X	X	X	X	X	X	X	X	X
X	X	X	X	—	X	X	X	X
X	X	X	X	X	—	X	—	X
X	—	—	—	—	—	X	X	—
X	X	X	X	X	X	X	X	X
—	—	—	—	—	X	—	—	—
X	X	X	X	X	X	X	X	X
X	X	X	X	X	—	X	X	X
X	X	X	X	—	X	—	X	X
X	—	—	—	—	X	X	X	X
X	X	X	X	—	X	X	X	—
X	X	X	X	X	X	X	X	X
X	X	X	X	X	X	X	X	X
X	X	X	X	X	X	X	X	X
X	X	X	X	X	X	X	X	X
X	X	X	X	X	X	X	X	X
X	X	X	X	X	X	X	X	X
X	X	X	X	X	X	X	X	X
X	X	X	X	X	X	X	X	X
—	—	—	—	—	X	X	—	—
—	—	—	—	—	—	X	—	—
X	X	X	X	X	X	X	X	X
X	X	X	X	X	X	X	X	X
X	X	X	X	X	X	X	X	X
O	X	X	X	X	X	X	X	X
O	X	X	X	X	X	X	X	X
X	X	X	X	X	X	X	X	X
X	X	X	X	O	O	X	—	X
X	X	X	X	X	X	X	X	X
O	X	X	X	X	X	X	X	X
—	—	—	—	—	—	—	—	—
X	X	X	X	X	X	X	X	X
X	X	X	X	X	X	—	X	X
X	X	X	X	—	X	—	—	X

Table 7.1   *Topics covered by the General Household Survey, 1971–81 – continued*

		1971	1972
Income	earnings (main, second, occasional jobs)	O	O
	unearnt income (rents, interest, etc.)	O	O
	tax and NI deductions	—	—
	state benefits (pensions, FIS, UB, etc.)	O	O
Health	chronic and acute sickness	X	X
	short-term and chronic health problems	—	—
	sight and hearing problems	—	—
	GP consultations	X	X
	hospital attendances and visits	X	X
	use of health and welfare service	X	X
	medicine-taking	—	O
	on hospital waiting lists	—	—
	smoking habits	—	X
	drinking habits	—	—
Other topics	(S) fertility and family formation	O	O
covered by	(S) leisure activities	—	—
a section (S)	(S) long-distance travel	X	X
	(S) elderly persons	—	—
or questions (Q)	(Q) proximity of relatives	—	—
	(Q) central heating	X	X
	(Q) heating fuel	—	—
	(Q) possession or use of car or van	X	X
	(S) driving licences and car usage	—	—
	(Q) house mortgages and loans	—	X
	(Q) house purchase intentions	—	—

Notes:
The table illustrates the range of information collected in the GHS, but does not list all topics or questions ever included. For further detail see the review of GHS topics 1971–8 in *Statistical News*, no. 46 (August 1979), pp. 23–6, or OPCS report on 1978 GHS, 1980, pp. 198–201. The depth of interviewing on topics, the number and wording of questions, varies over time. Some data are collected from certain groups (identified, for example,

1973	1974	1975	1976	1977	1978	1979	1980	1981
O	O	O	O	X	X	X	X	X
O	O	O	O	X	X	X	X	X
—	—	—	—	—	X	X	X	X
O	O	O	O	X	X	X	X	X
X	X	X	X	—	—	X	X	X
—	—	—	—	X	X	—	—	—
—	—	—	—	X	X	X	—	—
X	X	X	X	X	X	X	X	X
X	X	X	X	X	X	X	X	X
X	X	X	X	—	—	—	—	X
X	—	—	—	—	—	—	—	—
X	X	X	X	—	—	—	—	—
X	X	X	X	—	X	—	X	—
—	—	—	—	—	X	—	X	—
O	O	O	O	O	X	X	X	X
X	—	—	—	X	—	—	X	—
—	—	—	—	—	—	—	—	—
—	—	—	—	—	—	—	X	—
—	—	—	—	—	—	O	O	—
X	X	X	X	X	X	X	X	X
—	—	—	—	—	X	X	X	X
X	X	X	X	X	X	X	X	X
—	—	—	—	—	—	—	X	—
X	X	X	X	X	—	X	X	X
—	—	—	—	—	—	—	X	X

by age, household tenure, or employment status). Variations in the amount of data on each topic listed are indicated as follows:
X most extensive information (more detailed questions, or data for most groups)
O less detailed information (fewer questions, data for quarters or for some groups only)
— no information.

the employment section since 1974, questions on satisfaction with housing were included in 1978, and a section on potential movers collects information on the household's intentions of moving to another address. The GHS interviews involve all adult members of the household and are frequently carried out when all the family are present. There is therefore some limitation on the coverage of particularly sensitive topics. Self-completion questionnaires (as in the family information section introduced in 1979) are used to overcome this problem.

The GHS is also used as the source of samples for separate follow-up surveys. As the range of subject matter in the GHS is fairly wide, it allows sub-groups in the population to be identified and interviewed separately at a later stage if they are so willing. The survey has thus become a vehicle for a range of surveys going well beyond its own subject area. The 1975 GHS provided the sample for a follow-up survey of low income households for the Royal Commission on the Distribution of Income and Wealth (RCDIW, 1978: 104–34, 386–94), the Low Income Families Survey deposited at the SSRC Survey Archive by the RCDIW. The 1971, 1972 and 1973 GHS provided samples of public and private tenants for a follow-up survey on rent rebates and allowances for the Department of Environment and the Scottish Development Department for the purpose of providing estimates of the proportions of households eligible for rent rebates and rent allowances. An OPCS study of patients' attitudes to the hospital service carried out for the Royal Commission on the National Health Service was based on a follow-up survey to the 1976 and 1977 GHS (Royal Commission on the National Health Service, 1978).

The survey is organised in the form of four independent quarterly samples each designed to produce results that are representative of Great Britain. Quarterly results have been produced for some topics, such as job satisfaction and attitudes to pay. But almost all the analyses are based on annual data (that is, the aggregated results for four quarters), and the general report on each year of the survey does not contain any quarterly analyses. Each year of the survey is designed as a single survey in that major changes to the topic and question content occur between years, and the interview schedules for the four successive quarters are consistent from 1974 onwards. However, slight changes in the interview schedules and question wording were introduced from quarter to quarter before 1974. (For example, additional questions on aspirin-taking were included in the 1972 fourth quarter; in 1973 the GHS interviewers collected extra data on rates after revaluation in the second, third and fourth quarters.) Within each quarter interviews are carefully spaced out over the three-month period, in order to smooth out any seasonal variations, for example, in 'occupation last week'.

The GHS is based on a sample of about 15,000 addresses each year, with the sample for Scotland doubled to provide the minimum number of households necessary for separate analysis. For analyses covering Great Britain as a whole, the sample for Scotland is halved to give a national sample of just over 14,000 households (Table 1.2, p. 10). Unlike the FES, which reports results only for fully co-operating households, the GHS presents results for partially responding households. Partial response can take various forms: one person in a household may refuse to be interviewed, one question may be refused by a respondent, or proxy data may have to be collected on an absent member of the household (in which case information on certain questions such as income and opinions will not be obtained). Thus three response rates are quoted for the GHS: the *minimum* response rate includes only fully co-operating households, the *maximum* response rate accepts all partially responding households as respondents, and the most commonly quoted *middle* response rate includes households where information is missing only on some questions but excludes households with no information on one or more members of the household. In 1977, the rates were 74 per cent, 86 per cent and 83 per cent respectively.

A study of non-response bias to the 1971 GHS (second quarter) based on an analysis of the 1971 Census results showed the GHS to be very representative at the national level. As with the FES, families with young children are slightly over-represented. The two groups with the highest levels of significant non-response were single male and non-professional self-employed household heads. Overall non-response bias was limited to comparatively few variables, and was on the whole of a fairly small order even on these (Barnes and Birch, 1975). Further comparisons between GHS data and other sources confirm that the GHS gives good representation of the population in private households (OPCS, 1973a: 35–6, 75–7, 85–90). The census-based study of non-response will be repeated after the 1981 Census. Methodological papers on various aspects of the GHS are available from OPCS Social Survey Divison.

Response rates give only a broad indication of the proportion (and number) of households (or persons) for which usable results are available on any topic. For example, the income section usually obtains missing values or incomplete data for some 10 per cent of households, so that the number of household records with complete and usable income data is about 9,000 or 65 per cent of the Great Britain sample. On all other topics usable results are obtained for a higher proportion of households (and persons), often over 80 per cent, as indicated by the middle response rate. (However, OPCS does not publish response rates for individuals or for particular topics.) This means that the response rate of just under 70 per cent for the FES in the

1970s (which corresponds also to the proportion with usable data) compares favourably with the 65 per cent obtained on the GHS for income data. However, the larger GHS sample gives usable income data for 9,000 households compared with 7,000 from the FES. Secondary analysts should always check what the effective response rate (excluding missing values) is for the particular topic(s) of interest.

A general report on each year of the survey is published through HMSO, now usually available about eighteen months after the end of fieldwork, though some tables are available to government departments within six months after fieldwork. Starting with the 1978 GHS, early results of the survey have been presented, with commentaries, in a special GHS series of the *OPCS Monitors*. These are available free on request from the Information Branch of OPCS in London (see address on p. 60).

The GHS general reports, published annually, are invaluable sources of background information for secondary analysts. Each report contains the household and individual interview schedules for that year; the definitions and classifications applied to the survey results; and a list of tables identifying equivalent tables in earlier GHS reports. The main results of the survey are summarised both in tables and in accompanying commentaries. The *Introductory Report* on the first year of the survey describes the origin and development of the survey its purpose and potential applications (OPCS, 1973a). It gives notes on coding procedures and the fullest description of the sample design for the first four years of the survey. The sample design adopted from 1975 onwards is described in the 1975 and subsequent annual reports. The report for 1972 contains a chapter describing, with examples, the calculation of sampling errors associated with the original sample design, and a similar chapter appeared in the 1976 report in relation to the sample design used from 1975 onwards. The introductory report presents comparisons between GHS data and other sources on each topic, noting the reasons for non-comparability of the data in some cases, and indicating the relative merits of each source of data on the given topic. For example, the characteristics of the GHS, the FES, the DE New Earnings Survey, the Inland Revenue's Survey of Personal Incomes and other national sources of income data are compared. The relative merits of GHS data and other data sources on particular topics (such as health, income and earnings) are outlined in more detail in Maunder's review series (Vols 6, 9 and 13). The 1976 report studies trends in each topic over the period 1971–6 in some detail. The 1974 and 1977 reports present reviews of the secondary analyses of GHS data carried out by non-government users, and include articles by independent researchers on approaches to GHS secondary analysis (for example, Rothman, 1977).

The policy of actively encouraging non-government use of the GHS data and its potential for secondary analysis has been advertised through the SSRC Archive as well as in the general reports. OPCS recognises that the full potential of a multi-purpose household survey cannot be completely exploited by departmentally defined analyses. Apart from the published annual report, many unpublished tables are available to researchers. As for all government surveys, the only conditions are that the source of the data is fully attributed (as the data remain Crown copyright), and that departmental clearance is obtained both for the release of the data in question and for any proposed publication based on them.

Since the late 1970s the GHS microdata (that is, the anonymous but detailed results for households and their members) have been deposited after a lapse of time at the SSRC Survey Archive at Essex University, and are available for secondary analysis subject to the conditions applied to the release of unpublished tables. The Archive holdings are described both in its *Data Catalogue* and in its *General Household Survey Data Request Notes*. The Archive periodically holds workshops on secondary analysis of the GHS data at which the experience gained by users is shared and solutions to problems explored. The Survey Archive will also put people in touch with other GHS users or with specialists at OPCS who can assist with queries. One of the main problems encountered by users has been the lack of suitable software for the analysis of large hierarchical datasets such as the GHS (and FES) microdata. The Archive's solution so far has been to produce subsets of the GHS data in a flat (rectangular) file format suitable for analysis with SPSS, as this package is the most widely known and used by social researchers in universities. As noted in Appendix A, this solution carries certain limitations, and other packages are being assessed.

Three other potential problems in the analysis of the GHS microdata at the Archive should be noted. First, the tapes contain the basic raw data coded from the interview schedules, but none of the derived variables and recoding which form the basis of many OPCS tabulations. Some of the derived variables (such as the housing cost variables and bedroom standard) are not easy to re-create, if one is interested in producing tables comparable to those of OPCS. Secondly, the tape layout and content is not always identical for the four quarters of each year, in particular prior to 1974. Unless the user obtains a complete set of GHS tapes for a whole year, this difficulty is resolved by the Archive creating identical subsets of the data from each quarter. Thirdly, the amount of data for any person can vary enormously, from a dozen variables at one extreme to over 100 variables at the other. This arises in part from non-response from individual household members, but also because some GHS questions apply to all household members while others apply only to particular sub-groups in the population (for example, the economically active, or those suffering from health problems). The solution is, of course, to obtain data subsets containing only the variables of interest. If the analysis is to compare a particular group with the rest of the population, two data subsets will be required.

The Archive holds copies of datasets derived wholly or in part from the GHS, for example, datasets focusing primarily on the health information or the employment information in the GHS. It also holds *teaching packages* based on the GHS – subsets of GHS data specially designed to provide exercises for courses on data analysis, social statistics and statistical techniques. (The use of GHS datasets in social science methodology courses could stimulate wider non-government use of the GHS and other surveys.) The Archive has also produced special GHS documentation for secondary analysts, consisting of a standard codebook for each year and quarterly supplements on variables unique to a quarter.

While it has run for over a decade, the GHS is much 'younger' than the FES, and its potential for secondary analysis is less fully exploited as yet. As the next chapter will show, the potential for secondary analysis is also much wider than for the FES.

The Family Expenditure Survey

The FES is the longest-standing multi-purpose survey, and has now been running for over a quarter of a century. It has changed very little over this period, maintaining a primary focus on the income and expenditure of households in the United Kingdom, although there has been increasing detail in the income data collected.

There are a number of reports on the purpose, content, methodology and output of the FES (Kemsley, 1969b; DE, 1978; Kemsley *et al.*, 1980) and the annual Department of Employment reports on the FES results for each year also contain descriptions of the survey. The main reason, historically, for instituting the FES was to provide information on spending patterns for the Retail Price Index, and the development of the survey has always been heavily influenced by the requirements of producing weights for the RPI. But over the decades the use made of the results (both within government and by independent researchers) has progressively widened, and the FES is now effectively a multi-purpose survey. As it has been running continuously since 1957, it is frequently used as a source of information on the characteristics and circumstances of households for the period 1957 –70, before the GHS was instituted.

The origins of the FES go back to the turn of the century when the need for a measure of the effect of price changes on ordinary families became recognised. *Ad hoc* surveys on the expenditure of families were carried out in 1905 (with a follow-up inquiry in 1912 into 'the cost of living of the working classes'), 1937/8 and 1953/4 (Ministry of Labour, 1957). When considering the results of the 1953/4 survey, the Cost of Living Advisory Committee recommended that small-scale inquiries should be carried out at frequent intervals, rather than relying on large-scale exercises at lengthy intervals. In January 1957 the Family Expenditure Survey was initiated. For the first ten years (1957 to 1966) the FES was based on a sample of 5,000 addresses in Britain and between 3,000 and 3,500 households co-operated each year. From 1967 the sample was doubled to about 11,000 addresses in the United Kingdom, with roughly 7,000 households co-operating each year (Table 1.2). The main information collected has remained unaltered, though small modifications have been made over the years, to take account of changes in the goods and services consumed by households and the developing information needs of the multitudinous users of the data.

The FES data show how the expenditure patterns of different kinds of household vary, and the extent to which individual members of a household contribute to the household income. The basic unit of the survey is thus the household, rather than the individual; but for the household information to be complete, it is necessary that all members co-operate. The data are collected partly by interview and partly from expenditure diaries kept by each adult in the household. About 70 per cent of all households co-operate fully, an exceptionally high response rate for such a detailed survey. To build up a picture of total household expenditure, details of regular expenditure are obtained by interviewing all adult members of the household, and each individual aged 16 or over is then asked to keep diary records of his or her daily expenditure for fourteen consecutive days after the main interview. To set the spending information in perspective, detailed information is collected on the income of each adult member of the household. Basic information on the characteristics of household members, their relationship to the person designated as 'head of household', and on household durables (such as televisions, cars, washing machines) is also collected. The FES interviewers collect data on rateable values and rate poundage for households in the sample from local authorities, as is also done for the GHS.

The income and expenditure data collected for each household are very comprehensive. Regular expenditure data collected at the interview include housing costs, telephone bills, insurance payments, season ticket costs and certain types of credit. Individual expenditure data collected through the personal spending diaries include food and drink, clothes, fares, entertainment, books and newspapers, children's pocket money, gifts, contributions to charities, and any durable household goods bought in the two-week period. The primary concern of the FES expenditure diaries is to obtain a complete record of all household expenditure in the given fortnight, rather than to obtain expenditure on particular types of product (as in the National Food Survey) or on particular brands (as in many market research surveys). The income data collected at the interview are similarly designed to provide a complete picture of income from all sources, including earnings from full- or part-time work, casual earnings from all sources, pensions, unemployment benefit, supplementary benefits, means-tested benefits and the estimated value of income in kind. The focus is on the normal cash income of the household, so that certain types of income (such as legacies) are excluded, and normal earnings are also recorded for those whose income 'last week' was not typical (for example, employees temporarily absent from work).

The processing of the interview schedules and expenditure diaries for each household is complex. The household records are subjected to a series of detailed checks for inconsistency and identifiable errors. Missing or inadequate information is obtained if possible from the individual informant (by correspondence or by an interviewer revisiting the household) or the values are estimated and imputed. The household records are then edited and coded to conform to the concepts of definitions applied to the FES, for example, business expenditure is removed. Duplicate information is eliminated (for example, rent payments may be recorded both at the interview and in the expenditure diaries). Derived variables are created (for example, total household income and total household expenditure). Where necessary annual figures are converted to the weekly equivalent. Further validation checks are carried out on the computer before tables and statistics are produced. The resulting base tapes of FES data for each year of the survey provide a rich fund of information on the financial circumstances, budgets and standards of living of households in England, Wales, Scotland and Northern Ireland.

Responsibility for the operation of the FES is divided between the DE and OPCS, while the overall design and content of the survey are kept under review by an interdepartmental committee under the chairmanship of the Central Statistical Office. OPCS Social Survey Division is responsible for all stages up to the creation of the FES base tape, namely, the design and selection of the sample, design of the questionnaires, fieldwork, manual editing and coding of the completed household budgets. OPCS Social Survey Division also carries out operational research on the FES with a view to improving the methodology of data collection. The DE is responsible for the creation of the base tape, for processing and publishing the results, for controlling access to and the use made of the data by researchers, for any special analyses of the data, and for compiling the Retail Price Indices based on FES and other data. Reports on the conduct and methodology of the survey are most commonly produced by OPCS, while more general summaries of the methods and the main published analyses are produced by the DE.

An account of the sample design and techniques used for the first ten years of the FES (1957–66) is given in the Allen Committee Report (1965: 147–53). The sample design (for Great Britain) and field procedures used since 1967 (when the sample size was increased to about 11,000 addresses) are described in detail in the first technical handbook on the survey, *Family Expenditure Survey Handbook on the Sample, Fieldwork and Coding Procedures* (Kemsley, 1969b). This volume provides essential background information and documentation for researchers using the FES results. It describes the concepts and definitions applied to the FES data (for example, income, household); specifies the coding frames applied; and outlines the response, measures taken to ensure accurate information, and limitations on the accuracy of the FES. This first handbook is updated and extended by a second (Kemsley *et al.*, 1980). There are also a number of articles and papers by Kemsley on the FES methodology. Since 1962 separate reports on the FES results for each year have been published by HMSO for the Department of Employment, usually in the autumn of each year. There are also Ministry of Labour reports on the results for 1957–9, and for 1960–1. The annual reports provide summaries of the sample design, methodology, concepts and definitions applied to the survey; report the standard errors and numbers of households recording income or expenditure; present detailed expenditure data for different types of household and comparisons with the results for previous years; and provide an index to equivalent tables and charts in previous reports. Time-series of the more important tables from the survey are included in the DE's *Historical Abstract* and *Yearbooks of Labour Statistics*. Early results and summaries of each survey appear in the DE's *Employment Gazette*.

However, the volume of FES analyses is too great for all the tables to be published every year. The unpublished tables and statistical summaries held by the DE are freely available on request, subject to the reliability of the figures, and many requests for data from the survey can be met from tables already produced. (The more commonly requested information that can be met from unpublished tables is outlined in each annual report.) If the tables in the published annual reports do not provide the data required for a particular research project, it is worth checking with the FES team at the DE whether the data required can be made available from unpublished or special tabulations. The CSO's *Guide to Official Statistics* lists telephone numbers for FES inquiries (CSO, 1978: 10–11).

Until the early 1970s the only data available from the FES were the analyses and tables produced by the DE, thus limiting to some extent the range and detail of secondary analyses. Since then, the FES microdata have been deposited at the SSRC Survey Archive some two years after the results have been published. (By 1981 data for 1961–3 and 1968–79 were available and the data for 1965–7 was about to be deposited.) All requests for FES microdata from the Archive and any resulting publications must be cleared with the DE. This is to avoid inappropriate uses of the data, and to ensure that incorrect interpretations are not placed on the data, for the FES does not stand up to certain types of analysis. The more important of these are outlined in notes for intending users included in the FES documentation packages that can be obtained from the DE or the Archive. There is a separate package for each year of the survey since 1975, and each one specifies definitional and other processing changes as compared with previous years. Users should ensure they have the relevant documentation packages.

The basic unit in the FES is the household, not the family, and members of a household need not be related. Thus studies concerned with families more specifically need to exclude records for households of, for example, unrelated adults, and to sub-divide multi-family households into separate family units. The FES does not record intra-household transactions, so that the income and expenditure of lodgers, for example, cannot be separately identified, and the financial arrangements between husbands and wives cannot be studied. In general it is not possible to make a meaningful analysis of expenditure or income at a level below that of the household, although certain types of income, such as earnings from employment, can be analysed at the level of the individual (that is, for the head of household, wife of head, and all other household members combined). The FES tends to show higher economic activity rates than other surveys because part-time, occasional and seasonal work over the preceding year is included if the work is sufficiently regular. The FES earnings data are reliable, though less detailed than the New Earnings Survey data which are based on a much larger sample (Thatcher, 1968; see also Maunder's Vol. 6).

In the FES data on income and expenditure are built up from information covering different time-periods, and some types of income are excluded (for example, windfall income and money from the sale of goods). Household accounts in the form of an income-expenditure balance sheet for a specific period cannot be constructed, and measures of savings or dis-savings cannot be obtained. In general, the FES results show a tendency for expenditure to exceed income, and for this apparent dis-saving to diminish with income. Average expenditure tends to exceed average income in the lower income ranges, while in the higher income ranges average income substantially exceeds average expenditure. In general, grouping households by income is most reliable; total expenditure as defined in the survey is liable to random variations over time and so is less suitable as a general basis for classifying households.

The non-response rate to the FES is about 30 per cent. About a quarter of households in the sample choose not to take part in the survey, and the remainder are households that could not be contacted, or that do not complete the expenditure diaries. (Analyses of response for each year of the survey can be obtained from OPCS.) Response rates tend to be lower in Greater London and in provincial conurbations and highest in rural areas. Also, response rates appear to be lower among households living in dwellings with higher rateable values, among households without children and among the self-employed. A particular source of non-response bias is the tendency for response to decline with age (Kemsley, 1975). Non-response is greatest among households in the higher income ranges, and there is limited evidence that averages of household income recorded in the FES are on the low side (Thatcher, 1968). The main identified weaknesses in the survey have been found to be an understatement of earnings by women in part-time employment, and an erratic representation of the highest earnings groups, which are relatively minor defects. The FES does not accept any proxy data (as does the GHS for some topics) but values for income or expenditure are sometimes imputed for 'don't know' responses. There is no weighting of the results (to account for non-response) in either the published FES reports or the FES microdata at the Survey Archive.

The FES sample is relatively small for an incomes survey (about 7,000 fully co-operating households each year), and for particular types of household it can be very small. There are obvious dangers in drawing firm conclusions from the results for small groups of households because of the sampling error involved. The FES data cannot be used for analyses at sub-regional level because the sample is not balanced below regional level (except for Greater London). Some regional analyses are presented in the annual reports, but the more detailed of these are based on pooled results for two years. Similarly, more extensive analyses of the data for small groups of households could be based on pooled data for two or more years. More extensive data for Northern Ireland are available than are included in the FES data for the United Kingdom. Since 1967 the Northern Ireland Department of Finance has conducted its own survey, identical to the OPCS survey, but based on a larger sampling fraction. The Northern Ireland survey is based on a sample of about 1,000 addresses, from which 250 addresses are randomly selected for inclusion in the United Kingdom dataset. Analyses of the full results for Northern Ireland are published separately in the *Northern Ireland Family Expenditure Survey* reports. At present the Archive holds the FES tapes for the UK only; it may in the future hold separate tapes with the complete Northern Ireland sample.

The primary purpose of the FES is to provide information on patterns of expenditure for annual revision of the weights for the Retail Price Indices. Three price indices are in fact produced. The one most commonly used is the General Index, often simply referred to as the RPI. The other two indices exclude housing costs and relate to one-person pensioner and two-person pensioner households that are mainly dependent on state pensions and benefits (DE, 1979).

Since the late 1960s, when the sample size was doubled to facilitate secondary analyses by other government departments, the FES micro-data have been released to an increasing number of departments to allow them to do their own analyses rather than rely on the DE. The 1976 and subsequent FES reports list all major regular and occasional FES analyses published by other government departments, provide an annotated bibliography of related reports, and outline additional unpublished analyses that are available upon request from departments (with telephone contact points). These analyses provide a source of readily accessible FES analyses in addition to those presented in the main FES reports. Of particular interest to social scientists are the DHSS analyses of low income families (families with negative net resources in relation to their needs). The first analysis, based on 1968, 1969 and 1971 data, was published as a separate report with full methodological details (Howe, 1971); subsequent analyses have been published in *Social Trends* (for example, table 6.33 in no. 8, 1977: 116). The CSO itself regularly uses the FES to study the redistributive effects of taxes and benefits on household income. However, non-official secondary analyses of the FES on these and other topics are not reviewed in the FES reports – for example, studies by Nicholson (1965; 1976) and McClements (1978).

The FES data held at the SSRC Survey Archive are described in their *Data Catalogue* and *Family Expenditure Surveys Data Request Forms*. The Archive periodically holds workshops on secondary analysis of the FES which provide a forum for discussion between existing and intending users of the data. As with the GHS, the Archive releases FES tapes in a format suitable for analysis with SPSS. All tapes contain values converted to pence per week. The tapes do not contain area identifiers below regional level, both for reasons of confidentiality and because the sample is not balanced below regional level. The tapes for later years (1968 onwards) contain more derived variables than those for earlier years; but most of the derived variables can be re-created for 1961–7 by the user if necessary.

The Labour Force Survey and Other EEC Surveys

The biennial Labour Force Survey (LFS) is the most recent of the multi-purpose official household surveys. It has been carried out since 1973 as part of the United Kingdom's participation in the statistical programme of the European Economic Community. The original six member countries of the EEC held the first survey in 1960, and annual surveys were carried out in most countries between 1968 and 1971. A biennial programme was then established, with surveys in 1973 (with seven members participating), 1975 (with nine members participating), 1977, 1979 and 1981.

The primary purpose of the LFS is to provide statistics on the size and structure of the labour force on a comparable basis across the EEC as a contribution to community policy-making on such topics as regional development and foreign workers, and to provide an information base for the distribution of the social fund. It thus offers the most important source of data for comparative studies across the EEC after the population census. Its second main attraction is that it offers labour force data based on the methods and concepts that are current in other industrialised countries but have not yet been adopted in Britain. Thirdly, it offers data for a very much larger sample of households than in the GHS or FES (Table 1.2), thus allowing some topics and variables (such as unemployment and ethnic origin) to be analysed in much greater detail than with the other two surveys. Finally, it provides the first example of how EEC-wide surveys are conducted with a view to providing both the data required for EEC purposes and data that serve national (United Kingdom) information needs.

The United Kingdom is one of the few countries in the EEC and OECD to use labour force statistics derived from administrative records rather than household surveys. From 1948 to 1971 the annual series of employment statistics were based on quarterly counts of national insurance cards; from 1971 onwards statistics on employees in employment have been based on the Census of Employment which is essentially a survey of employers and their administrative records on their employees. Unemployment statistics have been derived from the records of the unemployment registers in local offices of the Department of Employment (or, since 1974, the Manpower Services Commission). Household surveys (and censuses) have three main advantages over employer surveys and administrative records as a source of labour force data. They cover a number of labour force minorities that are not covered by other sources (such as the self-employed, family workers and people who work at home). They avoid the difficulties of collating statistics from different sources on a compatible basis to provide an overall picture of the labour force. And information on labour force participation is supplemented by a range of other information on personal and household characteristics (Bosanquet and Standing, 1972; Hakim, 1980a). Thus the LFS is an important new source of data on the labour force and on the relationship between the social characteristics of people (or households) and their labour market behaviour.

As in the GHS, the LFS provides data on a number of standard topics included in each survey, and for which time-series can be developed, and a number of supplementary topics included periodically and offering little or no comparability across time. The main standard and supplementary topics are set out in Table 7.2. About half the topics are concerned with people's employment situation and the other half with education, training and qualifications; migration; housing; nationality; ethnic origin; and other basic information on household members including dependent children under school-leaving age. Many of these topics are covered by the GHS, with equal or greater detail in the information collected, and many are also covered in less detail by the population census. The LFS bridges the gap between the infrequent but universal censuses and the annual but much smaller GHS, and the LFS data are often used in conjunction with one or both of these sources. With a sample of over 105,000 households in the UK (about 0·5 per cent of the total) the LFS allows many variables and topics to be analysed at the national level in the same detail as in the census and is large enough to allow routinely for detailed regional analyses not possible with the GHS. For example, it is the only regular survey providing detailed data on ethnic minorities for the inter-censal period, including housing, household composition, migration, education and qualifications, economic activity rates, unemployment, occupational distribution and working conditions (such as shiftwork). As noted in Appendix B, the type of question on ethnic origin used in the LFS was that originally intended for the 1981 Census, but the classification of ethnic groups varies between surveys. The occupational classification used in the 1979 and following surveys is that used in the 1981 Census; but the 1973–7 surveys use the detailed KOS classification, with 400 occupations identified compared with the fifteen SEGs (or groupings of them) identified in the GHS tables (see Appendix B). The 1975 LFS collected data on travel-to-work patterns, and on housing mobility in relation to a change of job. The 1977 and 1979 surveys collected additional information on people who were not economically active, providing data on reasons for not working and on discouraged workers.

The design of the survey is a collaborative exercise between the Statistical Office of the European Community (SOEC) and the national statistical offices responsible for carrying out the survey in each country. In some countries, such as France, Italy and Germany, the LFS is accommodated within existing regular employment surveys (such as the German microcensus, see p. 39) and in some countries, such as Belgium and Germany, participation in the survey is compulsory. Where a new survey is instituted to provide the data required by the EEC, as in the UK, it is usually extended to collect other data of interest to the national government. To some extent there are two versions of the LFS for each country: the common EEC version and the more heterogeneous national versions incorporating a varying amount of additional information. For example, data on occupation only became an EEC requirement in 1981, but it was covered by the LFS in the UK and some other countries before then. The magnetic tapes transmitted by each country to SOEC contain only the microdata for the minimum required EEC topics, coded to standard EEC concepts, definitions and classifications, and laid out in a standard format. (For example, the EEC definition of a household differs from that used in British censuses and surveys by treating each person in a household of unrelated adults as a separate one-person household.) To each individual LFS respondent is attached a weighting, or grossing up, factor so that all LFS results are presented as national totals, both in SOEC publications and in OPCS reports. The SOEC reports present comparative LFS results for the UK and the other eight member countries and for the EEC as a whole; these are published regularly in the Eurostat series, with occasional reports on the supplementary topics covered in particular years (see OPCS, 1980d). The SOEC reports do not list the separate national reports published in each country which present the more comprehensive results for all the data actually collected in each survey. From time to time the European Commission sponsors more detailed analyses of LFS data on topics of current interest such as part-time employment (Robinson, 1979a, 1979b).

In the UK the survey includes questions intended to bridge the difference between UK and EEC definitions, and so yield data that are comparable with the statistics derived from administrative records and employer surveys which (as noted above) form the traditional basis of labour force data in Britain. (One result is that there are now three sets of figures on unemployment in Britain: the official EEC figures based on EEC definitions in the LFS; the British LFS figures based on international definitions and including both the registered and unregistered unemployed; and the DE figures derived from the unemployment register.) A variety of other questions are included on a regular or occasional basis to extend the utility of the LFS data to government departments. For example, the data on ethnic minorities are used by the DoE (in relation to housing), by the Home Office and the DE (in relation to employment). The data on vocational training are used by the MSC and data on pensions are used by the DHSS. The 1981 LFS

Table 7.2 Topics Covered by the Labour Force Survey in Britain, 1973–81

	1973	1975	1977	1979	1981
Household tenure	X	—	—	X	X
Type of accommodation (house, flat, etc.)	X	X	X	X	X
Possession of second home	X	X	—	—	—
Household composition	X	X	X	X	X
Sex, age, marital status	X	X	X	X	X
Whether registered disabled	—	—	X	X	X
Country of birth	X	X	X	X	X
Nationality	X	X	X	X	X
Ethnic group	—	—	—	X	X
Age completed full-time education	—	X	X	X	X
Qualifications held (all)	—	—	X	X	X
Qualifications obtained in full-time education	—	—	—	X	—
Vocational training (location, type, duration, subject, when started, financial assistance obtained, etc.)	O	O	—	X	—
Migration: – address one year previously	O	X	X	X	X
– in relation to change of job/employer	—	X	—	—	—
Economic activity status: – last week	X	X	X	X	X
– usual	X	X	X	X	X
– one year ago	X	X	X	X	X
Occupation and industry: – main or last job	X	X	X	X	X
– second job	X	X	X	X	X
– occasional work	—	—	—	—	X
– one year ago	X	X	X	X	X

Table 7.2 Topics Covered by the Labour Force Survey in Britain, 1973–81 – continued

	1973	1975	1977	1979	1981
Hours worked last week in main and second job	X	X	X	X	X
Current unemployment – duration	X	X	X	X	X
– whether registered	X	X	X	X	X
– whether receiving benefit	X	X	X	X	X
– reason for losing last job	X	X	X	X	X
– job-seeking activities	X	X	O	X	—
– discouraged workers	—	—	—	X	—
Unemployment after leaving full-time education	—	—	—	—	—
Job-seeking activities (people in employment)					
– different/additional job	X	X	X	X	X
– duration of search	X	X	X	X	X
Travel to work (time, distance, mode of transport	—	—	—	—	—
Homeworking	—	—	—	—	X
Working conditions (shift work, night work, type of workplace, noise levels, hygiene, safety)	—	X	—	—	—
Receipt of pensions (type, number, when started, etc.)	—	—	X	—	—

Notes:
The table does not distinguish between EEC required topics and topics covered by the survey in the United Kingdom. For details of topics which were EEC requirements (hence available for other countries), see the OPCS report (1980d). The table does not identify each separate question asked; variations in the amount of data collected on each topic are indicated as follows:

X most extensive information (more detailed questions)
O more limited information (fewer questions, or for some groups only)
— no information.

included questions on homeworking with a view to mounting a follow-up survey on this topic, and questions designed to assess the overlap with the 1981 Census. Because the LFS data differ significantly from the traditional system of labour force statistics in Britain, they were under-utilised in the 1970s, as a source of information on the labour force and also on other topics.

The LFS is carried out in a six-week period centred on May. Although most of the data are cross-sectional and time-specific, the survey also collects information on people's 'usual' economic activity status both at the time of the survey and one year before. The survey relies heavily on proxy interviews (see p. 8): 61 per cent of households gave proxy interviews in 1977. The methodology of the LFS was progressively improved over the first decade of its existence, particularly when it became the responsibility of OPCS Social Survey Division in 1980. The sample design, fieldwork procedures, response rates and grossing-up procedures are described in the first LFS report (OPCS, 1980d) in relation to the 1973–7 surveys, and in subsequent biennial reports. (Grossing up consists broadly of multiplying data for each respondent by 200.) The first report also discusses the purpose and content of the LFS in relation to SOEC requirements, presents illustrative results for 1973–7 with the emphasis on 1977 data for Great Britain, and considers the comparability of data from the LFS and other sources. The first three editions of the CSO's *Guide to Official Statistics* contain no references to the survey and the data available from it, though a brief description is given in OPCS (1977a) and some results are presented in the CSO *Social Trends* reports for 1977 and following years.

The numerous unpublished tables produced for government departments are available to other researchers subject to the usual conditions (p. 107). The 1973 LFS has already been destroyed, but the microdata for 1975, 1977 and 1979 were deposited at the Archive in 1981 and the tapes for subsequent years become available after a lapse of two years. Unlike the GHS and FES, the LFS tapes are censored with responses to some questions 'broad-banded' into a smaller number of categories. Access to the microdata now offers a major advantage for secondary analysis which was limited until recently to the tables and statistics produced by OPCS.

Apart from the LFS there are a number of other surveys in the EEC series that provide data on a reasonably comparable basis for all member countries (Barnes, 1979). The EEC survey on Consumer Attitudes and Buying Intentions was instituted in 1965 and covers all the countries of the Community. It has been carried out by OPCS in the UK in January, May and October each year since May 1974, with a total sample each year of 12,000 heads of households. The survey collects data on attitudes to the general economic situation, on ownership of durable goods, intentions on saving and on the purchase of durable goods. The microdata for this survey are sent to SOEC and SOEC publishes the comparative results for the EEC. Some results are presented in *Social Trends* (for example, no. 8, 1977: 130). OPCS has also carried out two rounds of the Social Indicators Survey for SOEC. The first, covering housing and health, was conducted in June/July 1977 in Britain with a sample of about 2,000 individuals. The second, on the quality of working life, was carried out in September 1978 with a sample of about 1,600 individuals. These SOEC surveys differ from other regular official surveys in collecting attitudinal data as well as factual data on the characteristics of individuals and households. For example, the survey on the quality of working life collected data on people's relative preferences for higher pay or shorter hours of work. The results are published by SOEC. The Archive holds all the EEC Eurobarometer polls which are commissioned by the Commission from opinion research agencies (in Britain usually Gallup). These are conducted on a six-monthly basis in spring and autumn of each year, with samples of about 9,000 for each survey across the EEC (or samples of 1,000–1,500 for the UK). They collect attitudinal data in the main – for example, on attitudes to the EEC, views on the status of women and satisfaction with the quality of life. For further details and a list of the Commission's reports, see the Archive's *Data Catalogue* (SSRC Survey Archive, 1980: 9). The range of EEC surveys may expand in future decades, thus offering a wider range of inter-nationally comparable social data on Britain and other member countries.

International Perspectives

All three of the multi-purpose national surveys described have counterparts elsewhere, although there are special features of equivalent surveys in each country that reflect national circumstances, needs and possibilities. In some cases the equivalent surveys are carried out on an *ad hoc* or periodic basis rather than at regular intervals. In industrialised countries they will usually be nationwide surveys while in developing countries they are often narrower in scope (for example, limited to urban population, rural population, selected cities, one or more provinces, certain social groups, or certain economic sectors). The separation observed in Britain of a labour force survey, a survey of income and expenditure and a survey covering both these and a wider variety of other topics is not necessarily observed elsewhere; elements of each may be present in different combinations in other national surveys, and the titles of regular surveys will vary accordingly.

Most directly comparable are the labour force sample surveys for other countries, especially other members of the EEC; comparable in concept and purpose, but less comparable in methodology are the Current Population Survey (CPS) of the United States, the Canadian Labour Force Survey and the 'microcensus' of the Federal Republic of Germany. The United States CPS has run continuously since 1947 and, as the first of many national labour force surveys, it has influenced the design of those developed elsewhere. It is a monthly survey with a rotating sample design. Supplementary questions are included in some months; from time to time additional questionnaires covering related topics are added to the survey and constitute in effect 'follow-up' surveys. Some of the CPS microdata tapes are available through data archives, and it has been suggested that Public Use Samples from the CPS for 1960 and following years be made available (Mason, Taeuber and Winsborough, 1977). The publications of the International Labour Office (such as their annual *Yearbook of Labour Statistics*) provide guides to the labour force survey data available for other countries.

As one of the first truly multi-purpose household surveys, the GHS still has relatively few direct counterparts elsewhere. The GHS *Introductory Report* notes that, in 1971, the closest equivalents were the national labour force surveys outlined above and the Indian National Sample Survey (OPCS, 1973a: 8–12). Since then a trend towards the development of multi-purpose household surveys has emerged, stimulated mainly by the United Nations emphasis on such surveys as a flexible means of updating decennial census results, and also by the OECD's interest in multi-purpose household surveys as a source of social indicators data. The OECD review of national multi-purpose household surveys in developing countries serves as a guide to the data available from them, although as yet probably few of the datasets are available in data archives (OECD, 1978). Despite its title, the United States General Social Survey is not an equivalent to the GHS as it is a non-official survey collecting attitudinal data in the main, as described in Chapter 10.

Household budget surveys are carried out in many countries on an *ad hoc* or regular basis. In concept and purpose they are comparable with the FES, but in approach and methodology there is a good deal of variation between countries so that precise comparisons with the FES results cannot always be made. To overcome the problem of the low response rates usually obtained in household budget surveys (as low as 14 per cent in some cases), some countries use samples based on households that have volunteered to participate rather than random samples. In some household budget surveys the reference period is one year, and households are asked to provide retrospective information on income and expenditure over a preceding year. The harmonisation of family budget surveys in the EEC countries only began in 1979; SOEC (1980) provides a review of the methods used and data collected in the EEC surveys in and around 1979; both the FES and the NFS were used to provide the relevant data for Britain. In some cases surveys are moving closer to the FES model. In the United States Consumer Expenditure Surveys were carried out on an *ad hoc* basis in 1950, 1960 and 1972; since 1979 a survey very similar to the FES has been initiated, using a fourteen-day period rather than one year as the reference period. An ILO report (1979) provides an introduction to the income and expenditure surveys carried out in some ninety countries in the period 1968–76 and illustrates the type of data collected in a number of comparative tables. Stark (1977) provides a detailed review of and guide to surveys and other sources of national data on income, earnings and expenditure for the USA, Canada, France, Germany, Ireland, Sweden, Japan and Australia; outlines their comparability with British sources (including the FES); and presents comparative analyses for various years. A less detailed review is also offered by Sawyer (1976) for OECD countries.

While surveys offering data comparable (to varying degrees) with the GHS, FES and LFS are increasingly available for many other countries, these are all cross-sectional studies, with their known limitations. In the future longitudinal and cohort studies, and surveys based on rotating samples, may become more common. Examples already exist for each of the fields covered by the LFS, FES and GHS. In the United States the National Longitudinal Surveys (NLS) provide longitudinal data on labour force participation for four samples, or cohorts (of men and women aged 15–25, women aged 30–44 and men aged 45–59 at first interview) who were repeatedly interviewed over a period of fifteen years. The extensive research literature based on secondary analysis of the data points to the value of longitudinal over cross-sectional data for studies in this field (Bielby *et al.*, 1979). Also in the United States the Family Income Dynamics Study has repeatedly interviewed a cohort (or panel) of 5,000 families for over a decade since 1968, collecting information on the changing pattern of family income and associated factors (Morgan *et al.*, 1974). Finally, in Britain the National Child Development Study is the longitudinal equivalent of the GHS in that it provides a multi-purpose survey of the life experiences of a particular age cohort (see p. 148). All of these studies are available at the Archive.

8

Using Multi-Purpose Surveys

The three multi-purpose surveys have over the years become part of the 'stock in trade' of social research, with an increasing number of secondary analyses carried out both in government departments and by independent researchers. Many secondary analyses are commissioned by government departments from independent researchers, so that the dividing line between government and non-government uses of the data becomes blurred. The FES, GHS and LFS have stimulated and facilitated greater interaction between social research inside and outside government. Some of the secondary research applications of the FES have become standard features and are regularly published in annual reports by the DHSS, CSO and other departments. The DE's annual reports on the FES from 1976 onwards include appendices describing the regular and *ad hoc* FES analyses of other departments (see p. 114). The GHS annual reports periodically include chapters on non-government uses of the data (see p. 106). A comprehensive review of all secondary research uses of the multi-purpose surveys is not attempted here. The range of existing and potential research applications is outlined more with a view to stimulating fuller use of these datasets.

Research on Distributional Issues

A secondary analysis of FES data for 1953/4 and 1960 carried out in the early 1960s effectively re-established poverty as an issue both for research and for social and economic policy. Two academics obtained the anonymised FES microdata from the then Ministry of Labour in the form of special sheets of coded information which were then processed entirely by hand. To reduce the sample of 13,000 respondents to the 1953/4 survey to manageable proportions for manual analysis, a 25 per cent sub-sample of households in the lowest income groups was drawn, yielding a sample of 1,400 low income households for detailed analysis. The full sample of 3,540 respondents to the 1960 survey was used although the detailed analysis focused on the 635 low income households. The secondary analysis was concerned to test the then-current assumption that poverty had been 'abolished'. The authors concluded that, on the contrary, the evidence suggested an increase in poverty between 1953/4 and 1960, and that (again contrary to popular belief) the majority of those living in poverty were children and adults of working age rather than the elderly (Abel-Smith and Townsend, 1965: 57, 64, 65). The study set the scene for research on distributional issues for the next fifteen years, leading to more extensive and regular secondary analyses of the FES (and in due course the GHS), to at least one major special survey on this topic (Townsend, 1979), and arguably to other official surveys as well (such as the DHSS Family Finances Survey). In particular the study created the precedent of secondary analysis of official survey data by academic researchers for purposes which often differed from the original applications of the data. The following years saw a great deal of collaborative work between researchers in central government departments and independent institutions; developments in the conceptualisation and methods of secondary analysis in relation to distributional issues; and a fuller exploitation of the FES data and, eventually, the GHS data.

The DHSS took up Abel-Smith and Townsend's suggestion that regular analyses of poverty be carried out after the FES sample size was doubled in 1967, with a first report by Howe (1971) and subsequent analyses reported in *Social Trends* (see p. 114). Recognition that the national assistance and, subsequently, supplementary benefit scales represented rough and ready definitions of the minimum income needs of families led to the development of income equivalence scales; these were intended to offer empirically based measures of the minimum income needs of families based on the FES results, but were eventually found to present relativities that do not differ markedly from those implicit in the supplementary benefit scales (Van Slooten and Coverdale, 1977: 28; Fiegehan *et al.*, 1977: 104–7). The NIESR study *Poverty and Progress in Britain 1953–73* (Fiegehan *et al.*, 1977) exploited more fully the FES potential for studies of changes over time, being in part a replication of the earlier study of change between 1953 and 1960.

The study was based primarily on secondary analysis of the FES data in published reports and the seven methodological appendices set out in some detail the procedures used to overcome discontinuities in the FES data over the twenty-year period, such as the regular changes in income-banding, changes in the pattern of household composition and changes in definitions. The 1971 microdata were also analysed and the results compared with those obtained from analyses of the published aggregate data; discrepancies between the two sets of results were small, suggesting that while secondary analysis of the published tables imposed limitations, the results were reliable. The study found that on the basis of a constant 1971 absolute living standard, numbers in poverty declined from about one-fifth of the population in 1953/4 to about one-fortieth in 1973. Real incomes of the poor increased by about 60–70 per cent over two decades. However, in relative terms there was little change over the period: the net income of the poorest fifth percentile was about the same proportion of the median income in 1953/4 and in 1973, so that the decline in the numbers in poverty as measured reflected a general improvement in living standards rather than a rise in the relative financial situation of the poor. The study also illustrates the importance of entity definitions (p. 22). For example, in 1971 twice as many tax units as households were below the poverty line (12·5 per cent compared with 7·1 per cent), the inability to maintain a separate household being itself an indication of poverty. Since the FES has (since 1960) collected data on both 'usual' and 'last week's' income, the study also showed that income instability was itself an indicator of deprivation, concentrated at the lower end of the income distribution (Fiegehan *et al.*, 1977: 19–31, 43–9, 111).

A study commissioned by the RCDIW, *The Causes of Poverty* (Layard *et al.*, 1978) illustrated the greater potential of the GHS for studying the social characteristics of those living in poverty. The study was based on secondary analysis of the 1975 GHS microdata in the main, though some use was also made of the microdata for 1972. The GHS for these years provides much less detail on income than in the FES, and the study illustrates how additional data can be estimated and imputed to supply the gaps in the data actually collected by a survey. For example, the 1975 GHS only collected data on gross incomes; tax liabilities and national insurance contributions for each tax unit were estimated and imputed in order to derive an estimated net income for each household. The poverty line was defined in relation to supplementary benefit income entitlement, which was also estimated and imputed for each household in the sample. To eliminate the impact of inflation on income data collected throughout 1975, incomes were scaled up to make them as close as possible to a comparable December 1975 position. (This conversion of data from a continuous survey to data for a single point in time features also in DHSS analyses of the FES.)

In order to carry out the complex calculations to derive the estimates of net relative incomes, households for which income data were incomplete or missing were excluded from the analysis, and a small number of other households were also excluded because they presented unusual characteristics. Thus the study was based on data for 8,600 households in Britain, or 61 per cent of the eligible GHS sample of 14,100 households. As noted earlier, response rates provide only a partial guide to the number (or proportion) of households for which usable data is available (pp. 105–6).

The study illustrates the effective marrying of theoretical approaches to explaining poverty (dual labour market theory) with policy-related concerns (the incentive versus equity issue) in the study of the joint interplay of the labour market and fiscal system in explaining poverty. It also illustrates how the GHS can be used to study population sub-groups and social minorities (the elderly, the sick and disabled, one-parent families, couples with children), and the relationships between topics, for example, the contributions of unemployment and ill-health to explanations of poverty. To explore the personal characteristics of the poor, the correlates and causes of poverty, a wider range of analytical techniques are applied to the GHS microdata than are used by OPCS in their original reports on the survey results: not only cross-tabulation, but also correlation analysis, path analysis and multiple regression.

In order to show the relationship between the labour market and fiscal policy, the significance of work-related factors is studied within each type of family (or tax unit): elderly people, couples with children, one-parent families and single people. For example, the study shows that while two-thirds of the families consisting of elderly people are in poverty, this is due not so much to 'old age' (as suggested by Fiegehan *et al.*, 1977: 62) as to labour market factors: 79 per cent of those who had retired without an occupational pension were in poverty compared with only 28 per cent of those who were still working. Regression analysis was used to show that financial circumstances in old age (in particular the likelihood of being in receipt of an occupational pension, the value of the occupational pension and home-ownership) were in large part predicted or explained by financial circumstances when working (the predicted wage during working life and its correlates such as educational level). Multiple regression is also used to study the determinants of earnings, and hence of low pay during working life, for men, single women and married women. In order to include the variable 'years of work experience', a proxy 'years since completing full-time education' is used, but while this works well for men and single women it overstates the work experience of married women and hence fails to distinguish accurately between those who have more or less work experience. Thus the equations explain 38 per cent of the variation of earnings for men, 44 per cent for single women, but only 23 per cent for married women. Similarly, multiple regression is used to study the determinants of women's participation and hours worked. These analyses are drawn together in a study of couples with children. Cross-tabulations are used to show the relative importance of husband's earnings and wife's earnings to total family income in relation to needs. The authors conclude that low pay is not the main cause of poverty. Most of those receiving low pay are married women, whose earnings ensure that the family is not among the poorest (Layard *et al.*, 1978).

Clearly secondary analysis based on microdata rather than published tables affords the researcher far greater control over the variables to be introduced, the specification of the variables and the complexity and detail of the analysis. However, the work involved is extensive and hence often limited to data for a single year. Unless a detailed analysis of the GHS microdata is envisaged, it is worth checking whether a reasonably equivalent table has already been produced, either in the OPCS report, or in other secondary analyses on the given topic. Previous analyses on a given topic will also give some indication of the likely problems, such as small cell sizes for particular sub-groups in the population, high levels of non-response, the limitations of the definitions incorporated in the coding, and so forth; but they also indicate the potential for further work.

Until the late 1970s the FES and GHS were usually analysed separately, mainly because they used different classifications of household composition and of socio-economic status or occupation, so that there was little possibility of conceptual bridges across the two sources. (As noted in Appendix B, the FES uses an occupational classification which is unique to it rather than the SEG classification applied to the GHS, census and other OPCS surveys.) While the two surveys are complementary in terms of their topic content, the potential for exploiting this complementarity in secondary analysis was enhanced from 1979 onwards when the GHS income section was revised to bring it conceptually closer to that of the FES (see Appendix B). The potential for secondary analysis of the two sources in conjunction with each other is thus greatly extended for the 1980s, particularly as the microdata are available at the SSRC Survey Archive.

Analytical Research

Analytical research concerned with establishing patterns of correlation and causation between social variables has been facilitated by access to survey microdata, and has been influenced by the North American research which developed as a result of the earlier access to microdata from household censuses and surveys. The GHS has been used to study the determinants of labour force participation, earnings and income, unemployment and the economic return to education. For example, Psacharopoulos (1977) used 1972 GHS data for male employees to assess the importance of personal characteristics as determinants of occupational status and social mobility (in relation to father's occupational status). The Hope-Goldthorpe scale of occupational status was applied to the GHS data on occupation. The results were compared with those of a similar study for the USA. Greenhalgh (1980) used GHS microdata for 1971 and 1975 to study the relative importance of sex and other personal and job characteristics as determinants of earning differentials at the beginning and end of the period of implementation of the Equal Pay Act. The results suggested a differential impact of the Act on the earnings of single and married women over the four-year period.

Analyses of the GHS data on health and education have looked at the relationship between social class (as indicated by SEG) and usage (or take-up rates) of public health and education services, to assess the importance of social class as a determinant of health care utilisation, and more generally to study the patterns and determinants of public service utilisation. For example, Forster (1976) used 1972 GHS micro-data to study the social class differentials in self-reported sickness and in general practitioner consultations. A *use to need ratio* was developed for each social class and this showed that the class differential in consultations was reversed when morbidity was taken into account, so that the level of usage relative to need declined with social class. Building on this work, Le Grand (1978a, 1978b) extended the analysis to the 1971, 1972 and 1973 GHS data on the use of hospital services and education services, to study the redistributive effects of the 'social wage'. He concluded that the higher socio-economic groups benefit most from NHS and education expenditure because of their greater propensity to use public services. This approach is now being used by the DES to study the distributional impact of education expenditure in more detail than has so far been done in CSO analyses of the FES.

The GHS has been used to study the determinants of migration and the relationship between housing tenure and labour mobility. The results suggested that council tenants and, to a lesser extent, private unfurnished tenants have a lower probability of migration than owner-occupiers, largely due to the way the housing market operates. The FES has been used by economists to estimate complete demand systems from household budget data. As yet there has been little analytical research based on the LFS as the microdata only became available at the SSRC Survey Archive in the early 1980s.

Studies of Social Groups

Analyses of FES and GHS data on one-parent families, pensioner families (or households) and families with children are now common-place, as illustrated above with reference to research on poverty. Since the proposal to include questions on ethnic origin in the 1981 Census was abandoned, the LFS and GHS will become increasingly important in the 1980s as the only regular sources of national data on ethnic minorities. GHS analyses by OPCS (see particularly the reports for 1976 and 1978) and CSO (in *Social Trends*) show that pooling data for two or more years allows more detailed analyses than are possible with data for a single year. The LFS offers data for a much larger sample than the GHS, based on a more detailed classification of ethnic groups (see Appendix B), although the topics covered are more limited than in the GHS. Both these surveys offer data to complement the information available from special surveys of ethnic minority groups.

The size of the LFS sample allows it to be used to study other small groups in the population. For example, it has been used by the DES as a source of data on the ethnic group and nationality composition of schoolchildren aged 5–16 years. It has been used by the DHSS as a source of data on pensioners, to estimate the effect (and cost) of the abolition of the earnings rule for retirement pensioners. It is regularly used as a source of data on the self-employed and on migrants.

Studies of Special Topics

As noted in Chapter 7, household surveys offer a number of advantages over administrative records as a source of data on employment and unemployment, and household surveys are most commonly used to provide labour force data in EEC and OECD countries. Thus the definition of unemployment in the GHS and the LFS is closer to international definitions, and these two sources are commonly used as the basis for comparative studies of unemployment in Britain and other countries. The international definition invariably yields a higher rate of unemployment than the statistics derived from administrative records, and both rates are normally quoted in CSO's *Social Trends* (see, for example, tables 5.13 and 5.15 in the report for 1977). The GHS and LFS are increasingly used in studies of the social aspects of the labour force (including especially the conditions of life and employment, the duration of employment, unemployment and underemployment). A comparative study of unemployment in nine member countries of the OECD made extensive use of GHS data on unemployment in addition to population census data and DE statistics on the registered unemployed (Sorrentino, 1979). A comparative study of part-time employment in EEC countries which argued that part-time workers could no longer be regarded as a marginal labour force was based primarily on the EEC Labour Force Surveys for 1975 (Robinson, 1979a, 1979b). The LFS data for the 1970s have been used to study trends in occupational segregation before and after implementation of equal opportunities legislation (Hakim, 1981).

Studies of the extent, nature and regional distribution of double job-holding in Britain have been based on the GHS and FES as well as the 1966 Census (Alden, 1977). The LFS also provides a suitable source for further research on second jobs (on moonlighting, as it is termed in the North American literature), overtime working and paid work by a wife, and their relative importance at each stage of the family life-cycle. It is generally thought that the FES provides no information on the 'hidden' economy, but the FES definition of economic activity (or of a worker) is more generous than in other sources, including anyone with regular earnings, however small, and however small the number of hours worked a week. Thus many people working part-time at home (such as homeworkers or sales representatives) are classified as working. The FES and 1981 LFS could be used further to study people who are only marginally attached to the labour force.

As noted earlier (p. 127) the GHS microdata have been used to study the relative importance of unemployment as a cause of poverty. The GHS microdata have also been used to study 'voluntary unemployment', that is, the disincentive effects of social security benefits on the propensity to regain work and hence on the duration of unemployment. For example, Nickell (1979a, 1979b) used 1972 GHS data to estimate the replacement ratio (the ratio of unemployment income to earnings from the last job held) for the 426 unemployed men in the GHS sample; the impact of the replacement ratio and other variables on the length of the unemployment spell was measured by regression analysis. The results suggested that benefits had some impact on the behaviour of unemployed men, although other factors (such as the local unemployment rate and age) were equally or more important. This work is being extended in the SSRC Research Programme on taxation, incentives and the distribution of income using the FES microdata for 1970–5 to study changes over time in the impact of taxation, social security benefits and other factors on housing tenure decisions, labour force participation and expenditure patterns.

Until the GHS was instituted, research data on leisure was largely restricted to data from administrative records and occasional local or national surveys (see Maunder's Vol. 4). The GHS data on leisure for 1973, 1977 and 1980 now provide an important new and regular source for research on the sociology of leisure. They have been used to monitor and forecast trends in leisure, to inform policies and facilitate planning for sports. The data can also be used, for example, to study the restriction in social and leisure activities resulting from unemployment, ill-health, or poverty, or the relationships between patterns of paid work and leisure, as well as sex and social class differences in leisure activities.

As noted in the ninth volume of Maunder's review series, the GHS data on reported ill-health and the utilisation of health care services present the essential basis of a health information system, offering major advantages over *ad hoc* sources. As noted earlier (p. 129) Forster used the GHS to show that the social class trend in utilisation of health services is reversed when health needs (as reflected in morbidity) are taken into account. Many studies use pooled data for two or more GHS years in conjunction with other sources such as census data, OPCS mortality data and data from routine health statistics. For example, aggregated GHS data for 1973–6 were used in conjunction with other data to assess the relationship between differential levels of demand and the distribution of general practitioners (Buxton and Klein, 1979). One study recoded GHS data on acute sickness to assess the relationship between symptomatology and survey data on restricted activity due to ill-health. Another study used GHS data on ill-health and health service utilisation, in conjunction with other sources, to consider the correlations between socio-economic and environmental indicators and health indicators. The results showed that social factors such as the level of unemployment are now more important determinants of sickness and mortality than environmental factors, such as poor household amenities (Forster, 1979). The research implications of the two different types of data on reported ill-health collected in 1977–8 and in other years are discussed in the GHS reports for 1971, 1978 and 1979. The DHSS report *Inequalities in Health* (1980) presents and reviews numerous secondary analyses of health data from official sources, including GHS data for 1973–6. Unusually, it offers a discussion of both theoretical and policy issues raised by the results.

Other Applications

This review of the existing and potential uses of the major national surveys in social research is necessarily limited and partial, but there are at least three other types of use that should be noted briefly.

There are an enormous number of studies that use national survey data only peripherally: to obtain a relatively small amount of data that is used in conjunction with other sources; to obtain background or comparative information to provide the national context for a smaller or local study; to conduct analyses of a single topic or question; or to explore the broad parameters of a topic during the development of a new survey. For example, the FES data is used by the Department of Energy to produce an annual report on patterns of household expenditure on fuel. Market researchers regularly use FES data on expenditure on particular types of goods and services to help assess the demand for specific products and to develop marketing policy. Some use has been made of the FES data on redundancy pay and on contributions to charities. The national surveys are frequently used simply to provide background information for an otherwise quite separate study as illustrated by Townsend (1979: 116–76). The implication here is that secondary analyses of national survey data are not always major studies; the surveys may provide useful information on a very limited aspect of social behaviour, on income from a particular source, or expenditure on a single type of item.

Another application is the extension and replication of the national surveys in other surveys, either of a geographically limited area or of a population sub-group. Surveys of this type carried out by OPCS were noted in Chapter 7. Multi-purpose household surveys, modelled to some extent on the GHS as well as the population census, have been carried out by a number of local authorities, usually on an *ad hoc* basis, though some (such as the Newcastle upon Tyne Household Survey noted in Table 1.1) are more regular. Simplified versions of the FES questions on income have been adopted by some social researchers for use in other surveys. The GHS health section, particularly the parts on disabilities and the use of services, have been replicated in local surveys, both to validate and further interpret GHS data, and to assess the utility of the GHS data for identifying deprived areas. The GHS health questions have been used in other surveys, for example, the DHSS cohort study of the unemployed, in order to measure the health problems of a particular group relative to that of the general population. This type of replication usually leads to secondary analyses of the national survey data, in order to compare the results of such studies with national averages or national patterns. If such applications become widespread, for example, by replicating the major classificatory questions and variables used in the GHS, LFS and FES, comparability between surveys will be increased, and their secondary analysis potential extended. The advantages of standard definitions and classifications of key variables in social research have already been argued (Stacey, 1969; Gittus, 1972) and the disadvantages of incompatible social classifications are evident (Reid, 1977: 32–49). Some surveys, however, have been influenced by both the strengths and the limitations of the multi-purpose surveys. The national survey of household resources and standards of living carried out in 1968/9 by Townsend was inspired in part by the earlier work of Booth and Rowntree, but also by the FES, and the lack of access to FES microdata for secondary analysis. While the FES provided a partial model, the survey attempted to extend the range of information collected (along lines similar to those later adopted for the GHS), as well as extending well beyond the range of information collected by both surveys. The study thus questioned some of the conceptual and other limitations of the FES and GHS as sources of data for studies of poverty (Townsend, 1979).

The third application is the use of national survey datasets for the development and testing of statistical tests and methodological procedures. Methodological work on the estimation of complete systems of demand equations using household budget data has been done in North America on the basis of FES data for the UK (Pollak and Wales, 1978). The GHS data have been used to obtain empirical measures of the effect of complex survey design on standard and widely used statistical tests such as chi-square tests, and to develop methods for the analysis of repeated surveys (Holt *et al.*, 1980).

International Perspectives

Comparative studies based on national survey data for Britain and other countries are a growth area in social research. The creation of national survey archives in Europe and North America has been an important factor in this development, by increasing awareness of, and access to, survey datasets across countries (see Chapter 11). The SSRC Survey Archive supplies the British multi-purpose survey datasets to researchers outside Britain and holds a number of important North American datasets, such as the National Longitudinal Surveys and the Family Income Dynamics Study (see p. 123). Both methodological and substantive research need no longer be constrained by the datasets available for a given country. As noted above, some methodological work has been developed by North American economists using FES data for Britain. As access to survey microdata was facilitated by the earlier emergence of survey archives in North America, some of the British analyses of the multi-purpose surveys have been influenced by the approaches and results of earlier North American work, and the comparable studies and datasources are usually referred to in reports. For example, Alden's analysis of the limited British data on double job-holding reviews the more extensive American datasources and literature on this topic (Alden, 1977). With the development of the SSRC Survey Archive in Britain, more extensive international comparative studies can be expected in the 1980s. Stark's (1977) comparative study of income distribution in Britain and seven other countries and Beckerman *et al.*'s (1979) study of the impact of income maintenance programmes on poverty in Britain and three other countries illustrate the potential for further comparative research.

Part Three

Other Surveys and Datasets

9

Other Official Surveys and Datasets

A wide range of other surveys and studies are carried out by government departments. These cover topics as diverse as occupational aspirations and educational attainment, unemployment, strikes, retirement patterns, women's employment, poverty, one-parent families, family formation patterns and the related use of contraception, health, work histories and related education and training histories, industrial relations, housing quality and factors related to housing choice, migration, mobility and leisure behaviour. Some of the more recent surveys, and the more important social datasets derived from administrative records, are listed in Tables 1.1 and 1.4. Space does not permit a review of all the major national surveys and social datasets; most are relatively specialised in their topic content and their interest for secondary analysis is thus narrower than with the three multipurpose surveys. The focus will be on a few illustrative examples and their use in secondary analysis. It is worth emphasising that the research community outside government tends to be ignorant of most *ad hoc* official surveys, and thus of their secondary analysis potential, and even within government researchers in one department may be unaware of surveys carried out by another department that may provide data suitable for certain secondary analyses. The availability of suitable official data sources can be explored through the CSO's Survey Control Unit, the CSO's *Guide to Official Statistics*, Maunder's fifteen-volume review series, lists of recent social surveys in the OPCS journal *Population Trends* and the listings of recent surveys in the published annual research reports of government departments. If a dataset of interest has been identified, the Archive can be asked to obtain it (if it does not already hold the data) but increasingly government departments are depositing their national survey data at the Archive after a certain lapse of time (sometimes before the main report is published).

Ad Hoc Surveys

The CSO's Survey Control Unit estimates that about 250 *ad hoc* surveys of individuals or households are carried out each year by government departments, and most of these fall into the broad category of social surveys. The characteristics of many of these surveys make them particularly attractive for secondary analysis.

Official surveys are commonly based on large samples (as compared with the local and frequently non-random samples that often form the basis of academic surveys), due to the need for nationally representative and reliable information for policy formulation and review. The size of the DoE's 1977/8 National Dwelling and Housing Survey (NDHS) is somewhat unusual in that it was designed to provide essential information on housing that would otherwise have been supplied by the cancelled 1976 Census for the distribution of rate support grant to local authorities and to provide sampling frames for three follow-up surveys. Unlike most *ad hoc* surveys, it collected a minimal amount of information for a very large sample of 415,000 households in England in the first phase. The survey was later extended to cover a further 200,000 households in the 1978 second phase, and a further 300,000 households in the 1979 third phase, so that the results for a total of 915,000 households provide complete coverage of all rate support grant 'needs' areas. The size of the survey made it attractive for secondary analyses as a census substitute. For example, the Department of Employment used it for a study of the employment and unemployment situation of ethnic minorities (Barber, 1981), and the Home Office used it for a study of ethnic minorities more generally (Field *et al.*, 1981), partly because the survey covered a much larger number of ethnic minority households than do smaller surveys (such as the LFS), and also because it incorporated the direct question on ethnic group originally tested for the 1981 Census and subsequently used in the LFS (see Appendix B). A number of local authorities have made use of the survey because the large sample ensured that the data could be analysed at sub-regional level: at local authority level, and even at ward level for urban areas. For example, the Greater London Council is using the 1977/8 NDHS data for the GLC area (a total of 200,000 households) to study the distribution of housing deprivation and unemployment, and for comparative studies of the socio-economic circumstances of ethnic groups.

Surveys by government departments are able to offer nationally representative data in part because they have access to administrative records which can provide sampling frames for surveys of particular groups in the population. (The special procedures used to preserve confidentiality when using administrative records as sampling frames are not discussed here.) For example, all national surveys of the unemployed have been based on samples drawn from the unemployment and benefit registers. In some cases censuses or surveys provide samples for follow-up surveys; the GHS is used in this way (p. 104), also the population census (p. 39) and, as noted in Table 1.1, the DE's Workplace Industrial Relations Survey is based on a sample drawn from the Census of Employment. A variety of other methods (such as household sifts, sometimes in conjunction with census SAS) are sometimes used in order to ensure that surveys provide nationally representative data on particular groups (for example, ethnic minorities), methods that are rarely used in academic surveys because of their costs. The typical sample size for national surveys (of individuals, households, or establishments) is between 2,000 and 5,000 compared with sample sizes in the hundreds typical of academic surveys. For example, the 1977 Retirement Survey carried out by OPCS for the DE and DHSS studied factors affecting decisions about retirement, and the socio-economic circumstances of those who had already retired, among 3,500 men and women aged 55 or 50 and over respectively. The Family Finances Survey carried out by OPCS for the DHSS was closely modelled on the FES but the sample of 3,000 concentrated on the low income families that are less well represented in the FES. It was primarily a survey of the factors contributing to financial poverty, and the information collected on the social characteristics of families went wider than that available in the FES.

While official surveys will have an immediate focus (usually policy-related questions and issues), they usually collect data on contextual topics, explanatory factors and related issues, which will only be used to shed light on the central policy issue in the main report. The contextual matter can be used as research data in its own right in secondary analyses. The OPCS 1976 Family Formation Survey collected detailed information on sexual behaviour, contraceptive use, family building intentions and attitudes towards family size, the results of which are reported in Dunnell (1979). The survey was to a large extent a replication of a 1967 OPCS Survey, and some comparative analyses of both surveys are included in the main report. In the course of collecting detailed fertility histories, the 1976 survey collected contextual information on other life events, including minimal work histories. Secondary analysis of the 1976 survey is being carried out at the London School of Hygiene and Tropical Medicine to examine the relationships between women's fertility histories and work histories, and to assess the influence of socio-economic factors on any links between the two histories. Similarly the MSC National Training Survey collected contextual data on membership of trade unions and professional organisations. It has been used as the only source of national data on the distribution of unionisation in the occupational structure (a topic on which rough estimates only were previously available), and union membership has been included as a factor in NTS-based secondary research on labour market segmentation and the determinants of income.

Until recently most official surveys were entirely *ad hoc* and hence time-specific, but from the 1970s onwards the surveys increasingly incorporated time as a variable and a degree of continuity and inter-connectedness began to emerge. For example, the DoE's 1977/8 NDHS was extended by three follow-up surveys on the private rented sector, on households sharing their accommodation with others and on households that had moved within the preceding eighteen months. The last incorporated time as a variable in that the housing situation of the movers at their previous address could be compared with their current housing, and the change related to their reasons for moving. The MSC 1975/6 National Training Survey collected retrospective data on work, unemployment, education and training histories from a national sample of 54,000 people, providing a second-best alternative to longitudinal data from cohort studies (such as the NCDS described in Chapter 10). The DHSS 1978/9 Cohort Study of the Unemployed provides true longitudinal data on a cohort of 3,400 newly registered unemployed men who were interviewed within four weeks of registration, at three months and at twelve months after registration. The Department of Employment 1980 Workplace Industrial Relations Survey provides time-specific data only but it follows a number of earlier surveys on the same topic, and is planned as a regular survey, to be repeated every three years with substantially the same design and content, so that it forms part of a series covering the 1980s, with the possibility of comparisons backwards to the 1970s. Sometimes surveys on a given topic are repeated periodically. For example, the DE's 1980 Survey of Women and Employment provides information on the work histories of a national sample of 5,500 women aged 16–59 and on factors related to their decisions to work or not, and the type of work chosen. The survey is a repeat (and extension) of a 1965 survey on the same topic and the two surveys together provide broadly comparable data on factors related to the changing pattern of women's employment. One of the limitations of the sample survey as a research technique is that it usually provides a *static* picture relating to a particular point in time, with little information on the social *processes* with which social scientists are concerned. This trend in official surveys makes the data far more attractive for secondary research since social processes and social change are tapped to a far greater extent in cohort studies, follow-up surveys, regular and replicated surveys.

Most official surveys are concerned with the current behaviour and attitudes of individuals, though sometimes retrospective data on the person's past behaviour and circumstances are collected, and sometimes data on other members of their family or household are also collected. Almost all the surveys are household-based, in the sense that interviews are conducted in households, and the survey topics relate to people in their private lives, as individuals, or as members of a household. Sometimes surveys relate to people in their public lives, with interviews carried out at an institution, such as the workplace, as illustrated by the OPCS survey for the DE of personnel managers' and line managers' policies and attitudes to women at work (Hunt, 1975) and by the DE's 1980 Workplace Industrial Relations Survey which collected data on 2,000 establishments, through interviews with management and employee representatives. In this case individuals are interviewed as public role-holders who provide information on the institution whose policies and activities are collectively determined by those who work in it. The difference between the two approaches is illustrated by using the information that a respondent's occupation is 'teacher' to assign him to a given social class and relate this to his other personal characteristics, or alternatively to analyse data on all respondents who are teachers to find out about the kinds of institutions that schools are. As most survey reports take the individual (occasionally the household) as the unit of analysis, one ready option for secondary analysts is to reanalyse the data using social institutions (such as the family, the household, the company, the trade union, or the school) as the unit of analysis.

More generally, the original reports on most official surveys (and typically those produced by OPCS on surveys for government departments) are in the nature of *survey reports* rather than *research reports*, that is, they provide detail on the survey methodology, numerous tables on the data collected and comment on the more striking findings – but they do not discuss the existing literature on the topic, or set the results in the context of social science theory and previous empirical work. One ready option for secondary analysts is thus to reanalyse the data (either the tables presented in published reports or the microdata available at the Archive) in the light of social science theory and the literature. For example, Brookes (1979) reanalysed part of the OPCS survey data on company organisation and worker participation reported on by Knight (1979). His reanalysis differs from the main report in that it sets the results in the context of previous research and existing theory on boards of directors within the management process, and the unit of analysis is the firm as a social institution rather than individuals. Similarly Hunt's (1975) survey of management attitudes and practices towards women might be re-analysed in the context of the literature on occupational segregation, to show how attitudes are determined by, reflect and support a structural feature of the labour market – a theoretically informed approach that would contrast with Hunt's own analysis which explained such attitudes somewhat tautologically in terms of prejudice towards women at work (MacIntosh, 1980). Hyman (1972) has illustrated how opinion poll data acquire new value when reanalysed in the framework of political science theory. Similarly, many official surveys could yield new or additional results if reanalysed within the framework of social science theory.

Government departments commission national surveys from OPCS, from independent research institutes, or from social and market research companies. The main reports are produced by OPCS or the department concerned and (most commonly, but not always) published by HMSO. Because of the pressure within departments for early results that can be fed into the policy process, the original report on a survey will never fully exploit the potential of the data beyond the immediate policy concern. More extensive (secondary) analysis by the original research team is unlikely because they will be quickly re-assigned to another survey with an equally tight timetable. The civil service practice of regularly re-posting people to different jobs within departments also ensures that the original research team is unlikely to do any secondary analyses. (By way of contrast, Townsend stayed with his poverty survey for some sixteen years to carry it through to a published report which exhausted the survey data's potential).

The secondary analysis potential of *ad hoc* official surveys needs to be emphasised because it is not an explicitly stated 'design feature' as with the multi-purpose surveys described in Chapter 7, but results rather from the characteristics of social research in government departments, with large, nationally representative, rich and complex survey data being collected and analysed within tight timetables to produce reports geared to a narrow and well-defined policy area, and the researchers moving on to other work even before the publication of the report. Sometimes more than one survey will be available on a given policy area (such as employment, unemployment, housing, health, education), presenting the secondary analyst with the opportunity to reanalyse the surveys to produce a more rounded picture than will be available from each survey in isolation. For example, a wide range of data on different aspects of unemployment are available from no less than four recent surveys: the MSC 1979 survey of the long-term unemployed, the DHSS 1978/9 cohort study, the DE 1980–1 two-stage survey of the long-term unemployed and the MSC 1980–1 cohort study of the unemployed. Sometimes surveys with different central concerns provide complementary data on a particular topic or social group. For example, a PhD student at London University is carrying out secondary research based on the 1977 Retirement Survey and the 1977 Family Expenditure Survey. The former provides detailed information on the attitudes, health, income and employment of a large sample of people around retirement age while the latter provides more detailed data on income for a rather smaller, but nationally representative sample of people in the same age groups. The two surveys are being used as complementary sources of data for a study of the labour force participation decisions of older families.

Access to official surveys for secondary analysis was until recently limited by the need to make special arrangements with the government department responsible for the survey. Access is now both easier and wider, as a result of data being available through the Archive at Essex University. Departments are increasingly adopting the practice of depositing national surveys at the Archive, and OPCS has adopted a policy aimed at routinising this procedure.

As the role of the SSRC Survey Archive in promoting secondary research became established, opportunities for secondary analysis began to be incorporated into the organisation and design of major surveys. Thus in the early 1980s social science research in Britain began to move towards the collaborative research model already established in North America, linking the research efforts of central government and the academic community to maximise the relative advantages of each (Hakim, 1982). For example, the new series of Workplace Industrial Relations Surveys (WIRS) are jointly funded by the Department of Employment, the SSRC and the Policy Studies Institute, with all three institutions playing a role in the design and analysis of the surveys. The data from the 1980 (and following) WIRS will be made available for secondary analysis by the academic community through the SSRC Survey Archive very shortly after the main report on the survey is published. It is expected that the survey will be used for policy-related studies within the DE, but will be approached from a more theoretical perspective by academic secondary analysts, thus maximising the utility of the data among all social science researchers.

Other Official Datasets

The focus on official surveys should not obscure from view the small (but increasing) number of social datasets derived from administrative records, or collected through the administrative system, that are becoming available at the Archive. At present the Archive holds the DE data on stoppages of work (known more commonly as the strikes data), which are collected through the administrative system for information but not for action. The data relate to establishments that are identified by size and industry but not by name, and provide information on the number and duration of stoppages of work in establishments. A number of university researchers have obtained the data through the Archive for secondary research on the distribution and causes of strikes which extend the primary analyses published by the DE (Smith *et al.*, 1978). For example, Prais (1978) analysed the strikes data using more detailed size-groups than were identified in DE analyses to assess whether the increased frequency of strikes of larger plants was in accordance with expectations and probability, or due to a greater degree of individual militancy in large plants.

As administrative records are increasingly computerised (for example, the unemployment registers) it becomes easier to extract (and render anonymous) random samples of all records or of selected groups, for statistical and research purposes. The number of non-survey social datasets available at the Archive will increase during the 1980s, as this form of data-release becomes established and replaces the special arrangements negotiated by individual researchers with departments. The content of such datasets is limited, as it is confined to the information already held in records, but they allow researchers outside government to do analyses additional to those carried out by departments, not all of which are published.

The Archive is pursuing an active policy of acquiring all major surveys and national social datasets derived from administrative records that can be released by government departments for use in secondary research by the academic community. Some departments (such as the CSO, DE and DoE) have developed policies of active collaboration with the Archive in this regard. No doubt data from other departments, such as the numerous DES datasets on education, will also become available at the Archive in due course. It is to be expected that the policy of encouraging secondary analysis that already operates in relation to the multi-purpose surveys will eventually be extended to *ad hoc* surveys and other datasets.

International perspectives

In countries where data archives are well established within the social science research community, many official surveys and datasets derived from administrative records are routinely available through archives. For example, in the USA data from national health surveys and social security records (such as the Continuous Work History Sample) are extensively used in secondary research by the academic community. In countries where archives are only recently established, or non-existent, access to such data is by special arrangement between the researcher and the government agency responsible for the data. *Ad hoc* surveys and official datasets are too varied in character for a review to be attempted here.

10

Non-Official Surveys

In terms of data content, non-official surveys offer the secondary analyst wider options than official sources but they also present greater variation in the quality of the data and there is more need to be selective in the choice of dataset. Non-official surveys are carried out by a wide range of organisations: market and social research organisations and opinion poll companies in the private sector (such as Gallup, NOP and BMRB); independent research agencies (such as SCPR and PSI); researchers in the academic community (in universities and polytechnics); and a range of other institutes which carry out research (such as the National Children's Bureau). The discussion here is centred on national studies within each of the types outlined in Table 1.1. Unless otherwise noted, all the surveys discussed are available at the SSRC Survey Archive.

Types of Social Data

Almost all the non-official continuous and regular surveys are carried out by opinion poll and market research companies, for example, the monthly surveys of Gallup, NOP (National Opinion Polls) and ORC (Opinion Research Centre). Collectively, they provide public opinion data on a wide range of social, political and economic issues as well as on attitudes to the government of the day and its policies (Table 10.1). The opinion polls resemble the GHS in that they contain some standard questions and topics; some topics that are rotated into the surveys periodically; and some topics included on an occasional basis (for example, opinion on current events). The central purpose of the National Readership Survey (NRS) is to provide detailed information on the newspaper and magazine reading habits of people in Britain. But it also collects information on the socio-economic characteristics and behaviour of respondents, including social class and income, household composition and tenure, qualifications obtained, smoking and drinking habits, cinema visiting, TV viewing, holidays away from home, ownership of stocks and shares, use of bank or savings accounts and data on the characteristics of the neighbourhood of residence. The NRS is similar to the FES in that it has been running continuously as a

Table 10.1 *Opinion Poll Data for Britain*

Topics, Issues	Sources
Satisfaction with the current government (policies, prime minister, opposition leader and policies)	Gallup, NOP, ORC
Political knowledge, interest and participation	ORC
Attitudes to political system, institutions, reforms	ORC
Salience (relative importance) of current issues and problems	NOP
Race relations, immigration	Gallup, NOP, ORC
Inflation, prices and incomes, cost of living	Gallup, NOP
Satisfaction with pay, savings	Gallup, NOP
Unemployment and its causes, the unemployed and benefits	Gallup, NOP
Role of women (duties, work outside the home, equal opportunities)	NOP, ORC
Attitudes to pornography	NOP
Foreign affairs and defence (Common Market)	NOP, ORC
Abortion, birth control, marriage	NOP
Drugs, gambling	NOP
Leisure activities and travel	NOP, ORC
Political parties and individuals	Gallup

Table 10.1 *Opinion Poll Data for Britain – continued*

Topics, Issues	Sources
Trade Unions	Gallup, NOP
Industrial relations (strikes, legislation)	Gallup, NOP, ORC
Crime and law	Gallup, NOP
Consumer confidence, buying intentions	Gallup, NOP
Nationalisation	Gallup
The media	ORC
Other special issues and events	Gallup, NOP
Voting intentions, electoral behaviour	Gallup, NOP, ORC
Religious beliefs	NOP
Family relationships	ORC

Classificatory variables always include age and sex. The following variables are often or occasionally included: occupation of head of household, employment status of respondent, social class or SEG, terminal education age, marital status, ethnic group, trade union membership, number of persons in household, number of electors and non-electors in household, number of children in household and car ownership.

Note:
The SSRC Survey Archive holds NOP surveys from 1963 onwards, Gallup political polls from 1970 onwards, and ORC surveys from 1971 onwards for Britain, and the British surveys of a number of Louis Harris International polls for 1970, 1971 and 1972.

quarterly survey since 1956 with a fixed design and content, although the sample was doubled in 1968. The quarterly sample size for the NRS is now 7,500 while the size of the opinion polls varies; but data for a number of quarters or years can often be combined to yield a larger dataset for more detailed analyses. Two time-series of the standard NOP questions for 1963–6 and 1967–70 have been created, and other time-series could potentially be developed. Another continuous survey of consumer behaviour, the BMRB's Target Group Index, is not currently available at the Archive although it is used extensively for secondary research in relation to Webber's socio-economic area classification (see p. 52) as illustrated by Bickmore et al. (1980).

The most important multi-purpose cohort study, the National Children's Bureau's NCDS (National Child Development Study, 1958 cohort), is available at the Archive, although its smaller predecessor, the Douglas 1946 cohort study, is not. The data consist of a number of files containing information on the cohort members' family background, experiences and behaviour at each age studied. The main topics covered are health (both of the cohort member and of the mother during the pregnancy); social adjustment during childhood; schooling and educational attainment at ages 7, 11 and 16; parent–child relationships at ages 1, 4, 7 and 11; social behaviour, attitudes and aspirations at age 16. The cohort of about 16,000 people born in one week in 1958 is large enough to allow detailed analyses of the cohort as a whole, of sub-groups within it such as first and second generation immigrants (numbering 350 and 1,120 respectively), or comparative studies of the males and females. The NCDS has now been extended to cover early adulthood with a fourth sweep of the cohort at age 23 (in 1981). There may be further sweeps of the cohort in adult life. The NCDS provides a unique source of longitudinal data not only on the development and life experience of people during childhood and adolesence but also, in due course, during adult life, all of which can be related to the characteristics of the family of origin.

The great majority of ad hoc studies consist of data obtained from samples of individuals. Some studies contain more complex data. For example, the NCDS files contain the results of interviews with parents; information supplied by teachers and schools; the results of tests of ability and educational attainment administered by teachers; information supplied by health visitors; examination results; and data from interviews with the cohort members themselves. Cartwright's study of patients and their doctors contains interview data for patients, the results of a postal survey of their doctors and data from DHSS records.

Because of the expense of large-scale surveys, many of the more important national surveys have been funded (in whole or part) by government departments as well as through the SSRC. For example, all the sweeps of the NCDS after the perinatal mortality study, and Kelsall's 1966/7 survey of 1960 graduates, were jointly funded by government departments and the SSRC. Many of the national surveys carried out by independent research institutes, such as the Policy Studies Institute (formerly PEP) and the Institute for Social Studies in Medical Care, have been commissioned by government departments: for example, Daniel's 1976 survey of the unemployed; Smith's 1974 survey of racial minorities; Cartwright's 1970 study of birth control services and her 1977 survey of patients and their doctors. The SSRC-funded studies include the quality-of-life surveys carried out by the SSRC Survey Unit; Boyle's 1973 social mobility follow-up survey to the Northern Ireland 1971 Census; Runciman's 1962 survey of social inequality; the Butler and Stokes electoral studies and the 1974 British Election Studies. National surveys carried out by the National Foundation for Educational Research, Social and Community Planning Research and a variety of other organisations as well as by individual researchers are available for secondary analysis along with surveys and datasets for other countries.

Approaches to Secondary Analysis

Secondary analysis does not necessarily imply that the focus of the study differs from that of the original analysis. Existing datasets can be reanalysed with the more sophisticated statistical techniques currently available, sometimes with a view to challenging the conclusions of the original researchers.

Mark Abrams carried out a 1966/7 survey on race prejudice for the Institute of Race Relations, as part of a wider study on the social situation of immigrants, the results of which were reported in Rose *et al.* (1969: 551–604). Abrams concluded that only 10 per cent of respondents (in the five boroughs sampled) could be classified as 'prejudiced', suggesting that the survey did not reveal a great deal of prejudice in the indigenous population towards coloured immigrants. His survey report was supplemented by secondary analysis of NOP and Gallup data on attitudes of the British public towards immigrants and immigration. Abrams's conclusions were subsequently challenged by a number of other researchers who carried out secondary analyses of the 1966/7 survey data. Schaefer's reanalysis illustrates some of the features of secondary analysis: it is based on more sophisticated analytical techniques than the simple cross-tabulations presented in Abrams's report; it challenges his conclusions; and it has a theoretical focus which contrasts with the essentially descriptive focus of the original report. The 1966/7 survey offered nearly fifty possible items for the development of a scale of racial prejudice, from which four were selected. These differed from the four items used in Abrams's analysis and reveal 30 per cent of the population to be prejudiced. A group of independent variables reflecting an individual's position in the social structure were identified; another group of intervening situational variables reflecting the degree of contact and interaction with ethnic minorities were also selected from the survey. Cross-tabulations of these two groups of variables with the prejudice scale revealed complex interactions between factors which were explored further through correlation analysis and multiple regression analysis. It was shown, for example, that downward social mobility was associated with lower (rather than higher) levels of prejudice, and higher levels of contact and interaction with immigrants were associated with higher levels of prejudice although the opposite had been observed in studies in the United States (Schaefer, 1974).

Lancaster's (1979) secondary analysis of Daniel's (1974) national survey of the unemployed also illustrates the use of multi-variate analysis where the primary analysis had relied on cross-tabulations, and the use of a large survey to obtain data for a particular sub-group of interest. Of the 1,500 respondents to Daniel's survey, Lancaster used only the data for the 479 British unskilled unemployed. His reanalysis was concerned specifically with assessing the relative impact of unemployment benefits on the duration of unemployment, or the disincentive impact of benefits on regaining work. He computed one new variable, the replacement ratio (the ratio of unemployment income to earnings from the last job held), and extracted three other variables (age, duration of unemployment and the local unemployment rate) from the survey data. Regression analysis was used to measure the relative and cumulative impact of these factors on the duration of unemployment.

Kelsall's 1966/7 survey of 1960 graduates (Kelsall et al., 1972) provided the model for a similar survey of 1970 graduates carried out by the Department of Employment in 1976/7 (Williamson, 1979). Analysis of the second survey was complemented by secondary analysis of the earlier survey, to indicate the extent of change over a decade in the early careers of highly qualified manpower. Access to two surveys on the same topic greatly extends the potential for further secondary research on the sociology of this elite group (perhaps in conjunction with the data from the 1973 Qualified Manpower Follow-Up Survey to the 1971 Census described on p. 41), in particular allowing time (or generation) to be added as a variable in the analysis. There are a number of other surveys which broadly replicate earlier surveys (for example, Cartwright's 1964 and 1977 health studies and a number of electoral studies) so that the type of research carried out with continuous surveys (such as the GHS) can often be carried out with more specialised surveys on particular topics as well.

Secondary analysis can be a useful adjunct to the analysis and interpretation of one's own original research, as exemplified by Abramson (1967). His own data consisted of the results of 330 interviews with 15-year-old boys attending various types of secondary school. Secondary analysis of a Gallup Youth Survey provided an important complement to this small-scale intensive study, allowing Abramson to set the results of his non-random survey in a broader national context. The Gallup Youth Survey was a four-wave panel study, with interviews in 1960–3 with a nationally representative sample of 1,800 young people aged 16–18 in 1960. Both studies used standard classificatory variables (such as type of school attended and social class of origin), and both collected information on attitudes towards social stratification (or social class), political party affiliation and parental party affiliation, although more detailed information on political attitudes was collected in Abramson's study. Thus there was sufficient overlap for the two sources to be used to complement each other, the Gallup survey providing the national picture on young people's political orientations and the intensive study illuminating the process of political socialisation at work in each type of secondary school. Both datasets were subsequently reanalysed to explore the effects of inter-generational mobility on political attitudes (Abramson and Books, 1971).

Sometimes new data are collected as an adjunct to secondary analysis of an existing dataset, as exemplified by Leggatt (1974). His study was based on a reanalysis of a survey of industrial companies, and new data on the commercial success of these companies that were extracted for the study from the annual reports deposited at Companies House. The study offers an example of secondary research based on a dataset combining survey information with data extracted from public records. The survey originally formed part of a NEDO study on the need and demand for management education and training in Britain. The secondary research was theoretical in orientation, seeking to identify management styles within companies and to assess the relationship between management styles and the commercial success of companies. Various items from the survey were selected to construct two scales of management flexibility and management autonomy, each defined in relation to the Weberian, bureaucratic, or mechanistic, model of management. Both measures were found to be negatively related to size of firm, although industry type was also a factor. A third scale, of the companies' commercial success, was constructed from data in company annual reports. However, the hypothesis that the less bureaucratic, more flexible and open-ended management styles would be associated with greater commercial success was not supported; on the contrary, size of firm was found to be the most significant variable, determining both management style and commercial success.

Some of the most successful secondary research relies entirely on existing datasets without collecting any new data. A cross-national comparative study of the class and status structure in industrialised countries carried out by Robinson and Kelley (1979) relied on two datasets: the NORC General Social Survey for the USA and the Butler and Stokes data on political change in Britain. The study illustrates many features of secondary analysis. The two datasets were quite different, the British survey being a single-purpose panel study carried out by academic researchers, the American survey being a multi-purpose annual survey carried out by an opinion research centre (see p. 155). Since the class and status structures investigated are not subject to rapid change, time was not a variable in the research and the researchers used data with a substantial ten-year difference in the fieldwork dates: the Butler and Stokes 1964 survey and the NORC surveys for 1973–6. Since the NORC General Social Survey data were available for more than one year, they merged the results for 1973, 1974 and 1976 into a single larger dataset; the 1975 data were not used because a key variable was not included that year. Another key variable, personal income and earnings, was available only for 1974 and 1976; to correct for inflation between the two years, all incomes were converted to 1975 dollars using the consumer price index.

In both cases sub-sets of the larger samples were used and the researchers carefully documented both the reasons for excluding parts of the samples and the implications (if any) for the representativeness of the resulting sub-sets. Women were excluded from the British dataset because the numbers were too small to permit separate analysis of this group and also because the data did not allow full-time workers to be distinguished. The American sub-set was also confined to people working full-time but aggregating results for three years gave sufficient numbers of women for this sub-group to be retained. Non-respondents on any of the variables used in the study were excluded but careful checks on the full and restricted samples showed that they were virtually identical on all other variables. Thus the sub-sets used in the analysis for the United States contained 1,100 men and 600 women; the analysis for Britain related to 700 men. The authors' interpretation of their findings bears in mind the relatively small numbers from each survey, but they note that the findings are consistently in the right direction and statistically significant (at least for men – women prove to be more intractable).

The study was an empirical quantitative test of the class theories of Marx and Dahrendorf, in itself an ambitious undertaking since the authors note that the theories have been subject to extensive theoretical analysis but few empirical studies. They also demonstrate how these conceptions of class can be combined with the Blau-Duncan status model dominant in much social science research. And they test the hypothesis that class position has a stronger impact on class identification and political attitudes in Britain than in the United States. Thus the two-nation study is in part a replication, to test the empirical evidence for theories about class structure in more than one industrial society, and in part a comparative study to assess the existence (and importance) of differences in the political culture between two societies. Operational definitions of the control and ownership of the means of production, the exercise of authority in the workplace, occupational status, class identification and political atti-tudes were applied to each dataset. Cross-tabulations, correlations between variables and regression analyses were used to test their hypotheses. The results showed two overlapping but distinct stratifica-tion systems, one a class system based on control of the means of production and authority, the other a status system based on education and occupational status, both having important consequences for income, political attitudes and class-consciousness. Position in one system was only modestly correlated with position in the other, each having significant and independent effects. The class factors increased by almost half the variance in men's income explained by the status factors alone. Control of the means of production was an important determinant of class-consciousness in Britain, whereas Americans were more attuned to status than to class distinctions (Robinson and Kelley, 1979).

Other Uses of Data in Archives

Surveys deposited in archives cannot provide the basis for follow-up surveys. Archives require that all identifiers (names, addresses and any other unique identifiers of persons, organisations, or other respon-dents) be removed from survey data before they are deposited, in the interests of ensuring the anonymity and confidentiality of the research information they hold. However, survey datasets held in archives are sometimes used to provide the model for a replication of an earlier study at a later point in time. Some secondary analysis of the earlier dataset will usually be carried out to provide analyses more closely comparable with those from the second (usually somewhat modified) survey. As noted earlier (p. 150), Williamson's survey of 1970 gradu-ates was modelled on Kelsall's earlier survey of 1960 graduates and contains comparative analyses of the two surveys. One of the advan-tages of a national archive is that earlier studies on a given topic will be retained for future use, rather than lost, as archives ensure that all relevant materials are available: questionnaires, coding frames, details of the design, sampling and data collection procedures, as well as the survey results themselves. In a sense archives become repositories of survey methodology (survey design, questionnaire design, coding and processing procedures) as well as depositories for survey results. Few survey reports contain the very detailed methodological information that is of interest for a later replication, as the main focus is usually on the results obtained.

A second use of data in archives that is not strictly speaking secondary analysis is in research on survey methodology, survey analysis and the statistical techniques applied to quantified social data. This type of use is more extensive in North America, but is developing also in Britain. For example, the NCDS and British Election Study data have been used to study the validity and reliability of chi-square tests and the analysis of correlations from survey data (Holt *et al.*, 1980).

International Perspectives

Since secondary analysis has a longer history and is more established among North American social scientists, it is not surprising that some secondary research based on British datasets has been carried out by North American researchers, often in cross-national comparative studies. The study by Robinson and Kelley (1979) discussed above is but one example of North American social scientists' ready appreciation of the value of the British research data available in archives. It is also an example of the type of cross-national comparative research that can be carried out with datasets whose titles and original purpose give no indication that they contain similar questions and variables making them suitable for the particular focus of the reanalysis.

The number and variety of North American studies based on secondary analysis of *ad hoc* and non-official datasets are too extensive for a review here. Hyman (1972) offers a very comprehensive guide to, and review of, secondary research in North America up to the early 1970s. Since then the range of suitable datasets has been extended and many more studies of this type have been carried out, as reflected in articles in most North American social science journals. Since Hyman's 'state of the art' review there have been three important developments. The idea of systematic replications of important earlier surveys held in archives for studies of social change has been established. The value of regular or continuous multi-purpose household surveys for academic and other social research has been established, most notably by the series of NORC General Social Surveys initiated in 1972. Finally, although social scientists have still not developed any comprehensive social theory around which social surveys and other data sources can be built, comparable to the economic base underlying the national accounts, there have been significant steps towards the design of social indicator models (Land and Spilerman, 1975) and the design of a system of social and demographic statistics (United Nations, 1975).

The NORC General Social Survey (GSS) is similar to the GHS in that it offers a regular multi-purpose household survey designed explicitly for secondary analysis with some standard topics and others included on a rotating or *ad hoc* basis. It is otherwise quite dissimilar, as the content of the survey is designed for use by the academic social science community, rather than for use in central government social policy and planning research, and includes attitudinal data as well as information on behaviour and the socio-economic circumstances of individuals. The GSS is the brainchild of James A. Davis (now Professor of Sociology at Harvard University); but the project has an advisory committee representing the American Sociological Association; the survey is carried out by a full-time staff at NORC; the data and codebooks are distributed through archives including the Roper Public Opinion Research Centre, the ICPSR and the SSRC Survey Archive (see Table 11.1); and the funding has been provided by independent foundations. The GSS is relatively small scale, offering interview data for a nationally representative annual sample of about 1,500 civilian non-institutionalised adults aged 18 and over, but data for two or more years are often merged to yield larger samples. From 1972 to 1978 the survey was annual; it became biennial in the 1980s. It has formed the basis for teaching packages on substantive topics (such as social stratification and mobility, attitudes, deviance) and methodological topics (such as question-wording and data analysis). It is argued that the GSS has provided not only the data for a wide range of secondary analyses but also the basis for a new era in social research, for example, in facilitating the movement away from a rigid deductive model of social research towards a more flexible and inductive model (Glenn *et al.*, 1978).

Secondary analysis of non-official datasets shows a very much more variable pattern in other European countries, influenced in part by the degree to which data archives are established institutions within the social science community and the related factor of access to computers. With the exception of the Zentralarchiv at the University of Cologne, established in 1960 as the first European archive making data available for secondary analysis, most archives were only created in the 1970s (in Norway, Holland and Denmark) and there are as yet no national data archives in France and Italy, for example (although other institutions disseminate official data). But other factors, such as the degree of development and organisation of empirical social research in each country, also play a part (Rokkan, 1976). Some European datasets are more readily accessible in North American archives, especially those specialising in international data. Language barriers present an important constraint on cross-national comparative studies, which explains in part the greater volume of comparative secondary research based on American and British data. It is possible that future years will also see a flowering of European comparative research.

Part Four

Archives and Secondary Analysis

11

The Survey Archive

The coming of age of secondary analysis as an established part of social research is closely connected with the recognition of data archiving as an important function within the social science community. The International Federation of Data Organisations for the Social Sciences (IFDO) was established in May 1977, becoming an associate member of the International Social Science Council a few months later, and holding its first international meeting in 1978. The founding members, four North American and seven European data archives (including the SSRC Survey Archive), reflected great diversity in their status, policies and operations, and many are still going through major stages in their development. It would be premature, therefore, to define or describe the role of data archives with references to any single archive. This chapter first considers the aims and functions of data archives taken as a group, noting those developments that have been actualised in some cases and remain as possibilities for others. It goes on to describe the role of the national British archive, the SSRC Survey Archive at the University of Essex, in greater detail. Finally, the practical aspects of using an archive are discussed.

The Role of Archives

The three major functions of data archives are the preservation and storage of data; the dissemination of data within the social science community; and the development of methods and procedures to stimulate the widest use of data. The degree of emphasis given to one or the other of these objectives in an archive's policy, and the methods adopted to further these aims, varies a good deal.

If the emphasis is on the first of these objectives, the archive is in effect a data library or a public records office for machine-readable information. A major part of the archive's resources will be devoted to the acquisition, preservation and storage of datasets. This will include, for example, developing procedures to guard against the decay of magnetic tapes; transferring data from media that are more liable to decay (such as computer cards, paper tape, or questionnaires) to magnetic tape; and ensuring that datasets are 'cleaned' before storage with full documentation. Acquisitions policies will vary between archives, as with libraries. Some archives are national reference libraries, with a broad acquisition policy covering all types of social science data; any dataset not already held will be obtained if a user request is received. Other archives specialise in particular types of data and operate a selective acquisition policy. They may specialise in data for a particular discipline or topic (such as political science or education), or in one particular type of dataset such as survey and other data relating to individuals, data on institutions, or what are termed 'ecological' datasets consisting of aggregate data for areas.

If emphasis is given to the second objective, resources will be devoted to ensuring easy access to the datasets held by the archive. For example, publications and catalogues describing the holdings will be produced; indexes to whole surveys, to the data topics, even to individual questions or single items of data, may be developed to facilitate the identification of suitable datasets by a prospective user; searchers for suitable datasets may be carried out by the archive on behalf of the user; the archive may create datasets from its holdings, either by producing data sub-sets suitable for a particular project, or by creating new datasets formed by linking or merging data from two or more of its existing holdings (for example, to create time-series or ecological datasets by combining items of information from a number of sources). Finally, a good deal of attention will be given to publicising the archive's holdings and its services, and to ensuring a rapid response to users' requests for data.

When the emphasis lies on the third objective, the archive is not so much a library as a type of teaching and research centre specialising in secondary analysis. In addition to holding datasets it will hold a software library and may actively develop new types of computer program. It will offer a consultancy service to data users, advising on the design of datasets for secondary analysis and on appropriate software; the consultancy service may be extended to researchers engaged in primary research who will eventually deposit their data at the archive. It will offer courses, seminars and workshops on data analysis, secondary analysis more specifically, on existing and potential applications of the archive's holdings. It may publish user manuals and handbooks on particular datasets, or types of data. It will devote resources to extending and educating the user community. It may offer a liaison service between depositors or originators of data and other users, between existing and potential users. Finally, it may offer a data analysis service based on its holdings and on its expertise in secondary analysis, and may publish research reports based on secondary analysis.

Few archives will offer all of this long list of potential services. Some, especially the major national archive for a country, will attempt to cover all three objectives to some extent. Frequently archives modify their policies over time, moving gradually from an emphasis on the library function in an early phase towards the secondary analysis centre at a later stage, as the archive becomes established, recognised and well funded. Some archives, however, have adopted a policy based on the third objective from the start; others have chosen to remain data libraries in the main. This brief outline demonstrates that it will almost always be possible for a user to suggest a desirable potential service that is not yet offered by a particular archive.

Another aspect of an archive's activities concerns its level of operations: regional, national, or international. To some extent local authorities in Britain function as data archives for the areas they serve – a function perhaps best exemplified by the Greater London Council. In France the regional offices of the national statistical office – INSEE – all function as regional archives for official data and statistics. Similarly, in North America there are regional offices functioning as archives and dissemination centres for official data. Some American universities provide public data archive services for their state, for example, the Social Science Data Library at the University of North Carolina. Other North American data archives operate at the national level, whether they specialise in a particular topic or function as general archives. In most countries there is one major general archive which liaises with other specialist archives and also with its counterpart in other countries. In Britain the SSRC Survey Archive fulfils this role.

The SSRC Survey Archive

The SSRC Survey Archive was established in the late 1960s at the University of Essex as the national archive for Britain. At first it attempted to give equal emphasis to all of the three policy objectives of an archive outlined above, until it was recognised that the limited SSRC resources devoted to the Archive entailed some limitation of its activities. The Archive's current policy still encompasses all three objectives, but the range of services offered within each type is necessarily limited. In the first decade of its development the overall emphasis was on the data library function: the acquisition, preservation and storage of datasets. In its second decade it is moving towards an emphasis on data dissemination, and in the longer term potentially the third objective.

The Archive's acquisitions policy is broad and non-selective, in keeping with its status as a national archive. It accepts all social science surveys and datasets, and its holdings cover sociology, political science, anthropology, education, social psychology, geography, history, economics, planning, health and labour force studies. However, the Archive uses a non-disciplinary classification of its holdings in its publications, one that differs from the classification of sources of social data presented in Table 1.1. Datasets are only declined when they are of transparently poor quality, are not computer-readable, do not have accurate and legible accompanying documentation, or when the likelihood of secondary analysis by other researchers is extremely small. Apart from these essential limitations, the SSRC Survey Archive accepts both small and large datasets (sample sizes for surveys range from 50 to 915,000); data for the whole country (the United Kingdom in some cases, more commonly Great Britain, occasionally for England and Wales only) or for particular counties, towns or other sub-regional areas; and data for the nineteenth and earlier centuries (the 1851 Census sample is described in Chapter 6), although the majority of its datasets relate to the 1960s and 1970s.

In addition to accepting those datasets offered to it, the Archive actively solicits surveys and datasets that are about Britain, have been conducted by British researchers, or are likely to be of interest to British researchers (Crewe, 1979). This policy is supported by the SSRC making the deposit of data in the Archive a condition of awarding a grant for social science research. Some research agencies, notably Social and Community Planning Research, National Opinion Polls Ltd and Social Surveys (Gallup) Ltd, automatically deposit their social and political surveys. Increasingly, government departments are depositing the data obtained from national surveys, especially those carried out by OPCS. If a particular dataset is requested by a potential user, the Archive will usually make special efforts to acquire it. But in general the Archive seeks to obtain a representative range of data on all aspects of British society. The SSRC Survey Archive is the largest social science data archive outside the United States. By 1981 it held nearly 2,000 data files, and was adding to its collection at the rate of about 200 a year. The Archive's holdings are described in its *Data Catalogue*, available in most university and polytechnic libraries, and in the Archive's quarterly *Bulletin*, which provides brief details on the most recent acquisitions and is available free on request.

As the national British archive, the SSRC Archive maintains links with other specialist archives in Britain, and also with other archives in Europe and North America (Table 11.1). It can deal with inquiries about any dataset that may be of interest to a user, whether British or foreign. In some cases it will refer the user to a specialist archive in Britain. In other cases it will seek to obtain the required dataset, either directly from the originator, or through a foreign archive. The Archive already holds a number of important foreign surveys, such as the NORC General Social Surveys for the USA (p. 155) and the American longitudinal studies described earlier (p. 123). It also holds a number of foreign surveys not available elsewhere (for Venezuela and Nigeria, for example), and some foreign census datafiles. The small specialist British archives with which it maintains links include the archive of education data at the University of Edinburgh; the Institute of British Geographers' census grid-square data archive at Durham University; the industrial relations archive at the London School of Economics and Political Science; and the data bank on organisations at the University of Aston in Birmingham.

The Archive's services are jointly funded by the SSRC and the University of Essex, and no charge is levied for the datasets supplied to researchers (with the exception of the census SAS – see pp. 55–7). A small charge is made to cover the reproduction costs of a dataset – that is, the tape (unless one is supplied by the user) and the accompanying documentation. The Archive supplies tapes in a format compatible with the researcher's local computer installation, to avoid the need for tape conversion work. Datasets have been 'cleaned' as far as possible by the Archive to eliminate (or at least flag) any discrepancies between the data and documentation; when released for secondary analysis, the dataset will be classified into one of six 'cleanliness' categories (or in the case of datasets obtained from the ICPSR, one of four cleanliness categories). As noted in Chapter 7, sub-sets of very large files (such as the GHS and FES) are produced containing only those variables actually required by the analyst, and in a consistent format. Thus datasets obtained from the Archive are ready for immediate use, and the majority are dispatched within ten days of being ordered. At present the identification of suitable datasets is a collaborative but *ad hoc* job involving both the Archive and the user; the Archive is developing a computer-based information retrieval system for its holdings in order to speed up the process of identifying a dataset suitable for a researcher's needs. In the long term it is possible that the identification of a suitable dataset and accessing the data will both be carried out on-line from a local terminal.

Other Archive activities help to develop secondary analysis in social research. Data-use workshops provide a forum for the exchange of information between data depositors, current and potential users, as described with reference to workshops on the GHS and FES (pp. 107, 114). The summer school in survey design and analysis at the University of Essex provides secondary analysts with practical skills in data analysis. Visting fellowships are offered to researchers wishing to carry out analysis of the Archive's datasets. A network of Archive representatives in universities and other institutions facilitates liaison with depositors and users. The Archives quarterly *Bulletin* provides a forum for the exchange of information between its depositors, users, and others with an interest in secondary analysis. The circulation of the *Bulletin* gives an indication of the increasing size of the Archive's user community: in 1980 it had a circulation list of 3,000.

How to Use an Archive

The identification of datasets suitable for a particular secondary research design is the key process in the successful use of a data archive. This process is in part a technical matter, but partly a more subtle process of interaction between the researcher's preconceived ideas and the available data. A researcher who has predefined notions of the type of sample and precise variables required for a research topic may well be lucky in finding a suitable dataset in an archive. More commonly, however, the successful secondary analyst approaches the identification of suitable datasets in a more open-minded and flexible way, allowing for some modification of the definition and selection of variables, even the type of sample, in the light of information already available in the archive. In some cases it may mean using different sub-sets from more than one survey, each offering partial but complementary data, for example, on the social group or topic of study. The identification of suitable datasets cannot be approached as a purely technical process, as it involves some degree of creativity on the part of the researcher.

The identification process commonly starts with the Archive's *Data Catalogue* and the updates issued in the *Bulletin*, but will usually involve advice from Archive staff. The use of suitable key-words can be crucial in this communication process, and broad variable concepts plus operational definitions and question examples can be helpful in making a data inquiry. The *Catalogue* classifies datasets into twenty-three broad subject categories such as: industrial relations, education, mass media studies, social structure and social stratification. Cross-references help identify studies relevant to more than one subject. For each dataset information is given on the content (the general purpose and a list of specific attitudinal and behavioural variables); the face-sheet of classificatory variables used; the date of fieldwork; the methodology (sampling method, sample size and method of data collection); and the original investigation (the principal investigators and resulting publications). In addition to the main subject classification of datasets, five indexes help identify sources of data for particular topics or groups (for example, journeys, apprentices, elites, or schools) or for particular areas (countries, regions, counties and towns).

Researchers should also bear in mind that if there is a specific user request the Archive can usually obtain datasets that have not already been deposited. Some archives have published indexes to all sources of data on a given topic or to all their own holdings, facilitating the search for suitable datasets from foreign sources; there are a number of official publications identifying regular and *ad hoc* official surveys on a given topic (p. 137) and the SSRC's *Newsletter* provides information on current and recent surveys that will be deposited at the Archive.

Table 11.1   List of Archives

Project TALENT Data Bank
AMERICAN INSTITUTE FOR RESEARCH
PO Box 1113
Palo Alto, California 94302

Alfred J. Tuchfarber, Jr. Director
BEHAVIORAL SCIENCES LABORATORY
University of Cincinnati
Cincinnati, Ohio 45221

Phillippe Laurent
BELGIAN ARCHIVES FOR THE SOCIAL
    SCIENCES
Place Montesquieu, 1 Boite 18
B-1348 Louvain-la-Neuve, Belgium

CELADE LATIN AMERICAN POPULATION DATA
    BANK
United Nations Latin American
    Demographic Center (CELADE)
Casilla 91
Santiago, Chile

Social Science Data Librarian
CENTER FOR SOCIAL ANALYSIS
State University of New York
Binghamton, New York 13901

CENTER FOR QUANTITATIVE STUDIES IN
    SOCIAL SCIENCES
117 Savery Hall
DK-45
University of Washington
Seattle, Washington 98195

Per Nielsen
DANISH DATA ARCHIVES
Odense University
Niels Bohrs Alle 25
DK-5230 Odense M
Denmark

Alice Robbin
DATA AND PROGRAM LIBRARY SERVICE
4451 Social Science Building
University of Wisconsin
Madison, Wisconsin 53706

Laine Ruus
DATA LIBRARY
Computing Centre
University of British Columbia
2075 Wesbrook Place
Vancouver, British Columbia
Canada V6T 1W5

Data Librarian
DATA LIBRARY
Survey Research Center
University of California
Berkeley, California 94720

DRUG ABUSE EPIDEMIOLOGY DATA CENTER
Institute of Behavioral Research
Texas Christian University
Fort Worth, Texas 76129

Librarian
Information Documentation Center
DUALABS, INC.
1601 N. Kent Street, Suite 900
Arlington, Virginia 22209

Stein Rokkan, Director
EUROPEAN CONSORTIUM FOR POLITICAL
    RESEARCH
Data Information Service
Fantoftvegen 38
N-5036 Fantoft-Bergen
Norway

Thomas Atkinson, Director
Data Bank
INSTITUTE FOR BEHAVIORAL RESEARCH
York University
4700 Keele Street
Downsview, Ontario
Canada

Assistant Director for Member Services
INTER-UNIVERSITY CONSORTIUM FOR
    POLITICAL AND SOCIAL RESEARCH
PO Box 1248
Ann Arbor, Michigan 48106

E. M. Avedon
LEISURE STUDIES DATA BANK
University of Waterloo
Waterloo, Ontario
Canada N2L 3G1

Reference Service
Machine-Readable Archives Division
    (NNR)
NATIONAL ARCHIVES AND RECORDS SERVICE
Washington, DC 20408

Table 11.1   *List of Archives – continued*

Patrick Bova
NATIONAL OPINION RESEARCH CENTER
University of Chicago
6030 South Ellis Avenue
Chicago, Illinois 60637

Lorraine Borman
NORTHWESTERN UNIVERSITY INFORMATION
    CENTER
Vogelback Computing Center
Northwestern University
Evanston, Illinois 60201

NORWEGIAN SOCIAL SCIENCE DATA SERVICES
Universiteet i Bergen
Christiesgate 15–19
N-5014 Bergen-Univ.
Norway

Robert Darcy
OKLAHOMA DATA ARCHIVE
Center for the Application of the Social
    Sciences
Oklahoma State University
Stillwater, Oklahoma 74074

Stuart J. Thorson
POLIMETRICS LABORATORY
Department of Political Science
Ohio State University
Columbus, Ohio 43210

POLITICAL SCIENCE DATA ARCHIVE
Department of Political Science
Michigan State University
East Lansing, Michigan 48823

Ronald Weber, Director
POLITICAL SCIENCE LABORATORY AND DATA
    ARCHIVE
Department of Political Science
248 Woodburn Hall
Indiana University
Bloomington, Indiana 47401

David K. Miller, Director
PROJECT IMPRESS
Dartmouth College
Hanover, New Hampshire 03755

Machine Readable Archives
PUBLIC ARCHIVES CANADA
395 Wellington Street
Ottawa, Ontario
Canada K1A 0N3

ROPER CENTER, INC.
Archival Developmental Activities:
Box U-164R
University of Connecticut
Storrs, Connecticut 06268
User Services Activities:
38 Mansfield Street
Yale University
New Haven, Connecticut 06520

SOCIAL DATA EXCHANGE ASSOCIATION
229 Waterman Street
Providence, Rhode Island 02906

SOCIAL SCIENCE COMPUTER RESEARCH
    INSTITUTE
621 Mervis Hall
University of Pittsburgh
Pittsburgh, Pennsylvania 15260

James Grifhorst
SOCIAL SCIENCE DATA ARCHIVE
Laboratory for Political Research
321A Schaeffer Hall
University of Iowa
Iowa City, Iowa 52242

JoAnn Dionne
SOCIAL SCIENCE DATA ARCHIVE
Social Science Library
Yale University
Box 1958 Yale Station
New Haven, Connecticut 06520

Sue Lewis
SOCIAL SCIENCE DATA ARCHIVE
Survey Research Laboratory
1005 W. Nevada Street
University of Illinois
Urbana, Illinois 61801

SOCIAL SCIENCE DATA ARCHIVES
Department of Sociology and
    Anthropology
Carleton University
Colonel By Drive
Ottawa, Ontario
Canada K1S 5B6

Table 11.1   *List of Archives – continued*

Everett C. Ladd, Jr
SOCIAL SCIENCE DATA CENTER
University of Connecticut
Storrs, Connecticut

James Pierson
SOCIAL SCIENCE DATA CENTER
University of Pennyslvania
353 McNeil Bldg CR
3718 Locust Walk
Philadelphia, Pennsylvania 19104

Sue A. Dodd
SOCIAL SCIENCE DATA LIBRARY
University of North Carolina
Room 10 Manning Hall
Chapel Hill, North Carolina 27514

Judith S. Rowe
SOCIAL SCIENCE USER SERVICE
Princeton University Computer Center
87 Prospect Avenue
Princeton, New Jersey 08540

Director
SSRC SURVEY ARCHIVE
University of Essex
Wivenhoe Park, Colchester
Essex, England

Jack Citrin, Director
STATE DATA PROGRAM, SURVEY RESEARCH
    CENTER
2538 Channing Way
University of California
Berkeley, California 94720

Robert M. deVoursney
STATE GOVERNMENT DATA BASE
Council of State Governments
Iron Works Pike
Lexington, Kentucky 40578

Cees P. Middendorp
STEINMETZ ARCHIVES
Information and Documentation Center
    for the Social Sciences
Royal Netherlands Academy of Arts and
    Sciences
Keizersgracht 569–572
Amsterdam, The Netherlands

ZENTRALARCHIV FUR EMPIRISCHE
    SOZIALFORSCHUNG
Universitat zu Koln
5 Koln
Bachemer str. 40
Federal Republic of Germany

International Perspectives

There is at present no complete guide to all data archives in Europe and North America. Table 11.1 lists the more important data archives. It is hoped that IFDO may at some point publish a guide to the various archives, their holdings and services, which, as noted earlier, vary a good deal, even between national archives.

The best available guide to the holdings and services of the European archives is currently an issue of the European Consortium for Political Research's *News Circular* (1979). A somewhat dated listing of North American archives is given by Hyman who also reviews their services, usage and influence on North American secondary research (Hyman, 1972: 1–34, 330–3). A more recent review is provided by Hofferbert and Clubb (1976). The SSRC Survey Archive has issued a leaflet describing the holdings and services of one of the most important of the North American archives – the ICPSR at the University of Michigan – which holds extensive material on Western and Eastern Europe and developing nations in addition to its American datasets; and the Archive holds copies of the ICPSR's annual *Guide to Resources and Services.*

The SSRC Survey Archive would be the initial contact point for queries regarding datasets that are known, or likely, to be held by other data archives. In most cases it can arrange acquisition of the required data and, if necessary, will convert the files to the user's requirements.

The SSRC Survey Archive is at the University of Essex, Colchester, Essex; tel. (0206) 860570 or 862286, Ext. 2244.

12

Secondary Analysis in Perspective

Secondary analysis will appeal to some researchers more than others. The creative but disorganised researcher is unlikely to do well as a member of a team carrying out a major survey; by specialising in secondary analysis the independent researcher can work alone while taking advantage of data collected by well-equipped teams (Glazer, 1963). Further, researchers whose primary interest is in assessing the empirical evidence for theories can avoid the practical difficulties of mounting a new data collection by relying on secondary analysis. Researchers interested in the development of social indicators and measures of social change will rely exclusively on secondary analysis of large national datasets. For others, the lack of resources (time and/or money) for new empirical research can be overcome by secondary analysis.

Secondary analysis may be particularly attractive at certain stages in a social scientist's career. Graduate students will often find secondary analysis an attractive alternative to the two standard solutions to their lack of research funds: the small local study carried out single-handed or the largely theoretical dissertation. Academics with large teaching loads and those unable to obtain research grants when funds become scarce may well turn to secondary analysis as an alternative avenue for continuing their empirical research. Social scientists who have successfully pursued a research career may find they are promoted to research administration jobs where the time and freedom to engage in new empirical research of their own are severely limited. Secondary analysis offers a means of continuing substantive work for research directors and administrators (whether in the public or private sector) who cannot afford to be tied down to the demanding timetable of a new data collection. Unlike a new survey, secondary analysis can be done in fits and starts, in available blocks of time, over a long period.

In some organisational settings secondary analysis becomes almost an obligatory research method because it can be done within a much tighter timetable than a new study, if results are needed quickly. In central and local government, briefings on, and summaries of, the available research evidence on a given topic have often to be produced in a very short time. Reanalysis of existing census or survey data to shed light on the particular question or issue will often be used to complement literature reviews for such work. Although the multi-purpose data collections are designed for this type of use in central government, which might, therefore, be designated as a primary application, those who do such analysis are in the same position as secondary analysts outside government: they are analysing data collected by others and must rely on the documentation and general reports provided by the data collecting agency. This is perhaps why secondary analysts outside government are able to do as much with national datasets as those in departments, particularly as they have a great deal more time at their disposal.

A major advantage of secondary analysis is that it is a great deal cheaper than empirical work that requires a new data collection. It will thus be additionally attractive to all researchers, in all organisational settings, in the seven lean years which follow the seven fat years. In periods when research funds are plentiful, great stores of survey and other data are collected. By preserving these data in archives, empirical research can continue on a more economical basis in periods when research funds are more restricted. But it is hoped that previous chapters have proved that secondary analysis does not consist merely of mopping up the leftovers from the original report on a data collection. The fresh perspective brought by another researcher (often from a different discipline) to an existing dataset allows original research to be produced by secondary analysis.

A greater emphasis on secondary analysis, as compared with purely theoretical work or empirical work based on new data, can also yield benefits for the development of social science. Secondary analysis allows for greater interaction between theory and empirical data because the transition from theory development to theory testing is more immediate. It may prompt greater emphasis on the inductive model of research instead of deductive theory constructed in isolation from any knowledge of the real world. It should facilitate a trend away from purely 'episodic research' on the topics or issues of the day towards more cumulative inquiry. It should allow theory to be informed by the dynamics of social change through the analysis of data for more than a single point in time (Glenn et al., 1978: 535 ff.). A greater emphasis on secondary analysis as against new data collections would contribute to a consolidating phase in social science research, with a rapprochement of theory and empirical evidence and the opportunity to explore their implications for social policy.

Surveys and other social datasets collected by government departments are likely to play a significant role in these developments. The perspective they offer on society and its processes is the 'bird's eye view' rather than the 'worm's eye view'. They provide data on the social structure, on trends over time, on the way different parts of the social structure interact and interrelate. Government surveys thus provide good material for empirically testing theoretical hypotheses and perspectives. However, large national surveys do not always provide information on how any group feel and experience their social reality, which is commonly the province of the small-scale study. Researchers who are familiar only with the small-scale study (and the majority of academic researchers in Britain fall into this category) may well feel uncomfortable working with large-scale survey data. The consolidation of theory and empirical research may necessitate a new orientation among social scientists in Britain, as well as the acquisition of more practical skills (for example, in data analysis).

The expansion of secondary analysis may also involve new approaches to methodology. An emphasis on tests of statistical significance is the product of researchers working always with a single dataset, usually an *ad hoc* survey or study. The use of replication tests to substitute for, or to complement, significance tests, may become a feature of secondary research. The simplest form of replication is to test the same hypotheses on two or more datasets of the same type – for example, two surveys of social mobility taken at different times. It can be argued that replication provides an even stronger test when hypotheses are tested against datasets based on different methodologies – for example, aggregate data, survey microdata and case study material on the same topic. If all the datasets independently yield the same results, the reliability and significance of the results is more solidly proved than if a single dataset had been used (with significance tests). The variety of datasets held by archives facilitates this methodological approach, and Finifter (1975) provides a systematic formulation of replication methodology for secondary analysts. Occasionally the results of a particular study are hotly disputed – as in the case of the National Children's Bureau's study of the effects of comprehensive secondary schools. As the study was based on the National Child Development Study, and the data are available at the Archive, a replication of (parts of) their analysis should demonstrate, far more conclusively than polemical debate, whether their findings were distorted or not. In some cases, replication has shown widely accepted research findings to be simply untrue, or the product of the particular techniques of analysis adopted.

Secondary analysis has its uses in teaching as well as research. Practical instruction in the techniques of data analysis is facilitated by the teaching datasets produced by survey archives. Fieldwork carried out by students may provide experience in data collection methodology but it does not often provide datasets of sufficient size and quality to form the basis for instruction in a wide range of analytical techniques. Multi-purpose surveys – such as the British General Household Survey or the American General Social Survey – have proved particularly successful among students (Glenn *et al.*, 1978: 541 ff.). One advantage of incorporating secondary analysis in the curriculum is that it promotes the integration of theory and empirical research and thus provides more comprehensive and solid training for professional social scientists.

More generally, secondary analysis is part and parcel of increasing specialisation in research work. Large national surveys and statistical exercises require large teams containing a variety of specialist skills, in sampling, fieldwork, statistics, programming, data analysis and report writing. There is already a clear division between those specialising in data collection and fieldwork and those specialising in data analysis and the production of research reports. With increasing specialisation, the dividing line between primary and secondary analysis may disappear. In future years, secondary analysts may come simply to be regarded as data analysts, using material collected by others which, through their efforts, is made to yield its fullest results.

Appendix A: Accessing Data

Computer-based analysis of existing datasets is for the most part no different from analysing data one has collected oneself, except that the time-lag between the conception of the study and data analysis is much shorter as there is no fieldwork to be done. As yet there are few general guides to computer-based processing of survey data, as much depends on the particular software used and the characteristics of the dataset. The SSRC Survey Archive summer school (see Chapter 11) offers an exceptionally wide range of courses on this topic, although software houses and computer bureaux run short courses on the uses of particular packages, and the Market Research Society, the Civil Service College and some research institutes also run courses on the applications of the more important packages or on aspects of survey data analysis. An increasing number of universities offer graduate courses in computer-based analysis of quantitative data, many of which use teaching packages created from data at the Archive, such as the GHS. Some of these teaching packages are listed in the Archive's *Data Catalogue* (SSRC Survey Archive, 1980: 22); others are listed in the Archive's *Bulletin*. A general guide to data analysis is beyond the scope of this appendix; it is intended only to point to the more common or important problems (and possible solutions) that crop up in secondary analysis, in particular of the large hierarchical datasets that are produced from the major national surveys.

Tape Conversion

The advantage of obtaining datasets for secondary analysis through the SSRC Survey Archive is that the tape is always supplied in a format compatible with the user's computer installation, so that it is ready for immediate use. Since the Archive does not charge for this tape conversion service (and, perhaps more important, the service of 'cleaning' the data and ensuring that the documentation is complete), it can be advantageous to go through the Archive even when the secondary analyst can obtain the data direct from the originator. The Archive currently supplies most data in an SPSS compatible format; other formats are possible, and may become more frequent as universities extend their range of standard packages for the analysis of social science data.

Datasets obtained direct from the originator often need to be converted. This is required, for example, for the datasets obtained direct from OPCS, such as the census SAS (see p. 55) and for data from commercial research agencies, which is commonly multi-punched. A number of computer bureaux offer a tape conversion service if the user's own computer department cannot handle this.

Software

SPSS is probably at present the most widely available package for the analysis of social science data, and it can be used on almost all the survey datasets supplied by the Archive or obtained from other sources. Problems arise mainly with census SAS and hierarchical datafiles such as the GHS and FES microdata. These can be overcome by re-formating the datasets as flat (rectangular) files which can be analysed with SPSS. But this approach had disadvantages. Very large datasets (such as the GHS and FES) become even larger, as the data is stored less efficiently, and processing costs increase. It may be necessary to restrict the analysis to a predetermined sub-set of the data, which reduces flexibility in the range of variables used. The Archive itself re-formats the GHS and FES tapes by converting them to flat SPSS files in which the individual or the household is the unit of analysis; as a result the links between persons in a household may be lost, so that it is impossible to discover, for example, whether a particular husband has a working wife. The loss of information contained implicitly in heirarchical files (by virtue of their structure) can be overcome by adding new variables, which state explicitly the linkages between persons in each family or household, when the tapes are re-formatted to SPSS flat files, as has been done by some GHS users (see the Archive *Bulletin*, no. 16, p. 1, and no. 17, p. 1). There are a number of other packages available, but most have limitations of one sort or another. In general, packages with extensive file-handling capabilities (which allow the unit of analysis to be variably defined) tend not to offer extensive statistical capabilities; as such, any file-handling package which can interface with a statistical package (such as SPSS) would be very attractive to users of social science data.

One of the more promising packages appears to be CENTS-AID, a package developed by a census agency in the United States, DUA-Labs, for the analysis of the large hierarchical 1 per cent census Public Use Sample tapes, and now widely used on both census and other data in North America and elsewhere. This is essentially a tabulating system, but the latest version (3·0) can interface with SPSS in that a correlation matrix can be processed further with SPSS. Another advantage is that tabulation requests are written in the SPSS format now familiar to many researchers. CENTS-AID has been acquired by the CSO (for use by government departments) and by the GLC (for the analysis of GHS microdata).

Other packages capable of analysing hierarchical datasets are SIR

Appendix B: A Guide to Standard Classifications

The secondary analysis potential of data is greatly enhanced if standardised methods of collecting and coding 'facesheet' or 'classificatory' variables are applied. Standard or compatible definitions and classifications of basic social variables facilitate comparative research (across time or space, or simply between datasets) and allow linkages to be made between datasets in order to create richer multi-source datasets. The creation of the SSRC Survey Archive in the late 1960s led the British Sociological Association, in conjunction with the SSRC, to develop guidelines for the collection and coding of key variables in social research, with a view to ensuring the secondary analysis potential of new research data, improving data comparability, and facilitating the interplay of theory and empirical research. The resulting volumes (Stacey, 1969; Gittus, 1972), although now somewhat dated, provide comprehensive reviews of the theoretical significance of key variables, of actual and recommended operational definitions and classifications for each: income, occupation, education, family and household, housing, religion and locality. It is regrettable that the original intention of extending and updating this work quinquennially has not been implemented by either the BSA or the SSRC. In the absence of more recent reviews, I shall simply note the more important characteristics of, and recent developments in, the classifications currently in use. The focus is on official classifications, not only because these are used in most of the datasources discussed earlier. Official classifications have a number of advantages over the variety of *ad hoc* classifications used in particular studies, and were recommended (where they existed) in the BSA/SSRC reviews. (For some topics, such as religion and politics, none exists.) With the exception of much housing data (see below), most official classifications are multi-purpose or open-ended in the sense that they have no single predetermined purpose and the entity problem (see p. 22) is thus smaller than with highly purposive academic research. They are used extensively in non-official research, and detailed information on them is readily available in published reports. In recent years the comparability of official classifications has been improved in order to facilitate comparisons across datasets, a development that has proceeded more quickly than the implementation of the recommendations of the BSA (in Stacey, 1969; Gittus, 1972), and is due largely to the prompting of the CSO.

Occupation

Up to 1972 the Registrar General's (or OPCS) *Classification of Occupations*, prepared and updated primarily for use in coding census results, was the only classification used in official statistics. It has a social bias in that the classification aims to identify groups of occupations that are reasonably homogeneous in terms of the type of work, but also in terms of the degree of skill involved, the environmental conditions and the socio-economic status associated with the occupation, so that the occupation unit groups can be aggregated to the Registrar General's (or OPCS) Socio-Economic Group (SEG) and Social Class classifications (see below). In 1972 the DE published CODOT, the *Classification of Occupations and Dictionary of Occupational Titles*, which was designed for use in local employment offices (jobcentres) and hence had an economic or labour force bias. For statistical purposes a condensed version, Key Occupation Statistics (KOS), was used, for example, in the New Earnings Survey (NES) and LFS results. From the late 1970s the DE and OPCS classifications were linked by creating a new intermediate classification of 161 major occupation groups which can be sub-divided into either the 549 census occupation units or the KOS 404 occupation units. This new common occupational classification was applied from 1979 in the LFS, from 1983 in the NES, and in the 1981 population census (OPCS, 1980c).

The advantages of the common occupational classification of 161 major groups in all official data sources cannot be overemphasised, especially for secondary analysis. From 1981 onwards it is possible to create multi-source datasets on the occupational structure, and to relate DE data on the characteristics of occupations (such as weekly or hourly earnings) to the OPCS data on the social characteristics of people in these occupations (for example, age, sex, marital status, ethnic group and educational qualifications). To some extent the lack of income data in the British census can be overcome, by attributing people in an occupation with the average earnings of the occupation as shown by the NES. Comparability with the 1971 Census classification has largely been preserved at the 549 occupation unit level, and a series of tables produced from the 1971 1 per cent sample tapes shows the precise relationship between the 1971 and 1981 classifications and the impact of the change on the OPCS social class classification (Boston, 1980).

The OPCS occupational classification, and the derived socio-economic classifications, are widely used outside government. *The Classification of Occupations* lists over 20,000 separate occupation titles, so that coding of census or survey results to the 223 occupation units (in 1971) or 549 occupation units (in 1981) is relatively straightforward. The social status and prestige classifications devised by academic social scientists, such as the Hall-Jones and the Hope-Goldthorpe classifications, can then be applied to the census-coded results. However, the prestige scales were developed in relation to the occupations typically held by men, so that the coding of typically female occupations (which constitute one-quarter of the OPCS occupation units) may be both unreliable and invalid.

Socio-Economic Status: Class and SEG

The OPCS Social Class classification has been used since the 1911 Census, and provides the basis for most inter-censal comparisons. It is widely used in non-official data collections. The SEG classification was introduced in the 1951 Census, was extensively amended in 1961, amended again in 1981 in order to offer comparability with other EEC censuses, and commonly provides the basis for international comparisons. The OPCS classifications are used in all census output and in census-related statistics produced by OPCS, such as the statistics on occupational mortality and fertility. Both full and collapsed versions of SEG are used in the GHS output. But all the FES results are based on a separate and unique classification of eleven occupation groups that was adopted at the survey's inception and has so far remained unchanged.

The rationale of the OPCS Social Class classification, as described in the 1970 *Classification of Occupations*, is to create groups that are 'homogeneous in relation to the basic criterion of the general standing within the community of the occupations concerned. This criterion is naturally correlated with, and its application conditioned by, other factors such as education and economic environment, but it has no direct relationship to the average level of remuneration of particular occupations' (OPCS, 1970: x). It has been argued that the Social Class classification is in fact concerned with status, as defined by sociologists (Nichols, 1979: 159). In practice, researchers have used it as the equivalent to socio-economic status (SES) as identified in many North American datasets in comparative studies (see, for example, Robinson and Kelley, 1979: 50). The publication of the Hope-Goldthorpe scale (Goldthorpe and Hope, 1974) has produced attempts to compare the two classifications (Bland, 1979). It is notable, however, that although the Hope-Goldthorpe classification ranks occupational groups on the basis of empirical research on their prestige (or standing), the final classification of seven socio-economic status groups or classes was not based solely on these prestige scores but took account of the theoretical (or subjective) considerations of the researchers and did not have an entirely hierarchical ordering. The SEG classification does not incorporate an explicit ranking in terms of social status. But it is arguable that a status gradient of sorts is implicit in the collapsed version of SEG that is used in the GHS; indeed, this version is sometimes referred to as a 'social class' or 'socio-economic class' variable.

The most important classification of socio-economic status outside government is the social class classification widely used by market research and opinion poll companies and applied in many of the datasets deposited at the Archive, including the National Readership Surveys and opinion poll data described in Chapter 10. This differs in detail rather than rationale from the OPCS Social Class classification, as described by Monk (1970).

Further details on the OPCS social classifications are given in Boston (1980), CSO (1975), Leete and Fox (1977) and in the reference works published in the year before each census (for example, OPCS, 1970, 1980c). A discussion of the various socio-economic classifications applied in official and non-official sources is provided by Reid (1977). A discussion of the relationship between the existing classifications and the theoretical concerns of sociologists is offered by Nichols (1979).

Until recently the family, not the individual, has been taken as the appropriate unit of analysis for studies of social stratification, and thus data on families and their members have been presented with reference to the social class of the head of household, family head, or chief economic supporter, who is usually male. With the increasing number of working women, the majority of families now have two earners (both husband and wife) and there has been increased interest in sex as a factor in social stratification. Reference to the husband's occupation alone as the determinant of a family's social class is now questioned (Gittus, 1972: 103; CSO, 1975: 9–12; Reid, 1977: 65; OPCS, 1978c: 32). In the USA research is under way to obtain composite measures and operational definitions of the socio-economic status of households and families, with reference to the characteristics of all members (for example, Sampson and Rossi, 1975), but there is no equivalent research in Britain.

Industry

The Standard Industrial Classification is applied both in official data sources (such as the population census) and, where appropriate, in other large national surveys. It has recently been revised to allow new industries, such as those connected with North Sea oil and computers, to be more readily identifiable.

Housing

Until recently there was a tendency for official data on housing to focus on indicators of bad housing (especially in the census), but the housing information from the GHS and FES is more wide-ranging, including household durables and central heating among the amenities, for example. Housing tenure is increasingly used as the operational definition of 'housing classes' (Gittus, 1972: 53–7, 85–6; Goldblatt and Fox, 1978). There is a trend towards finer differentiation within, and between, the three main tenure groups (owner-occupation, council tenancy, private tenancy) and the residual group. For example, accommodation held with a job or business and the new forms of tenure in housing association schemes are identified in the GHS and the 1981 Census. An increasing problem for both surveys and the census is the definition of the boundary line between a private household and an institution, which arises from the increasing number and types of partly shared accommodation (such as student accommodation, sheltered housing for the elderly, flat-sharing in urban areas). Standard definitions and classifications cannot always readily cope with new forms of social organisation.

Household and Family Composition

This trend also creates a problem for the definition of a household and for classifications of household composition. Definitions of the household are based on *de facto* income-sharing, as evidenced by members taking meals together (the common cooking-pot criterion), but the utility of this single criterion is increasingly questioned in relation to households of non-related members. The definition of the family most commonly relates to the nuclear family in official statistics, based on the assumption of *de jure* income-sharing. There are two main types of household composition classification: those based on the *familial structure* of the household (identifying the number, size and types of families in the household) and those based on the *age–sex structure* (identifying the numbers of children, adults and sometimes also persons of pensionable age). The census uses both types. Different versions of the second type are used in published reports on the FES and GHS results, but the coding in FES and GHS microdata allows other classifications to be applied by secondary analysts. It should be noted that the selection of the head of household is left to respondents in the census; therefore the census definition of the 'chief economic supporter' (identified at the coding stage) corresponds more closely to the definition of household (or family) head in the GHS and FES.

Country of Birth and Ethnic Group

Until the 1970s immigrants and ethnic minority groups could only be identified somewhat indirectly from population census and other official datasources through information on a person's country of birth. The limitations of this indicator are well documented in analyses of census country-of-birth data (see Chapter 4). In the 1970s various direct questions on ethnic group were tested for inclusion in the 1981 Census. The results of the pilot studies are reported by Sillitoe (1978). Although not adopted for the 1981 Census, the simplest type of question, which had proved most successful in field tests, was used in the DoE's National Dwelling and Housing Survey, and in the 1979 and following Labour Force Surveys (Bulmer, 1980a). The question asks respondents to identify (from a show-card) to which of a dozen racial or ethnic groups they belong, but the groups listed vary slightly between surveys. The classification used in the NDHS and (with small modifications) the 1981 LFS lists: white; West Indian; Indian; Pakistani; Bangladeshi; Chinese; Turkish; other Asian; African; Arab; other; mixed origin. The classification used in the 1979 LFS lists: English, Welsh, Scottish or Irish; Polish; Italian; other European; West Indian; African; Indian; Pakistani; Bangladeshi; Arab; Chinese; other or mixed. The numbers recorded in some groups (such as Turkish or Chinese) are small, so that most analyses are based on aggregating the groups into a smaller number of categories.

The only other standard source of data on ethnic groups, the GHS, does not rely on a direct question. Since its inception in 1971, GHS interviewers have been required to record, for each household member actually seen, whether they were 'white' or 'coloured'. The latter category includes all non-whites, such as Negroes, Indians and Pakistanis, Chinese and Japanese. The classification is regarded as reasonably consistent and meaningful, although clearly not as precise as that obtained from a direct question. Since the GHS (like the FES) excludes households with no member resident in Britain, and is based on a relatively small sample, the number of 'coloured' persons identified in any one year is small – just over 1,000 persons in 1978. Interviewers' assessment of colour, when cross-tabulated against the person's country of birth and/or parents' country of birth, provides an adequate measure of ethnic origin (see, for example, table 4.21 in the 1976 report and table 2.21 in the 1978 report).

Income

The FES questions on income are often taken as the prototype for collecting income data in household surveys. They are more detailed than any other set in specifying all sources of income (earned and unearned, although windfalls are excluded), precise amounts and the period of time to which the data relate (for example, last week's earnings and usual earnings are often both recorded). The data are collected in sufficient detail for the gross and net incomes of different income units (household, family and tax unit) to be identified at the analysis stage. Kemsley (1969a) has designed a simplified version of the FES questions for use in other surveys; they were recommended by the BSA and SSRC (Stacey, 1969: 76–9), and are often used as the basic model by social and market research organisations such as Social and Community Planning Research. The income section of the GHS has always been less detailed than the FES, although it has been extended and amended, particularly from 1979 onwards, to offer greater comparability with the FES by collecting sufficient detail to calculate both gross and net *current* (and usual) income instead of *annual* income as in 1971–8. An evaluation of the GHS income questions used from 1979 onwards appears in the 1979 GHS report.

Area Coding

Coding of the characteristics of the locality or neighbourhood in which survey respondents (and non-respondents) live is as yet not extensive, either in official or non-official surveys, and is usually limited to only one or two of the variables recommended by the BSA: rateable values and census ED identification code or ED characteristics (Gittus, 1972: 144). For both the GHS and FES the rateable value of the home is collected for all households in the samples (but not the average local rateable value). Some researchers have added 1971 Census SAS-derived indicators on the neighbourhoods of persons in their samples into the survey data. Some market research surveys are now regularly coding the 1971 Census social area classification (or ACORN) type (see pp. 52, 57–8) for survey respondents. This approach is being adopted by departments for some national surveys carried out in the years around the 1981 Census – such as the DE's 1980 Survey of Women's Employment and the 1980–1 survey of the long-term unemployed (see pp. 140 and 142) and the NCDS (see p. 148). More extensive area-type coding in surveys, both national and local, would enhance their secondary analysis potential, as argued in Gittus (1972: 140) and in Chapter 5 above (pp. 80–1).

International Perspectives

Most of the standard classifications used in official datasources in Britain are compatible with the standard international classifications (for example, of industries and occupations). *Compatible* means that the basic coding applied to data allows both national and international classifications to be applied separately, *or* one can be aggregated from the other. There are as yet no standard international classifications of many social variables, such as household composition, for example. But increasingly there are conventions on the tabulation of results from population censuses and major types of household survey (such as household budget surveys) which ensure that results are reasonably comparable for cross-national comparative studies.

Bibliography and Author Index

All the sources listed are followed by page references, to show where they are mentioned or discussed in the text.

Abel-Smith, B. and Townsend, P. (1965) *The Poor and the Poorest* (London: Bell). p. **125**.

Abramson, P. (1967) 'The differential political socialisation of English secondary school students', *Sociology of Education*, vol. 40, no. 3, pp. 246–69. p. **151**.

Abramson, P. and Brooks, J. (1971) 'Social mobility and political attitudes: a study of intergenerational mobility among young British men', *Comparative Politics*, vol. 3, pp. 402–28. p. **151**.

Airey, C. *et al.* (1976) *A Technical Report on a Survey of Racial Minorities* (London: Social and Community Planning Research). p. **24, 79**.

Alden, J. (1977) 'The extent and nature of double jobholding in Great Britain', *Industrial Relations Journal*, vol. 8, no. 3, pp. 14–33. p. **130, 134**.

Allen Committee Report (1965) *Committee of Inquiry into the Impact of Rates on Households*, Cmnd 2582 (London: HMSO). p. **111**.

Almond, G. A. and Verba, S. (1965) *The Civic Culture* (Boston, Mass.: Little, Brown), p. **20–1**.

Anderson, M. *et al.* (1977) 'The national sample from the 1851 Census of Great Britain – an interim report on methods and procedures', *Historical Methods Newsletter*, vol. 10, no. 3, pp. 117–21. p. **52, 89**.

Bain, G. S. and Elsheikh, F. (1979) 'An inter-industry analysis of unionisation in Britain', *British Journal of Industrial Relations*, vol. 17, no. 2, pp. 137–57. p. **65**.

Baldwin, J. (1974) 'Social area analysis and studies of delinquency', *Social Science Research*, vol. 3, pp. 151–68. p. **80**.

Banks, J. A. (1978) 'The social structure of nineteenth century England as seen through the census', in *The Census and Social Structure*, ed. R. Lawton (London: Frank Cass), pp. 179–223. p. **86**.

Barber, A. (1981) *Labour Force Information from the National Dwelling and Housing Survey*, Research Paper no. 17 (London: DE). p. **138**.

Barnes, B. (1979) 'Household surveys in the United Kingdom', *Population Trends*, no. 16, pp. 12–16, p. **120**.

Barnes, R. and Birch, F. (1975) 'Estimating the characteristics of non-respondents in the General Household Survey', *Statistical News*, no. 30, pp. 17–19, p. **105**.

Beckerman, W. (1979) 'The impact of income maintenance payments on poverty in Britain, 1975', *Economic Journal*, vol. 89, no. 354, pp. 261–79. p. **134**.

Beckerman, W. *et al.* (1979) *Poverty and the Impact of Income Maintenance Programmes in Four Developed Countries* (Geneva: ILO). p. **134**.

Benjamin, B. (1958), 'Intergeneration differences in occupation', *Population Studies*, vol. 11, pp. 262–8. p. **71**.

Benjamin, B. (1970) *The Population Census* (London: Heinemann). p. **27–8**.

Beresford, M. (1963) 'The unprinted census returns of 1841, 1851, 1861 for England and Wales', *The Amateur Historian*, vol. 5, pp. 260–9. p. **83**.

Bickmore, D., Shaw, M. and Tullock, T. (1980) 'Lifestyles on maps', *Geographical Magazine*, vol. 52, no. 11, pp. 763–9. p. **79–80, 148**.

Bielby, W. T. *et al.* (1979) *Research Uses of the National Longitudinal Surveys*, US Department of Labor R & D Monograph No. 62 (Washington, DC: US Government Printing Office). p. **123**.

Blake, J. and Donovan, J. J. (1971) *Western European Censuses 1960: An English*

Language Guide (Berkeley, Calif.: University of California, Institute of International Studies; repr.,Westport: Greenwood Press, 1976). p. **44, 59**.

Bland, R. (1979) 'Measuring social class: a discussion of the Registrar General's classification', *Sociology*, vol. 13, no. 2, pp. 283–91. p. **179**.

Bogue, A. G. (1976) 'The historian and social science data archives in the United States', *American Behavioural Scientist*, vol. 19, no. 4, pp. 419–42. p. **94**.

Booth, C. (1886) 'Occupations of the people in the United Kingdom 1801–1881', *Journal of the Royal Statistical Society*, vol. 49, no. 2, pp. 314–44. p. **3, 86**.

Bosanquet, N. and Standing, G. (1972) 'Government and unemployment 1966–1970: a study of policy and evidence', *British Journal of Industrial Relations*, vol. 10, no. 2, pp. 180–92. p. **62, 116**.

Boserup, E. (1970) *Women's Role in Economic Development* (London and New York: Allen & Unwin/St Martin's Press). p. **64, 74**.

Boston, G. (1980) 'The classification of occupations', *Population Trends*, no. 20, pp. 9–11. p. **178, 180**.

Boulding, E. *et al.* (1976) *Handbook of International Data on Women* (New York: Wiley). p. **64**.

Brennan, M. E. and Lancashire, R. (1978) 'Association of childhood mortality with housing status and unemployment', *Journal of Epidemiology and Community Health*, vol. 32, pp. 28–33. p. **80**.

Brookes, C. (1979) *Boards of Directors in British Industry*, Research Paper No. 7 (London: DE). p. **141**.

Bulmer, M. (1979) 'Parliament and the British census since 1920', in *Censuses, Surveys and Privacy* ed. M. Bulmer (London: Macmillan), pp. 158–69. p. **28**.

Bulmer, M. (1980a) 'On the feasibility of identifying "race" and "ethnicity" in censuses and surveys', *New Community*, vol. 8, nos. 1–2 (Spring–Summer), pp. 3–16. p. **43, 182**.

Bulmer, M. (1980b) 'Why don't sociologists make more use of official statistics?', *Sociology*, vol. 14, no. 4, pp. 505–23. p. **3**.

Butler, R. (1978) *Employment of the Highly Qualified 1971–1986*, Research Paper No. 2 (London: DE). p. **66–7**.

Buxton, M. J. and Klein, R. E. (1979) 'Population characteristics and the distribution of general medical practitioners', *British Medical Journal*, vol. 1, no. 6161, pp. 463–6. p. **132**.

Buxton, N. K. and Mackay, D. I. (1977) *British Employment Statistics: A Guide to Sources and Methods* (Oxford: Blackwell). p. **8, 28, 86**.

Byrne, D., Williamson, B. and Fletcher, B. (1975) *The Poverty of Education: A Study in the Politics of Opportunity* (Edinburgh: Martin Robertson). p. **79**.

Carley, M. (1981) *Social Measurement and Social Indicators* (London: Allen & Unwin). p. **76**.

Carter, P. G. (1976) *US Census Data for Political and Social Research: A Resource Guide* (Washington, DC: American Political Science Association). p. **44**.

Castles, S. and Kosack, G. (1973) *Immigrant Workers and Class Structure in Western Europe* (London: OUP). p. **70**.

Chenoweth, L. C. and Maret, E. (1980) 'The career patterns of mature American women', *Sociology of Work and Occupations*, vol. 7, no. 2, pp. 222–51. p. **22**.

Cheshire, P. C. and Weedon, R. (1973) *Regional Unemployment Differences in Great Britain and Inter-regional Migration Models* (Cambridge: CUP). p. **73**.

CIPFA (1979) *Community Indicators* (London: CIPFA). p. **7, 76–7, 79**.

Clark, S. (1981) 'Packages for the analysis of large social science datasets, research report to the SSRC', University of Essex. p. **175**.

Collet, G. E. (1908) 'The social status of women occupiers', *Journal of the Royal Statistical Society*, vol. 71, pp. 513–15. p. **85**.

Collison, P. (1960) 'Occupation, education and housing in an English city', *American Journal of Sociology*, vol. 55, no. 6, pp. 588–97. p. **75**.

Collison, P. (1967) 'Immigrants and residence', *Sociology*, vol. 1, no. 3, pp. 277–92; repr. in Peach (1975), pp. 266–82. p. **68, 75**.

Collison, P. and Mogey, J. (1959) 'Residence and social class in Oxford', *American Journal of Sociology*, vol. 54, no. 6, pp. 599–605. p. **75**.

Coombes, M. G. *et al.* (1978) 'Towards a more rational consideration of census areal units: daily urban systems in Britain', *Environment and Planning A*, vol. 10, pp. 1179–85. p. **65**.

Crewe, I. (1979) 'The SSRC Survey Archive', *Statistical News*, no. 45, pp. 8–11. p. **162**.

Crewe, I. and Payne, C. (1971) 'Analysing the census data', in D. Butler and M. Pinto-Duschinsky, *The British General Election of 1970* (London: Macmillan), pp. 416–36. p. **72, 80**.

CSO (annual from 1965) *Regional Statistics* (London: HMSO). p. **73**.

CSO (annual from 1970) *Social Trends* (London: HMSO). p. **20, 83, 114, 120–1, 125, 129–30**.

CSO (1975) 'Social commentary: social class', *Social Trends*, no. 6, pp. 10–32. p. **180**.

CSO (1976) *Guide to Official Statistics*, no. 1 (London: HMSO). p. **8, 33, 54, 120, 137**.

CSO (1978) *Guide to Official Statistics*, no. 2 (London: HMSO). p. **8, 33, 54, 111, 120, 137**.

CSO (1980) *Guide to Official Statistics*, no. 3 (London: HMSO). p. **8, 33, 54, 120, 137**.

Daniel, W. W. (1974) *A National Survey of the Unemployed* (London: Political and Economic Planning). p. **150**.

Daniel, W. W. (1981) *The Unemployed Flow* (London: Policy Studies Institute). p. **5**

Davidoff, L. (1979) 'The separation of home and work? Landladies and lodgers in nineteenth and twentieth century England', in *Fit Work for Women*, ed. S. Burman (London: Croom Helm), pp. 64–97. p. **84**.

Davidson, R. N. (1976) 'Social deprivation: an analysis of intercensal change', *Transactions*, vol. 1, no. 1, pp. 108–17. p. **79**.

Davies, C. (1980) 'Making sense of the census in Britain and the USA: the changing occupational classification and the position of nurses', *Sociological Review*, vol. 28, no. 3, pp. 581–609. p. **84**.

DE (1971) *British Labour Statistics: Historical Abstract 1886–1968* (London: HMSO). p. **86, 111**.

DE (1972) *Classification of Occupations and Dictionary of Occupational Titles* (London: HMSO). p. **178**.

DE (1976) 'The unregistered unemployed in Great Britain', *Department of Employment Gazette*, vol. 84, no. 12, pp. 1331–6. p. **66**.

DE, Unit for Manpower Studies (1977) *The Role of Immigrants in the Labour Market* (London: DE). p. **66**.

DE (1978) 'Family expenditure: a plain man's guide to the Family Expenditure Survey', *Department of Employment Gazette*, vol. 86, no. 2, pp. 137–47. p. **108**.

DE (1979) 'The Family Expenditure Survey and annual revision of the weights for the retail price indices', *Department of Employment Gazette*, vol. 87, no. 3, pp. 236–40. p. **114**.

Denham, C. (1980) 'The geography of the census: 1971 and 1981', *Population Trends*, no. 19, pp. 6–12. p. **49, 52**.

Denton, F. T. and George, P. J. (1973) 'The influence of socio-economic variables on family size in Wentworth County, Ontario, 1871: a statistical analysis of historical microdata', *Canadian Review of Sociology and Anthropology*,, vol. 10, no. 4, pp. 334–45. p. **94**.

Department of Finance (annual since 1968) *Northern Ireland Family Expenditure Survey* (London: HMSO). p. **113**.

DES (1971) *Survey of Earnings of Qualified Manpower in England and Wales 1966–67*, Statistics of Education Special Series No. 3 (London: HMSO). p. **43, 66**.

DHSS (1976) *Sharing Resources for Health in England* (London: HMSO). p. **67**.

DHSS (1980) *Inequalities in Health* (London: DHSS). p. **2, 132**.

Dinwiddy, R. and Reed, D. (1977) *The Effects of Certain Social and Demographic Changes on Income Distribution*, RCDIW Background Paper No. 3 (London: HMSO). p. **72**.

DoE (1975) *The Use of Indicators for Area Action*, Area Improvement Note 10 (London: HMSO). p. **67, 75–6, 78**.

DoE (1976) *British Cities: Urban Population and Employment Trends 1951–1971*, Research Report No. 10 (London: HMSO). p. **65**.

DoE (1979) *Directory of Local Authority Surveys 1978: Housing and Population* (London: DoE). p. **5**.

Dogan, M. and Rokkan, S. (eds) (1969) *Social Ecology (Quantitative Ecological Analysis in the Social Sciences)* (Cambridge, Mass.: MIT Press). p. **81**.

Donnison, D. and Soto, P. (1980) *The Good City* (London: Heinemann). p. **74, 78**.

Dunn, E. S. (1974) *Social Information Processing and Statistical Systems – Change and Reform* (London: Wiley). p. **22–3**.

Dunnell, K. (1979) *Family Formation 1976* (London: HMSO). p. **139**.

Durant, M. (1978) 'The General Household Survey 1971–78', *Statistical News*, no. 42, pp. 10–13. p. **99**.

Dyos, H. J. (ed.) (1968) *The Study of Urban History* (London: Edward Arnold). p. **93**.

Edwards, B. (1974) *Sources of Social Statistics* (London: Heinemann). p. **8, 33, 41**.

Edwards, S. L. and Pender, M. (1976) 'Indicators of local prosperity, databank', *Statistical News*, no. 32, pp. 3–7. p. **75**.

Ehrenberg, A. S. C. (1975) *Data Reduction: Analysing and Interpreting Statistical Data* (London: Wiley). p. **59**.

European Consortium for Political Research (1979) 'Data archives', *ECPR News Circular*, no. 33, pp. 4–44. p. **167**.

Evans, A. (1977) 'Notes on the changing relationship between registered unemployment and notified vacancies: 1961–1966 and 1966–1971', *Economica*, vol. 44, no. 174, pp. 179–96. p. **66**.

Fiegehan, G. C., Lansley, P. S. and Smith, A. D. (1977) *Poverty and Progress in Britain 1953–73* (Cambridge: CUP). p. **125–7**.

Field, S. *et al.* (1981) *Ethnic Minorities in Britain: A Study of Trends in their Position since 1961*, Home Office Research Study No. 68 (London: HMSO). p. **138**.

Finifter, B. M. (1975) 'Replication and extension of social research through secondary analysis', *Social Science Information*, vol. 14, no. 2, pp. 119–53. p. **2, 11, 17, 171**.

Flaherty, D. H. (1977) 'Access to historic census data in Canada, a comparative analysis', *Canadian Public Administration*, vol. 20, no. 3, pp. 481–98. p. **94**.

Flaherty, D. H. (1979) *Privacy and Government Databanks. An International Perspective* (London: Mansell Scientific). p. **54**.

Flowerdew, R. and Salt, J. (1979) 'Migration between labour market areas in Great Britain 1970–1971', *Regional Studies*, vol. 13, no. 2, pp. 211–31. p. **65**.

Fogel, R. and Engerman, S. (1974) *Time on the Cross* (Boston, Mass.: Little, Brown). p. **94**.

Fonda, N. and Moss, P. (eds) (1976) *Mothers in Employment* (London: Brunel University). p. **67**.

Forster, D. P. (1976) 'Social class differences in sickness and general practitioner consultations', *Health Trends*, vol. 8, no. 2, pp. 29–32. p. **129, 131**.

Forster, D. P. (1979) 'The relationship between health needs, socio-environmental indices, general practitioner resources, and utilisation', *Journal of Chronic Diseases*, vol. 32, pp. 333–7. p. **132**.

Foster, J. (1974) *Class Struggle and the Industrial Revolution* (London: Weidenfeld & Nicolson). p. **90–2**.

Fox, A. J. (1979) 'The role of OPCS in occupational epidemiology: some examples', *Annuals of Occupational Hygiene*, vol. 21, pp. 393–403. p. **43, 71**.

Frankel, M. R. (1971) *Inference from Survey Samples: An Empirical Investigation* (Ann Arbor, Mich.: University of Michigan, Institute for Social Research). p. **24**.

Frey, W. H. (1980) 'Black in-migration, white flight and the changing economic base of the central city', *American Journal of Sociology*, vol. 85, pp. 1396–1417. p. **65**.

Gales, K. E. and Marks, P. H. (1974) 'Twentieth century trends in the work of women in England and Wales', *Journal of the Royal Statistical Society*, series A, vol. 137, pt 1, pp. 60–74. p. **63, 86–7**.

Gibson, J. A. S. W. (1979) *Census Returns 1841, 1851, 1861, 1871 on Microfilm – A Directory of Local Holdings* (London: Gulliver Press). p. **88, 93**.

Gillespie, A. (1977) *Journey to Work Trends within British Labour Markets, 1961–1971* (London: London School of Economics, Department of Geography). p. **65**.

Gittus, E. (ed.) (1972) *Key Variables in Social Research: Religion, Housing, Locality* (London: Heinemann). p. **76, 133, 177, 180–1, 183**.

Glass, D. V. (1973) *Numbering the People: The Eighteenth-Century Controversy and the Development of Census and Vital Statistics in Britain* (Farnborough, Hants: Saxon House). p. **28**.

Glazer, B. G. (1963) 'Retreading research materials: the use of secondary analysis by the independent researcher', *American Behavioral Scientist*, vol. 6, no. 10. pp. 11–14. p. **169**.

Glenn, N. D. (1976) 'Cohort analysts' futile quest: statistical attempts to separate age, period and cohort effects', *American Sociological Review*, vol. 41, pp. 900–8. p. **19**.

Glenn, N., Converse, P. E., Cutler, S. J. and Hyman, H. H. (1978) 'The General Social Surveys', *Contemporary Sociology*, vol. 7, no. 5, pp. 532–49. p. **155, 170–1**.

Goldblatt, P. and Fox, J. (1978) 'Household mortality from the OPCS Longitudinal Study', *Population Trends*, no. 14, pp. 20–8. p. **43, 71, 181**.

Goldstone, L. (1977) 'Improving social statistics in developing countries', *International Social Science Journal*, vol. 29, no. 4, pp. 756–71. p. **59**.

Goldthorpe, J. H. and Hope, K. (1974) *The Social Grading of Occupations* (London: OUP). p. **179**.

Gray, P. and Gee, F. A. (1972) *A Quality Check on the 1966 Ten Percent Sample Census of England and Wales* (London: HMSO). p. **39**.

Greenhalgh, C. (1980) 'Male–female wage differentials in Great Britain: is marriage an equal opportunity?', *Economic Journal*, vol. 90, no. 360, pp. 751–75. p. **128**.

Gwartney, J. D. and Long, J. E. (1978) 'The relative earnings of blacks and other minorities', *Industrial and Labor Relations Review*, vol. 31, no. 3, pp. 336–46. p. **74**.

Haber, S. (1973) 'Trends in work rates of white females 1890 to 1950', *Industrial and Labor Relations Review*, vol. 26, pp. 1122–34. p. **87**.

Hakim, C. (1977) *Census-Based Area Profiles: A Review*, Occasional Paper No. 2 (London: OPCS). p. **58, 76**.

Hakim, C. (1978a) *Census Confidentiality, Microdata, and Census Analysis,* Occasional Paper No. 3 (London: OPCS). p. **54, 58**.

Hakim, C. (1978b) *Social and Community Indicators from the Census*, Occasional Paper No. 5 (London: OPCS). p. **46, 58, 76–7**.

Hakim, C. (1978c) *Census Data and Analysis: A Selected Bibliography*, Occasional Paper No. 6 (London: OPCS). p. **54, 58**.

Hakim, C. (1978d) *Data Dissemination for the Population Census; A Data Users' Guide*, Occasional Paper No. 11 (London: OPCS). p. **45, 47–8, 54, 58, 79, 88, 93**.

Hakim, C. (1979a) 'The population census and its by-products: data bases for research', *International Social Science Journal*, vol. 31, no. 2, pp. 343–52. p. **5, 37, 39**.

Hakim, C. (1979b) 'Census confidentiality in Britain', in *Censuses, Surveys and Privacy*, ed. M. Bulmer (London: Macmillan), pp. 132–57. p. **37, 39, 54, 88**.

Hakim, C. (1979c) *Occupational Segregation*, Research Paper No. 9 (London: DE). p. **64, 86–7**.

Hakim, C. (1980a) 'Social aspects of employment: data for policy research', *Journal of Social Policy*, vol. 9, no. 1, pp. 77–98. p. **62–3, 116**.

Hakim, C. (1980b) 'Census reports as documentary evidence: the census commentaries 1801–1951', *Sociological Review*, vol. 28, no. 3, pp. 551–80. p. **13, 36, 84, 86–7, 90**.

Hakim, C. (1981) 'Job segregation: trends in the 1970s', *Department of Employment Gazette*, vol. 89, no. 12, pp. 521–9. p. **130**.

Hakim, C. (1982) 'Secondary analysis and the relationship between official and academic social research', *Sociology*, vol. 16, no. 1, pp. 12–28. p. **3, 24, 143**.

Hall, P. (1973) *The Containment of Urban England* (London: Allen & Unwin). p. **65**.

Harrison, I. R. (1976) 'Poplar genealogy: the resources of a dockland parish', *The Genealogist's Magazine*, vol. 18, no. 7, pp. 352–3. p. **88**.

Herbert, D. (1972) *Urban Geography: A Social Perspective* (Newton Abbot: David & Charles), p. **78**.

Hindess, B. (1973) *The Use of Official Statistics in Sociology: A Critique of Positivism and Ethnomethodology* (London: Macmillan). p. **13**.

Hofferbert, R. I. and Clubb, J. M. (eds) (1976) 'Social science data archives: applications and potential', *American Behavioral Scientist*, vol. 19, no. 4, pp. 381–488. p. **167**.

Holt, D. *et al.* (1980) 'Chi-squared tests with survey data', *Journal of the Royal Statistical Society*, series A, vol. 143, pp. 303–20. p. **133, 154**.

Holtermann, S. (1975) 'Areas of urban deprivation in Great Britain: an analysis of 1971 Census data', *Social Trends*, no. 6, pp. 33–47. p. **67, 75–6**.

Howe, J. R. (1971) *Two Parent Families: A Study of their Resources and Needs in 1968, 1969 and 1970*, DHSS Statistical Report Series No. 14 (London: HMSO). p. **114, 125**.

Hunt, A. (1975) *Management Attitudes and Practice Towards Women at Work* (London: HMSO). p. **141**.

Hyman, H. H. (1972) *Secondary Analysis of Sample Surveys: Principles, Procedures and Potentialities* (New York: Wiley). p. **3–4, 11, 16–19, 21, 141, 154, 167**.

ILO (1979) *Household Income and Expenditure Statistics, No. 3: 1968–1976* (Geneva: ILO). p. **123**.

Imber, V. (1977) *A Classification of the English Personal Social Services Authorities*, DHSS Statistical and Research Report Series No. 16 (London: HMSO). p. **67, 75–6, 80**.

Irvine, J., Miles, I. and Evans, J. (1979) *Demystifying Social Statistics* (London: Pluto Press). p. **13**.

Johnston, R. J. (1976) 'Areal studies, ecological studies, and social patterns in cities', *Transactions*, vol. 1, no. 1, pp. 118–22. p. **76, 81**.

Jones, G. K. and Roper, S. (1974) 'Planning a nursery programme', *Greater London Intelligence Quarterly*, no. 27, pp. 51–61. p. **77**.

Jones, K. and Smith, A. D. (1970) *The Economic Impact of Commonwealth Immigration* (Cambridge: CUP). p. **68–70**.

Kelsall, R. K., Poole, A. and Kuhn, A. (1972) *Graduates: The Sociology of an Elite* (London: Tavistock/Methuen). p. **17, 150**.

Kemsley, W. F. F. (1969a) *Income Questions – a Simplified Version of the FES Questions for Use in Other Surveys*, Government Social Survey Methodology Paper No. 147 (London: OPCS). p. **183**.

Kemsley, W. F. F. (1969b) *Family Expenditure Survey Handbook on the Sample Fieldwork and Coding Procedures* (London: HMSO). p. **108, 111**.

Kemsley, W. F. F. (1975) 'Family Expenditure Survey: A study of differential response based on a comparison of the 1971 sample with the Census', *Statistical News*, no. 31, pp. 16–21. p. **113**.

Kemsley, W. F. F. *et al.* (1980) *Family Expenditure Survey Handbook* (London: HMSO). p. **108, 111**.

Kish, L. (1979) 'Samples and censuses', *International Statistical Review*, vol. 47, no. 2, pp. 99–109. p. **38**.

Knight, I. B. (1979) *Company Organisation and Worker Participation* (London: HMSO). p. **141**.

Knox, P. L. (1975) *Social Well-Being: A Spatial Perspective* (London: OUP). p. **78**.

Knox, P. L. (1978) 'Territorial social indicators and area profiles', *Town Planning Review*, vol. 49, no. 1, pp. 75–83. p. **76**.

Lammermeier, P. J. (1973) 'The urban black family of the nineteenth century: a study of black family structure in the Ohio Valley, 1850–1880', *Journal of Marriage and the Family*, vol. 35, no. 3, pp. 440–56. p. **94**.

Lancaster, T. (1979) 'Econometric methods for the duration of unemployment', *Econometrica*, vol. 47, no. 4, pp. 939–56. p. **150**.

Land, K. C. and Spilerman, S. (eds) (1975) *Social Indicator Models* (New York: Russell Sage). p. **155**.

Law, C. M. (1967) 'The growth of urban population in England and Wales, 1801–1911', *Transactions*, vol. 41, pp. 125–43. p. **86**.

Lawton, R. (ed.) (1978) *The Census and Social Structure: An Interpretative Guide to the 19th Century Censuses for England and Wales* (London: Frank Cass). p. **28, 85–6, 88–90, 93**.

Layard, R. *et al.* (1978) *The Causes of Poverty*, RCDIW Background Paper No. 5 (London: HMSO). p. **126–7**.

Lee, C. H. (1979) *British Regional Employment Statistics 1841–1971* (Cambridge: CUP). p. **86**.

Lee, T. R. (1977) *Race and Residence* (London: OUP). p. **68, 78**.

Leete, R. and Fox, J. (1977) 'Registrar General's social classes: origins and uses', *Population Trends*, no. 8, pp. 1–7, p. **180**.

Leggatt, T. (1974) 'Management style and economic success in industry' in *Sociological Theory and Survey Research*, ed. T. Leggatt (London: Sage), pp. 185–205. p. **151**.

Le Grand, J. (1978a) 'Who benefits from public expenditure?', *New Society*, vol. 45, no. 833, pp. 614–16. p. **129**.

Le Grand, J. (1978b) 'The distribution of public expenditure: the case of health care', *Economica*, vol. 45, no. 178, pp. 125–42. p. **129**.

MacIntosh, A. (1980) 'Women at work: a survey of employers', *Department of Employment Gazette*, vol. 88, no. 11, pp. 1142–9. p. **141**.

Market Research Society (1976) 'Response rates in sample surveys', *Journal of the Market Research Society*, vol. 18, no. 3, pp. 113–42. p. **1**.

Marsh, D. C. (1958) *The Changing Social Structure of England and Wales 1871–1951* (London: Routledge & Kegan Paul). p. **86**.

Martinotti, G. (1978) 'Data processing, government and the public: reflections on the Italian case', *International Social Science Journal*, vol. 30, no. 1, pp. 146–63. p. **60**.

Mason, K. O. *et al.* (1973) 'Some methodological issues in the cohort analysis of archival data', *American Sociological Review*, vol. 38, pp. 242–51. p. **19**.

Mason, W. M., Taeuber, K. E. and Winsborough, H. H. (eds) (1977) *Old Data for New Research* (Madison, Wis.: University of Wisconsin, Centre for Demography and Ecology). p. **10, 54, 122**.

Maunder, W. F. (ed.) (1974–81) *Reviews of United Kingdom Statistical Sources*, 15 vols (London and Oxford: Heinemann/Pergamon):

No. 1 *Personal Social Services* by B. P. Davies and G. J. Murray.

No. 2 *Central Government Routine Health Statistics* by M. Alderson and F. Whitehead.

No. 3 *Housing in Great Britain and Northern Ireland* by S. Farthing and M. Fleming.

No. 4 *Leisure and Tourism* by F. M. M. Lewes, S. R. Parker and L. J. Lickorish.

No. 5 *General Sources of Statistics* by G. F. Lock.

No. 6 *Wealth and Personal Incomes* by A. B. Atkinson, A. J. Harrison and T. Stark.

No. 7 *Road Passenger and Road Goods Transport* by D. Munby and A. Watson.

No. 8 *Land Use, Town and Country Planning* by J. T. Coppock and L. F. Gebbert.

No. 9 *Health Surveys and Related Studies* by M. Alderson and R. Dowie.

No. 10 *Ports, Inland Waterways and Civil Aviation* by R. E. Baxter and C. Phillips.

No. 11 *Coal, Gas and Electricity* by D. J. Harris, H. Nabb and D. Nutall.

No. 12 *Construction and the Related Professions* by M. C. Fleming.
No. 13 *Wages and Earnings* by A. Dean.
No. 14 *Rail and Sea Transport* by D. H. Aldcroft and D. Mort.
No. 15 *Crime Statistics* by M. A. Walker.

p. **8, 13, 106, 112, 131, 137.**

Mayhew, K. and Rosewell, B. (1978) 'Immigrants and occupational crowding in Great Britain', *Oxford Bulletin of Economics and Statistics*, vol. 40, no. 3, pp. 223–48. p. **13, 64, 70.**

McClements, L. D. (1978) *The Economics of Social Security* (London: Heinemann). p. **114.**

Merritt, R. L. and Rokkan, S. (eds) (1966) *Comparing Nations. The Use of Quantitative Data in Cross-National Research* (New Haven, Conn.: Yale University Press). p. **81.**

Midwinter, E. (1977) 'Education statistics: the social factor', *Where*, no. 126, pp. 80–1. p. **79.**

Miller, W. L., Raab, G. and Britto, K. (1974) 'Voting research and the population census 1918–71', *Journal of the Royal Statistical Society*, series A, vol. 137, pt 3, pp. 384–411. p. **73, 80.**

Ministry of Labour (1957) *Household Expenditure 1953–54, Report of an Enquiry* (London: HMSO). p. **109.**

Mitchell, B. R. and Deane, P. (1971) *Abstract of British Historical Statistics* (Cambridge: CUP). p. **86, 90.**

Monk, D. (1970) *Social Grading on the National Readership Survey* (London: Joint Industry Committee for the NRS). p. **180.**

Montagna, P. D. (1977) *Occupations and Society: Towards a Sociology of the Labor Market* (New York: Wiley). p. **2, 63.**

Morgan, J. N. *et al.* (1974) *Five Thousand American Families* (Ann Arbor, Mich.: University of Michigan, Survey Research Centre). p. **123.**

Morris, V. and Ziderman, A. (1971) 'The economic return on investment in higher education in England and Wales', *Economic Trends*, no. 211, pp. 20–31. p. **43, 66.**

Moser, C. A. (1972) 'Statistics about immigrants: objectives, sources, methods and problems', *Social Trends*, no. 3, pp. 20–30. p. **13.**

Moser, C. A. and Scott, W. (1961) *British Towns* (Edinburgh: Oliver & Boyd). p. **73, 78.**

Nakamura, M. *et al.* (1979) 'Job opportunities, the offered wage and the labor supply of married women', *American Economic Review*, vol. 69, pp. 787–805. p. **74.**

Newman, D. (1978) *Practical Problems of Sampling in the Census of Population and Techniques for Ensuring the Confidentiality of Census Information in Great Britain*, Occasional Paper No. 4 (London: OPCS). p. **39, 46, 58.**

Nichols, T. (1979) 'Social class: official, sociological and Marxist', in *Demystifying Social Statistics*, ed. J. Irvine *et al.* (London: Pluto Press), pp. 152–71. p. **179–80.**

Nicholson, J. L. (1965) *Redistribution of Income in the United Kingdom in 1959, 1957 and 1953* (London: Bowes & Bowes). p. **114.**

Nicholson, J. L. (1976) 'Appraisal of different methods of estimating equivalence scales and their results', *Review of Income and Wealth*, series 22, no. 1, pp. 1–11. p. **114.**

Nickell, S. (1979a) 'The effect of unemployment and related benefits on the duration of unemployment', *The Economic Journal*, vol. 89, no. 353, pp. 34–49. p. **131.**

Nickell, S. (1979b) 'Estimating the probability of leaving unemployment', *Econometrica*, vol. 47, no. 5, pp. 1249–66. p. **131.**

Norris, G. (1978) 'Unemployment, subemployment and personal characteristics', *Sociological Review*, vol. 26, pp. 89–108 and 327–47. p. **22.**

O'Dell, A. and Parker, J. (1977) *The Use of Census Data to Identify and Describe Housing Stress* (Garston, Watford: DoE Building Research Establishment). p. **76, 78.**

OECD (1978) *Multi-Purpose Household Surveys in Developing Countries* (Paris: OECD). p. **122.**

OPCS (1970) *Classification of Occupations* (London: HMSO). p. **42, 54, 178–80.**

OPCS (1973a) *The General Household Survey: Introductory Report* (London: HMSO). p. **105–6, 122**.

OPCS (1973b) *Cohort Studies: New Developments*, Studies on Medical and Population Subjects No. 25 (London: HMSO). p. **43**.

OPCS (1977a) 'Labour Force Survey', *Population Trends*, no. 7, pp. 15–17. p. **120**.

OPCS (1977b) *1971 Census Grid Square Statistics: Explanatory Notes* (London, OPCS). p. **49**.

OPCS (1978a) *1971 Census General Report, Part I: Definitions* (London: HMSO). p. **39, 54**.

OPCS (1978b) *1971 Census Income Follow-up Survey*, Studies on Medical and Population Subjects No. 38 (London: HMSO). p. **41, 72**.

OPCS (1978c) *Occupational Mortality*, Series DS No. 1 (London: HMSO). p. **68, 180**.

OPCS (1979) *Immigration Statistics: Sources and Definitions*, Occasional Paper No. 15 (London: OPCS). p. **13, 58**.

OPCS (1980a) *1971 Census of Population: A Guide to Published and Unpublished Material* (London: OPCS). p. **45**.

OPCS (1980b) *Libraries in the UK Holding Census Volumes* (London: OPCS). p. **46, 88, 93**.

OPCS (1980c) *Classification of Occupations and Coding Index* (London: HMSO). p. **54, 178, 180**.

OPCS (1980d) *Labour Force Survey 1973, 1975, 1977* (London: HMSO). p. **120**.

OPCS (1980e) *People in Britain: A Census Atlas* (London: HMSO). p. **49, 57, 76**.

OPCS and GRO(S) (1977) *Guide to Census Reports, Great Britain, 1801–1966*, (London: HMSO). p. **28, 31, 33, 54, 86, 93**.

Payne, G. (1977) 'Occupational transition in advanced industrial societies', *Sociological Review*, vol. 25, no. 1, pp. 5–39. p. **62, 86**.

Peach, C. (ed.) (1975) *Urban Social Segregation* (London: Longman), p. **68**.

Pickett, K. G. (1974) *Sources of Official Data* (London: Longman). p. **8, 33**.

Pollak, R. A. and Wales, T. J. (1978) 'Estimation of complete demand systems from household budget data: the linear and quadratic expenditure systems', *American Economic Review*, vol. 68, no. 3, pp. 348–59. p. **133**.

Prais, S. J. (1978) 'The strike proneness of large plants in Britain', *Journal of the Royal Statistical Society*, series A, vol. 141, pp. 368–84. p. **143**.

Price, R. and Bain, G. S. (1976) 'Union growth revisited: 1948–1974 in perspective', *British Journal of Industrial Relations*, vol. 14, no. 3, pp. 339–55. p. **86**.

PRO (1971) *Records of Interest to Social Scientists 1919–1939: Introduction*, PRO Handbook No. 14 (London: HMSO). p. **83**.

PRO (1975) *Records of Interest to Social Scientists: Unemployment Insurance 1911 to 1939*, PRO Handbook No. 16 (London: HMSO). p. **83**.

Psacharopoulos, G. (1977) 'Family background, education and achievement: a path model of earnings determinants in the UK and some alternatives', *British Journal of Sociology*, vol. 28, no. 3, pp. 321–35. p. **128**.

RCDIW (1978) *Lower Incomes*, Cmnd 7175 (London: HMSO). p. **104**.

Redfern, P. (1981) 'The Census 1981 – an historical and international perspective', *Population Trends*, no. 23, pp. 3–15. p. **36, 43**.

Reid, I. (1977) *Social Class Differences in Britain: A Sourcebook* (London: Open Books). p. **67–8, 133, 180**.

Robinson, O. (1979a) 'Part-time employment in the European Community', *International Labour Review*, vol. 118, no. 3, pp. 299–314. p. **117, 130**.

Robinson, O. (1979b) 'Part-time employment in the EEC – a marginal labour force?', *The Three Banks Review*, no. 122, pp. 61–76. p. **117, 130**.

Robinson, R. V. and Kelley, J. (1979) 'Class as conceived by Marx and Dahrendorf: effects on income inequality and politics in the United States and Great Britain', *American Sociological Review*, vol. 44, pp. 38–58. p. **152–4, 179**.

Robson, B. T. (1969) *Urban Analysis: A Study of City Structure* (Cambridge: CUP). p. **78**.

Rokkan, S. (1976) 'Data services in Western Europe: reflections on variations in the conditions of academic institution-building', *American Behavioral Scientist*, vol. 19, pp. 443–54. p. **60, 94, 155**.

Rose, E. J. B. *et al.* (1969) *Colour and Citizenship, A Report on British Race Relations* (London: OUP). p. **68–9, 149**.

Rothman, J. (1977) 'The development of an income surrogate', in OPCS, *General Household Survey 1974*, OPCS (London: HMSO), pp. 19–26. p. **13, 106**.

Royal Commission on the National Health Service (1978) *Patients' Attitudes to the Hospital Service*, Research Paper No. 5 (London: HMSO). p. **104**.

Runnymede Trust (1975) *Race and Council Housing in London* (London: Runnymede Trust). p. **78**.

Rutter, M. *et al.* (1979) *Fifteen Thousand Hours* (London: Open Books). p. **16, 80**.

Salathiel, D. (1977) 'The use of social indicators in the distribution of rate support grant', paper presented to the Royal Statistical Society Social Statistics and Survey Methodology Group. p. **67, 75**.

Sampson, W. A. and Rossi, P. H. (1975) 'Race and family social standing', *American Sociological Review*, vol. 40, pp. 201–14. p. **180**.

Sawyer, M. (1976) *Income Distribution in OECD Countries*, OECD Economic Outlook Occasional Studies (Paris: OECD). p. **123**.

Schaefer, R. T. (1974) 'Correlates of racial prejudice', in *Sociological Theory and Survey Research*, ed. T. Leggatt (London: Sage), pp. 237–64. p. **149–50**.

Scott-Samuel, A. (1977) 'Social area analysis in community medicine', *British Journal of Preventive and Social Medicine*, vol. 31, pp. 199–204. p. **80**.

Sharpe, L. J. (1978) 'The social scientist and policy-making in Britain and America', in *Social Policy Research*, ed. M. Bulmer (London: Macmillan), pp. 302–12. p. **23**.

Shaw, M. (1979a) 'Wolverhampton 1871 and 1971', *Population Trends*, no. 18, pp. 17–23. p. **93**.

Shaw, M. (1979b) 'Reconciling social and physical space: Wolverhampton 1871', *Transactions*, new series, vol. 4, no. 2, pp. 192–213. p. **93**.

Shepherd, J. *et al.* (1974) *A Social Atlas of London* (Oxford: Clarendon Press). p. **76**.

Shevky, E. and Bell, W. (1955) *Social Area Analysis* (Stanford, Calif.: Stanford University Press). p. **52**.

Sillitoe, K. (1978) 'Ethnic origin: the search for a question', *Population Trends*, no. 13, pp. 25–30. p. **37, 182**.

Smart, M. W. (1974) 'Labour market areas: uses and definitions', *Progress in Planning*, vol. 2, pp. 239–353. p. **65**.

Smith, C. T. B. *et al.* (1978) *Strikes in Britain*, Manpower Paper No. 15 (London: HMSO). p. **143**.

SOEC (1978) *Census of Population in the Community Countries 1968–1971* (Brussels: SOEC). p. **44**.

SOEC (1980) *Methodology of Surveys on Family Budgets* (Luxembourg: SOEC). p. **122**.

Sorrentino, C. (1979) *International Comparisons of Unemployment*, Bulletin of the US Department of Labor, Bureau of Labor Statistics (Washington, DC: US Government Printing Office). p. **130**.

SSRC Survey Archive (1980) *Data Catalogue* (Colchester: University of Essex). p. **107, 114, 121, 147–9, 162, 164, 173**.

Stacey, M. (ed.) (1969) *Comparability in Social Research* (London: Heinemann). p. **133, 177, 183**.

Stark, T. (1977) *The Distribution of Income in Eight Countries*, RCDIW Background Paper No. 4 (London: HMSO). p. **123, 134**.

Stevens, P. and Willis, C. F. (1979) *Race, Crime and Arrests*, Home Office Research Study No. 58 (London: HMSO). p. **68, 70**.

Stilwell, F. J. B. (1970) 'The regional distribution of concealed unemployment', *Urban Studies*, vol. 7, no. 2, pp. 207–14. p. **66, 73**.

Thatcher, A. R. (1968) 'The distribution of earnings of employees in Great Britain', *Journal of the Royal Statistical Society*, series A, vol. 131, pp. 133–80. p. **11, 112–13**.

Townsend, P. (1979) *Poverty in the United Kingdom* (London: Allen Lane). p. **2, 8, 10, 16, 125, 132–3, 142**.

United Nations (1975) *Towards a System of Social and Demographic Statistics*, Studies in Methods Series F, No. 18 (New York: Statistical Office of the United Nations). p. **23, 155**.

Van Slooten, R. and Coverdale, A. G. (1977) 'The characteristics of low income households', *Social Trends*, no. 8, pp. 26–39. p. **21, 125**.

Visvalingam, M. (1978) *A Locational Index for the 1971 Kilometre-square Population Census Data for Great Britain*, Working Paper No. 12 (Durham: University of Durham, Census Research Unit). p. **77**.

Wabe, J. S. (1969) 'Labour force participation rates in the London metropolitan region', *Journal of the Royal Statistical Society*, vol. 132, pp. 245–64. p. **63, 80**.

Webber, R. J. (1975) *Liverpool Social Area Study* (London: Centre for Environmental Studies). p. **76**.

Webber, R. J. (1977) *The National Classification of Residential Neighbourhoods: An Introduction to the Classification of Wards and Parishes* (London: Centre for Environmental Studies). p. **52, 77**.

Webber, R. (1978a) *Parliamentary Constituencies: A Socio-Economic Classification*, Occasional Paper No. 13 (London: OPCS). p. **52, 73, 77**.

Webber, R. (1978b) 'The new geography of party allegiance', *New Society*, vol. 45, no. 834, pp. 682–3. p. **73, 80**.

Webber, R. (1979) *Census Enumeration Districts: A Socio-Economic Classification*, Occasional Paper No. 14 (London: OPCS). p. **52, 58, 77**.

Webber, R. J. and Craig, J. (1978) *A Socio-Economic Classification of Local Authorities in Great Britain*, OPCS Studies on Medical and Population Subjects No. 35 (London: HMSO). p. **52, 77**.

Williamson, P. (1979) 'Moving around in the room at the top', *Department of Employment Gazette*, vol. 87, pp. 1220–8. p. **17, 150**.

Subject Index